open

open

open

editorial

JORINDE SEIJDEL

(IM)MOBILITY
EXPLORING THE BOUNDARIES
OF HYPERMOBILITY

This issue came into being in collaboration with guest editor Eric Kluitenberg, a media theorist, writer and organizer of projects concentrating on culture and technology. In 2010, Kluitenberg organized the 'ElectroSmog International Festival for Sustainable Immobility'. ElectroSmog arose out of criticism of the 'growing worldwide mobility crisis' and began as a 'search for an alternative lifestyle that is no longer dominated by speed and continuous mobility'. The festival took place in several international cities simultaneously and was streamed live on the Internet. The idea that communications technology can resolve the conflict between ecology and mobility was by no means confirmed during ElectroSmog, but once again problematized, not in the last place by the recognition of different 'regimes of mobility' that are active on the local and global levels and affect one another.

Sustainability and ecology is merely one dimension of mobility as a social question. In the light of globalization, the new technology and sociopolitical developments on the local and global levels, it is equally about mobility versus immobility in terms of people, data, capital and products. It is also about mobility privileges and the freedom of movement, or lack thereof, of population groups and individuals, about incessant flows of data, the enticements of capital and free commodity markets.

This issue of *Open* explores the internal contradictions of prevailing mobility regimes and their effects on social and physical space. Advanced communications technology, rather than revealing itself to be a clean alternative for physical movement from place to place, seems to pave the way for an increase of physical and motorized mobility. The accelerating flows of data and commodities stand in sharp contrast to the elbowroom afforded to the biological body, which in fact is forced to a standstill. And while data, goods and capital have been freed of their territorial restrictions, the opposite is true for a growing portion of the world's population: border regimes, surveillance and identity control are being intensified at a rapid pace. In short, on the one hand there is a question of an uncurbed and uncontrolled increase of mobility, while on the other, segregating filtrations are taking place.

Kluitenberg explores the contradictory regimes of (im)mobility in his introductory essay and searches for a perspective of intervention. He provisionally arrives at a 'general economy' of mobility, whereby the boundless longing for freedom of movement intensifies to the point of a 'fatal worldwide standstill'. Following the example of Saskia Sassen, he concludes by turning to the local as a context from which effective counterforces can be generated on the global level. From another line of approach, namely the rhizomatics of Deleuze and Guattari, philosopher and jurist Marc Schuilenburg argues for connectivity with the local, introducing a new term in this regard: *terroir*, a contextualized approach to place and identity in which the emphasis lies on the dynamic relation between objects and people.

Charlotte Lebbe, architecture researcher, and Florian Schneider, media artist and filmmaker, each address the ambivalence of the present border regimes. Lebbe analyses how the external borders of the Schengen Area are being more and more strictly guarded with the help of new digital techniques, in order to regulate mobility. She sees the rise of a *dispositif* surveillance, the Ban-opticon. Schneider, seeking a new theory of borders and a different approach to mobility, argues in favour of abandoning the concept of the nation-state and advances the notion of 'transnationality'. Architecture theorist Wim Nijenhuis presents a 'dromological' history of mobility, leading to the topical question of what exile means in today's 'exit city'.

Culture critic Brian Holmes examines the technological and cultural side of the capitalist mobility system: he analyses the intermodal distribution and transportation industry, in particular container shipping and the system of just-in-time production, drawing among other things upon Ursula Biemann's video work *Contained Mobility*. Political sociologist Merijn Oudenampsen and architecture researcher Miguel Robles-Durán interviewed the social geographer David Harvey, who theorizes on the spatial effects of capital accumulation.

John Thackara, design critic, reflects upon the limitations of mobility as a challenge for designers, who ought to seek new ways of using space and time. Through a problematization of the mobility of food and its tracking, media theorist Tatiana Goryucheva investigates the preconditions for a democratic design of technology. Architect Nerea Calvillo expounds upon the project *In the Air*, which focuses on collecting data to visualize invisible elements in the urban atmosphere and aims at being a tool for increasing the awareness and participation of city inhabitants. The contribution by design and research collective Metahaven is about the mobility of money. In *Mobile Money*, they envisage new forms of money and capital.

Last but not least, in the column, media theorist Joss Hands, whose @ is for Activism: Dissent, Resistance and Rebellion in a Digital Culture recently appeared, discusses the mobilizing capacity of social media in the recent events in the Middle East, and how they can trespass on space, time, movement and personal will.

Eric Kluitenberg

Extreme Displacement

Survey of the Emerging Regimes of (Im)Mobility

A worldwide explosion of mobility versus bodiless inter-action in digital networks; hyper-mobility of flows of capital and goods versus the immobility of the biological body; the pres-sure of ecological and energetic depletion versus the desire for total freedom of movement: our present-day mobility regimes are characterized by deeply rooted contradictions. Media critic Eric Kluitenberg seeks a perspective for intervention to achieve ecolog-ical and social stability.

It is exactly eleven o'clock in the morning, 18 March 2010. We are speaking with architect Daan Roggeveen through a rather poor Skype connection. Right now he is in the departure hall of Xi'an International Airport, waiting for his flight to Shanghai. He has just enough time to give a presentation on Go West, a research project that he and journalist Michiel Hulshof are currently undertaking in Central and West China.[1] The topic is the explosion of mobility in the new metropolises that China is stamping out of the ground with astounding speed.

1. www.gowestproject.com.

The setting for this curious talk is the opening programme of the ElectroSmog Festival for Sustainable Immobility.[2] The idea of the Festival is to investigate new forms of connectivity through digital networks as alternatives for physical travel. In the auditorium of De Balie in Amsterdam, and through live streams of the Festival on the Internet, Roggeveen's story is supported by a slideshow of empty highways, ghostly new urban landscapes and desolate shopping centres.

2. For documentation on the festival, see: www.electrosmogfestival.net/documentatie.

Wuhan, the most recent object of Hulshof and Roggeveen's research, is a medium-sized city in central China. We ask how many cars are added to the flow of traffic there each day. The estimate is approximately 500. As we speak, over 30 cities of comparable size (between one and three million inhabitants) are being constructed in China, not counting the areas of the larger urban agglomerations (Beijing, Shanghai, Shenzhen/Hong Kong/Guangzhou).

A quick calculation tells us that a cautious estimate would have to reckon on 15,000 new cars per day. And then we receive comparable reports from Delhi, Dhaka and Nairobi through video chats with Internet activists, designers, filmmakers – a dizzying panorama of out-of-control hypermobility throughout the entire world.

After this, the departure point of the Festival, a search for sustainable immobility, seems almost laughable. After all, we haven't even begun to talk about the explosion of air traffic, which shows a comparable exponential growth. This headlong rush towards a worldwide traffic jam can also be taken, however, as a convincing call to seriously look for viable alternatives for the persistent compulsion for motorized transportation.

The 'Network of Things' and the Electronic Cottage

Owing to the new developments in information and communication technologies and the transference of physical production to low-wage countries, the Western economies, including the Netherlands, have been transformed into primarily service and logistics oriented economies. This has given rise to new regimes of mobility, but also of immobility. Nowadays, increasingly complex flows of transportation are being coordinated by equally complex flows of data in order to achieve optimal, just-in-time efficiency. An ever-finer-meshed tracing net is being flung over the physical space in which RFID-tagged objects move as nodes in

Empty motorway near Xi'an, Daan Roggeveen, project *Go West: The Changing Face of China's Invisible Cities*, 2010.

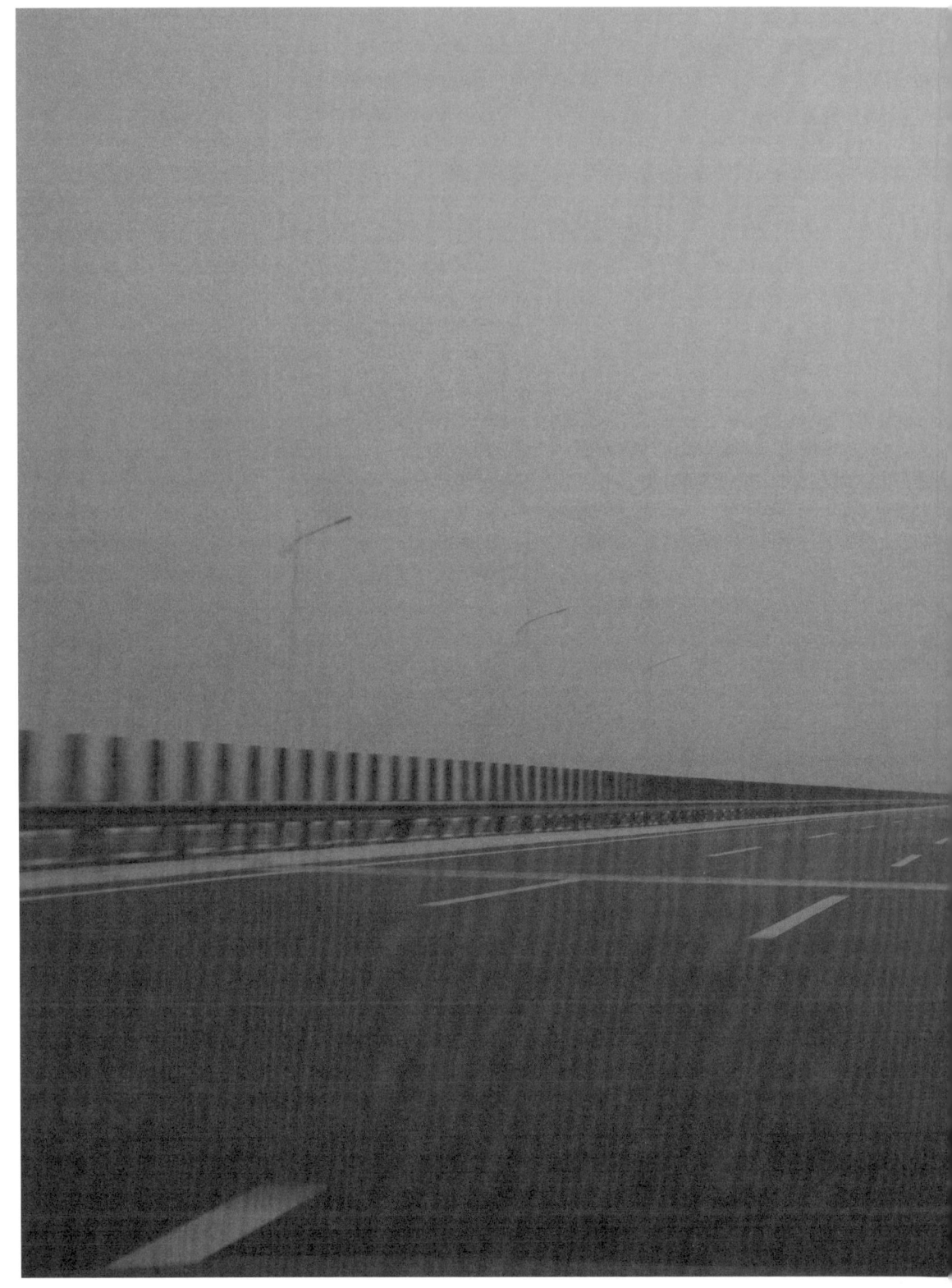

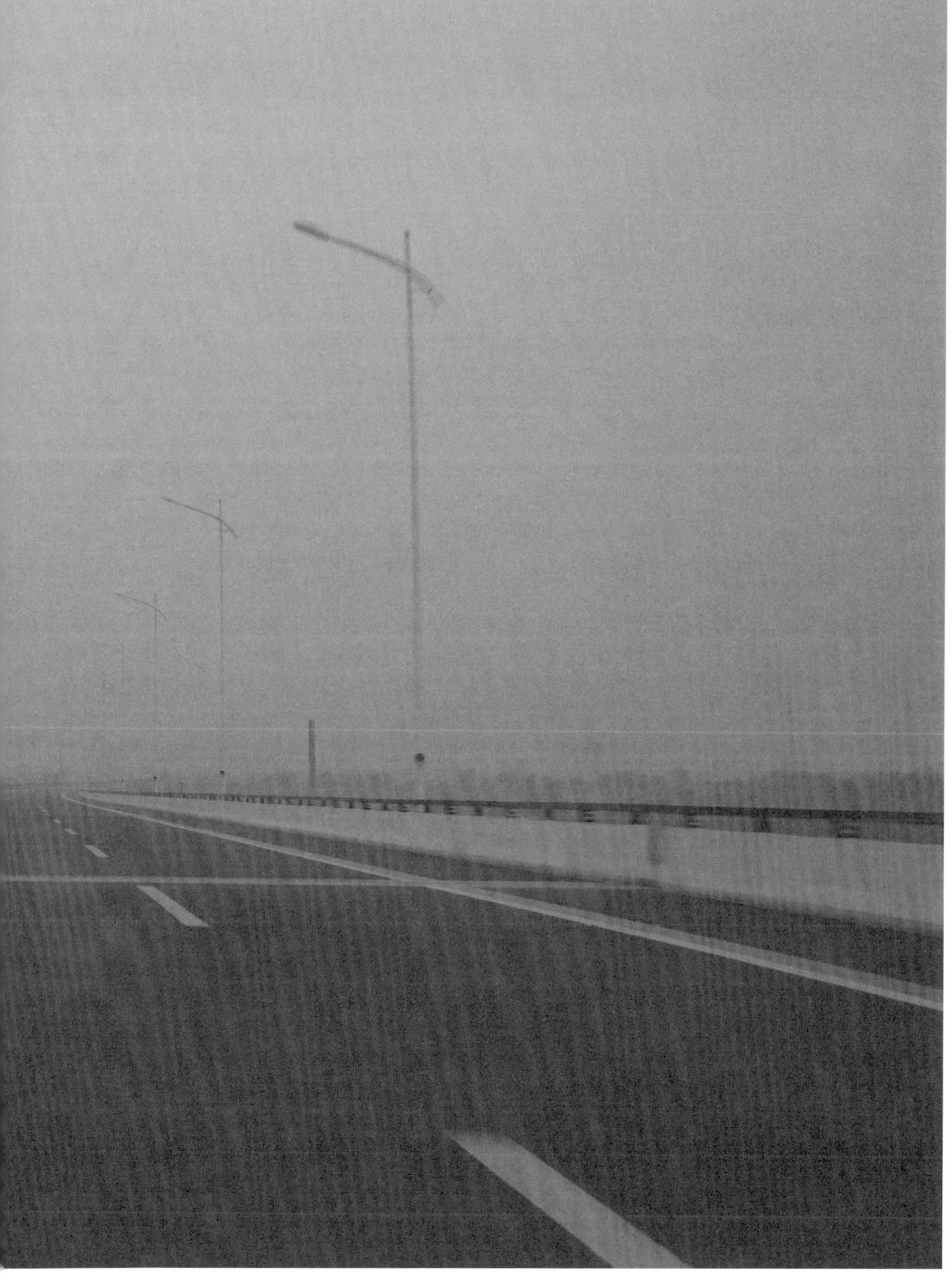

a 'network of things'. In the meantime, workers are increasingly becoming glued to their computer screens as the complexity of the logistic operations grows.

The informationalization of society and the economy leads to the rise of counterforces, however.[3] Dematerialized labour, production and distribution create the desire for physical connectivity and interaction. Body culture, nightlife and tourism are recognizable expressions of this. They also are the most common socially-accepted forms of satisfying that desire. The great promise of the information age was that with the increasing possibilities of information and communication technology, the necessity and desire for physical contact – and accordingly mobility – could be drastically reduced, and thus ecological sustainability strengthened. Considering the above, this promise must be called into serious question.

Among other things during the ElectroSmog Festival, the ideas of the American futurologist Alvin Toffler were critically revaluated. In his adulated book *The Third Wave*, on 'the coming information age' written at the beginning of the 1980s, Toffler developed a vision that has become reality only in part.[4] One of Toffler's most attractive notions was the rise of a new type of living and work environment called 'the electronic cottage', a fusion of living and working made possible by advanced communication networks and an economy primarily oriented to information processing capacities. According to him, it was patently obvious that that the home/teleworker in the electronic cottage would have a mobility-reducing effect. For Toffler, another aspect was at least equally important: the saving of time. What with travelling to and from work having become unnecessary, time could be freed up for private life. This would lead to a revitalization of the *oikos* (family, the home) and, in a broader sense, to a revitalization of (local) community life.

The history of teleworking shows the opposite, however. Even after more than 30 years of research, endless series of pilot projects and massive investments, such a revitalization still has not got off the ground. The refinement of information technology, the rise of a new (under) class of information workers, and in particular the mobilization of high-quality information technology (laptops, WiFi, third and fourth generation wireless communications networks, smartphones, tablets and other handhelds) have not led to relief in the private sphere or to a revitalization of family and community life. The *oikos* has fallen hostage to the continual obligation to produce and the abolition of the separation between work and private life. And nowadays, the most advanced corporate practices are dominated by the 24-hour economy and just-in-time production and distribution methods. Mobility researchers have ascertained that in zones where the density of communication is greatest, mechanized mobility actually demonstrates the

3. 'Informationalization' refers to the dominance of information processing systems in society and the economy, of which 'computerization' is only one part. See: Manuel Castells, *The Rise of the Network Society* (Malden, MA: Blackwell Publishers, 1996).

4. Alvin Toffler, The Third Wave (New York: Bantam Books, 1980).

highest intensity.[5] Moreover, in the real-time economy, the shutting off of the ubiquitous flow of information is a strategic risk over which the lower echelons in the hierarchy of information workers have no say whatsoever.[6] Exit or sabotage are in principle the only possibilities they have to choose from.

5. For further elaboration of this idea, see among other things my essay 'Distance versus Desire' in the ElectroSmog Festival blog: www.electrosmogfestival.net/2010/11/28/distance-versus-desire-clearing-the-electrosmog.

6. For an introduction to this concept, consult the survey by *The Economist*, www.economist.com/node/949071?story_id=949071.

Polar Inertia

The concept of polar inertia can be described an accelerated modernity where everything happens at the speed of light without the need to go anywhere. As Paul Virilio, the philosopher of speed, so beautifully put it, the biological body itself is increasingly in a state of polar inertia in the midst of swirling data flows. As the flows of information are accelerated to immediacy, the point where the time it takes to transfer information is no longer perceptible, the body is forced into a state of total immobility. People who work at call centres will immediately recognize this experience. Architect Wim Nijenhuis even speaks of a 'compulsion to remain seated', which leads to countless physical aberrations, RSI, muscle deterioration, pain in the joints, bulging physical contours, or even hair loss caused by electronic screens lacking adequate protection from radiation!

The emerging regimes of mobility and immobility are characterized by extreme internal contradictions. The causes are so complex that attempts to put them into an unequivocal and linear perspective are doomed to fail from the start. At the same time, there is a great ecological and social pressure to find solutions for the disruptive forces released by these emerging regimes of mobility and immobility. What considerably complicates their analysis is the fact that they cannot be treated separately from the sweeping transformation to a global economy in a network society. In financial markets, for example, we have the picture of an almost completely autonomously functioning hypermobile system. At the same time, the opposite has proven true in the area of migration. Borders are opened only selectively, on the basis of specific socioeconomic criteria, but are increasingly closed to a majority of the world's population. The changing border regimes are producing new forms of mobility and immobility that have far-reaching ethical and political implications.

The causes and effects of the above are the subject of intense social debate and scientific research, and motivation for countless international activist movements. Out of the boundless desire for complete freedom of movement ('sovereign mobility') rise the contours of what Georges Bataille describes as a 'general economy' of im/mobility.[7] According to him, man is not a rationally thinking being. He is sooner led by abundance rather than wishing to let himself be limited

7. I borrowed the concept of 'general economy' from: Georges Bataille, *The Accursed Share: An Essay on General Economy*, Volume I, Consumption (originally, *La Part Maudite* [Paris: Les Éditions de Minuit, 1967]; here: New York: Zone Books, 1991).

by the force of economic circumstances. Such an ethic principle contrasts sharply with the political reality of the emerging regimes of mobility and immobility. Moreover, this political reality is at odds with the pursuit of ecological stability. A thorough analysis of both the emerging global political constellations and the desire for sovereign mobility is therefore necessary in order to avoid a crash and escape global gridlock.

Borders and Assemblages in a Worldwide Digital Age

In her book *Territory, Authority, Rights*, sociologist Saskia Sassen analyses the new worldwide constellations of territory, authority and rights (TAR) that have arisen hand-in-hand with digital networks.[8] Sassen shows how extremely complex interactions between local actors, authorities, economic players, transnational and institutional arrangements, in combination with new technologies and communicative capacities, play a role in the forming of new 'assemblages' in the age of digitalization and globalization. She concentrates her analysis in particular on two 'social arenas' that are also of crucial importance for the emerging regimes of mobility and immobility: the global financial system and new forms of international politics that are rooted in local places in the worldwide data networks.[9]

The global financial system seems mainly to be characterized by a combination of placelessness and hypermobility, caused by the emergence and integration of electronic data networks, according to Sassen. With their mix of speed and interconnectity, says Sassen, it is not easy to demonstrate that these markets are embedded in anything social. There seems to be a possibility of an almost purely technical domain that for the most part functions autonomously and separately from the social context. Its autonomy is further reinforced by the growing role played by academic financial economics in the invention of new derivatives, the most widely used instrument in contemporary financial markets, as well as softwaring that carries out the actual transactions.[10]

In such an autonomously functioning system of networks that give real-time access (without any loss of time) to all relevant financial data, the location from which these activities are developed no longer seems to play a role. However, as Sassen points out, the structure of this financial system is much more emphatically differentiated than the above picture would suggest. First of all, the increasing complexity of the instruments and the technological knowledge that is necessary in order to let these markets function are of such a nature that they raise the need for what Sassen calls 'cultures of interpretation'.

This expertise is not available to the same degree everywhere, so that the financial centres where it is abundantly at hand become more important. The academic embeddedness of the financial system also has its limitations. It does not give a completely adequate picture of the dynamics of derivatives trading, which is also partly influenced by local factors. What's more, it is not always

8. Saskia Sassen, *Territory, Authority, Rights: From Medieval to Global Assemblages* (Princeton, NJ: Princeton University Press, 2006).

9. Ibid., 343.

10. Ibid., 348.

possible to unequivocally determine the accuracy of risk assessment models and the effectiveness of individual firms.[11] Blindly trusting [11. Ibid., 355.] in software instruments is thus not wise. Financial centres where academic institutions, businesses, financiers, technological firms, local authorities (supervisors) and technological infrastructures form nested communities are therefore becoming increasingly important. Only together, and in mutual interweaving, do they have the possibility of operating effectively in this new global financial system.

The fact that the financial centres do not function autonomously is also shown by the guiding principle of derivative trading: the individual risks connected with investing in specific companies and projects are shared by multiple players in the market. Moreover, these are also shared between different territories and economic zones within the global financial network. Business risks are thus absorbed in the system as 'market risks'.

Because of this, the market as a whole is considered better capable of covering local risks and absorbing eventual disappointing results. The problem that arises here, as the recent financial crisis has shown, is that if all of these local risks become too great when taken together, the hypermobility and interwovenness of transnational capital flows is precisely what can threaten the functioning, even the continued existence, of the financial system as a whole. Likewise, the increased importance of local financial centres such as Wall Street, City of London, Tokyo and Frankfurt

a/M that operate in a global financial market paves the way to the creation of hypermonopolies or oligopoly. If they are too strongly affected by risky derivatives, they can suddenly tumble and set off a cataclysmic downward spiral in markets across the globe (in real-time). This happened, for example, in 2008, after the failure of Lehman Brothers Holdings Inc.

One specific firm localized in one specific territorial context can thus spark a worldwide financial crisis (although the present crisis sooner demonstrates a systemwide failure of the derivatives trade). Regional and territorial authorities, particularly national and local financial supervisors, thereby gain extraordinary importance for the functioning of the global financial system. Thus the financial system must be characterized as a hybrid type marked by electronic networks (placeless) and territorial insertions (place-determined). Their mutual connectivity generates a social arrangement in which the global system ultimately is embedded.[12] [12. Ibid., 349.]

While the global financial system seems to have become borderless, it thus by no means has become placeless. Paradoxically enough, the very same authority that traditionally is responsible for policing the borders and the machinery of the state is now playing a crucial role in the functioning of this global system – as supervisor and risk manager.

Cross-Border Horizontal Network Connections

Sassen points out that the local can be multiply scaled. According to her, specific local phenomena, organizations and actions can be constituted on several levels simultaneously – in a particular local setting, but also in different countries or regions, or within one country in different sectors or on different levels of society. This can generate global formations that develop as a network of horizontal connections. These horizontal networks contrast strongly with the hierarchal vertical arrangements typical of transnational entities such as the International Monetary Fund and the World Trade Organization and that generally come about through the (vertical) authority of the nation-state.[13]

13. Ibid., 365.

These horizontal networks lead to possibilities for a new type of cross-border politics that is at once deeply local and digitally connected on a global scale. Telecommunications create new linkages across space that bypass the traditional hierarchies of scale: local to national to international. Locally rooted actors gain immediate access to one another, independent of where they are located, and form networks of relations around shared issues, interests and identities. Concrete examples include local human rights and environmental movements that are mainly active locally but through the 'network of relations' around shared social issues can work and communicate directly with one another and exert greater pressure on local authorities. These sorts of local movements become, as Sassen puts it, 'global through the knowing multiplication of local practices'.[14]

14. Ibid., 375.

Although this kind of cross-border, horizontal network connection is generally less formalized than the hierarchical organizational structures of the WTO type – the traditional target of anti-globalization protesters – this does not mean that these horizontal ties are only reserved for informal civilian and activist initiatives. Nor do they play a marginal role in the new transnational politics and economic constellations of the globalized world. Influential actors such as multinational enterprises, international lobby groups, NGOs and transnational institutionalized political movements can also avail themselves of these ties and accordingly bypass traditional hierarchical (control) structures. The mix of digital networks, platforms and transactions with their own social logics guides the use of new technologies. According to Sassen, this signals the existence of complex assemblages that form specific spatiotemporal orders, each with their own capacities, possibilities and vulnerabilities. These are hybrid constellations of local, territorially-bound elements and networked, place-less electronic connections. They form the basis for the emerging regimes of mobility and immobility in (transnational) physical and social exchange.

From Now On, the Border is Omnipresent

Contrary to what is often assumed, with the advent of the new global constellations – or assemblages, as Sassen calls them – the nation-state and its borders are by no means disappearing. On the contrary, they are undergoing a fundamental transformation. Of note in this regard is that Sassen character-izes institutions like the IMF and the WTO as temporary indicators of that transformation, not as the embodiment thereof, as alter-globalists and protest actions around summit meetings generally suggest. According to her, the nation-state actually plays a crucial role in this transformative process and in the functioning of the new political and territorial assemblages that are arising from it. Guaranteeing the sovereignty of the national territory and guarding the border was always the privilege of the nation-state; it is also the privilege of the state to give it up. Countries are opening their doors for foreign investment and flows of capital, and governments are developing specific visa regimes for knowledge workers, or conversely, for unskilled and low-paid work. They are also making agreements with other governments for the transference of the production of goods and services to low-wage countries. Through this selective opening of the border, new forms of mobility and immobility are emerging with respect to knowledge, capital and labour. Digital networks are making such selective openings possible and operational, and creating new spatial orders, such as the special economic zones in China, as well as new temporal orders, such as temporary work and residence permits and differentiated visa regimes.

The exclusive right to a territory for a homogenized population (language, culture, ethnicity), the classical project of the nineteenth-century nation-state, is being relinquished in favour of a more differentiated social, economic and technological profile. Privileges such as the right of establishment and/or residence,

access to knowledge, infrastructure and services are granted to certain actors (often multinational enterprises that want to open new branches), or to certain social groups (knowledge workers), while these are denied to other groups, such as migrants and civilians who do not fit the desired profile.

The governance and control over this process requires new informational systems that enable a ubiquitous regime of information, access, administration, profiling and data surveillance. Sassen speaks in this regard of a shift from geographical borders to 'embedded bordering capabilities' operating both subnationally – for example, around special investment zones – and transnationally, in international trade agreements. Specific rights and juridical protection provisos are being de-nationalized. In this regard, the international human rights organization offers much weaker provisos for protection than do the WTO regulations, which protect the cross-border circulation of professionals.[15]

The border, once considered the geographical demarcation of a territory, and the means by which the state asserted exclusive authority over its physical domain, is folding inward, as it were, and transforming into a filter that only gives certain groups access to civil privileges and rights. The emerging border regimes operate both inside and outside the nation-state and its territory, and are dependent on the application of networked data profiles and an omnipresent surveillance infrastructure. Consequently, every person, as a professional, citizen or migrant, can

15. Ibid., 417.

be granted or denied access to specific rights and privileges, and also to territories that no longer are only nationally determined, but can assume any desired form or scale, from local to global. With the help of new tracing technologies such as RFID and biometric scanning, freedom of movement is determined by the representation (the profile) of the biological body in the database. At the same time, however, the possibility also arises for individual citizens to free themselves of 'state capture' by making use of the new 'denationalized' rights and privileges.

Through the coupling of data files, such as in the Netherlands' euphemistically named 'citizen service number' (BSN), the 'data body' functions as a filter for the state-sanctioned national social and economic traffic. At the same time, it operates supranationally, on account of the new database systems that have been set up for the purpose of controlling international passenger traffic, such as the 'Schengen Information System' developed for the European Schengen Area. The privilege of freedom of movement from place to place within this area is granted to citizens of the Schengen countries and holders of a valid visa, while the same databases that sanction this privilege are used to prevent undesirable 'aliens' from crossing the outer border or track them down within the territory of the Schengen Area.

Sovereignty and the Economy of Abundance

A returning question in regard to the emerging regimes of mobility and immobility is whether mobility should be considered a right or a privilege, by which the ecological perspective collides with the ethical principle of freedom of movement. Attempts to change the direction of the growth curve of hypermobility in advanced and developing economies have met with virtually no success. And influencing behaviour by enhancing ecological (self) awareness also offers no effective counterbalance to people's desire to move around freely and travel without restriction. Various practical interventions to achieve a more even distribution of mobility have by no means proven capable of curbing this exponential growth. Only one mechanism seems capable of activating an immediate attitude of behavioural correction: the imminent scarcity of (energy) sources. Once their price threatens to grow too high and the ecological limits become apparent, the logic of the market unrelentingly sets in and forces a change of behaviour for economic reasons.

Unfortunately, human behaviour has proved to be anything but rationally determined. The strongest criticism of the utilitarian logic of rational economic theory, which is based on the division of scarce means for the benefit of maximum satisfaction of demand, is formulated by the French philosopher and writer Georges Bataille in his essay on 'general economy'.[16] In the first part of that essay, Bataille contrasts his notion of a 'general economy' with what he terms the 'classical economy'. Bataille brilliantly substitutes 'sovereignty' for the utilitarian logic

16. See: Georges Bataille, *La Part Maudite* (Paris: Les Éditions de Minuit, 1967).

directed at efficiency, and 'abundance' for (the economy of) scarcity. He makes short work of the utilitarian principle. An activity with practical usefulness always derives its significance from what it is useful for, after all, not from the activity itself. To a large extent, therefore, that activity is also intrinsically meaningless or valueless. Bataille observes that, on the contrary, in natural processes the most crucial activities, such as reproduction, are characterized by an excessive expenditure of energy. Not efficiency but abundance is the guiding principle here, not production but (boundless) consumption. 'Life beyond utility is the domain of sovereignty,' according to Bataille. Only by ridding our activities of the yoke of that utility is it possible to come in contact with what really – intrinsically – is of 'sovereign' importance for us.

The technical philosopher Lewis Mumford also observes that human beings, with their excessively developed brains, always have an extreme surplus of (mental) energy that must be 'displaced' in one way or another.[17] Rational criteria play only an extremely limited role in the expending of this abundant (life) energy. Suppression of these essentially libidinal forces inevitably turns against the social order and can even eclipse the urge for self preservation.

17. See: Lewis Mumford, *The Myth of the Machine: Technics and Human Development* (New York: Harcourt Brace Jovanovich Inc., 1966), 14-47.

The freedom of movement (the right to unlimited mobility) is a constituting element of this 'sovereignty' in the Bataillian sense. 'Sovereign mobility' is a cherished achievement of the affluent and the self-emancipating sectors of the global society. It is soon considered an acquired right and not a privilege that simply could be given up in the face of material limitations. The sovereign body wants to be able to move freely, and the cost of that mobility will ultimately hardly form an effective restriction in curbing the boundless desire to move freely from place to place. The boundlessness of this desire also explains why the character of the human relation with the automobile is much more libidinal and excessive than utilitarian and rational.

Fault Lines in the Emerging Regimes of Worldwide Hypermobility

In the search for a responsible development of mobility, the balance between ethics, sovereignty and sustainability is extremely precarious. The desire for sovereign mobility and the necessity of attaining ecological and energetic stability are advancing straight towards a head-on collision. Such a crash scenario has incalculable consequences for the ecology, the economy and society. However, we should not resign ourselves to doom scenarios, which are based on the impossibility of taking action in the emerging global constellations. Doing nothing, not intervening, is not an option, nor do attempts to deny the desire for sovereign mobility lead to solutions.

The internal contradictions in the emerging regimes of mobility and immobility elicit tensions that ultimately will turn against them. Possibilities for intervention present themselves precisely where the contradictions become manifest. These are the collision points where local realities and global dynamics collide, where people are confronted with the fact that they are excluded from the privileges of sovereign transnational hypermobility. More than anything, the nature of these intervention possibilities is local. The complexity, intransparency and ungovernable quality of the emerging global assemblages of territory, authority and rights that Sassen analyses reinforces the importance of the local as an anchorage point both for transnational organizations and local civic movements.

The immediate effects of the emerging global regimes manifest themselves at the local level: guarding of the border, migration, registration, surveillance and identity checks, the flows of capital, energy, goods and people (or their absence). This intensified role of the local is further strengthened by the growing importance of organization at the city level compared to that at the national level. This is the preeminent place where the forces that produce and guide the emerging global consolations converge.

In this new urban context of intense and digital global connectivity, it is possible for local initiatives, municipal and regional governments, citizens' initiatives, activist groups, NGOs and other non-state actors to connect up with similar initiatives at other locations. They can share methods, knowledge and experience with each other, coordinate actions, or collectively exert pressure on national and transnational institutions. The particular strength of horizontally organized network connections is that these local actors have direct access to one another and to each other's knowledge, methods and local capacities. Whereas in former times, international influence could only be exerted through national authorities, nowadays traditional hierarchical constructions of authority are being bypassed. Out of what Sassen calls the deliberate multiplication of local practices – the multiscalar nature of the local – global consolations can arise that generate an effective counterforce for combating undesirable effects of globalization.

The local level is the logical starting point for a nonlinear search for a balance between the desire for sovereign mobility and the necessity for ecological and social stability. The detention camps for undesirable aliens are built locally and deportation centres burn in the local memory. Traffic clogs the streets in front of our doors, but our own cars are often parked there too, while above us in the polluted atmosphere the deafening roar of the air transport continues unabated. The emerging regimes of mobility and immobility take root in the local, and they can be addressed in the multiplicity of languages and dialects spoken there.

The crash scenario cannot be ruled out just like that, however. The alarming picture that emerged from the opening discussion of the ElectroSmog Festival, of a planet hurtling at breakneck speed towards global gridlock, permits no resignation. The crash of the present system of hypermobility can as yet end in a fatal worldwide standstill.

Burning cell, K wing, Schiphol-East Detention Center, 27 October 2005, still from the campaign video *Free Ahmed Isa*.

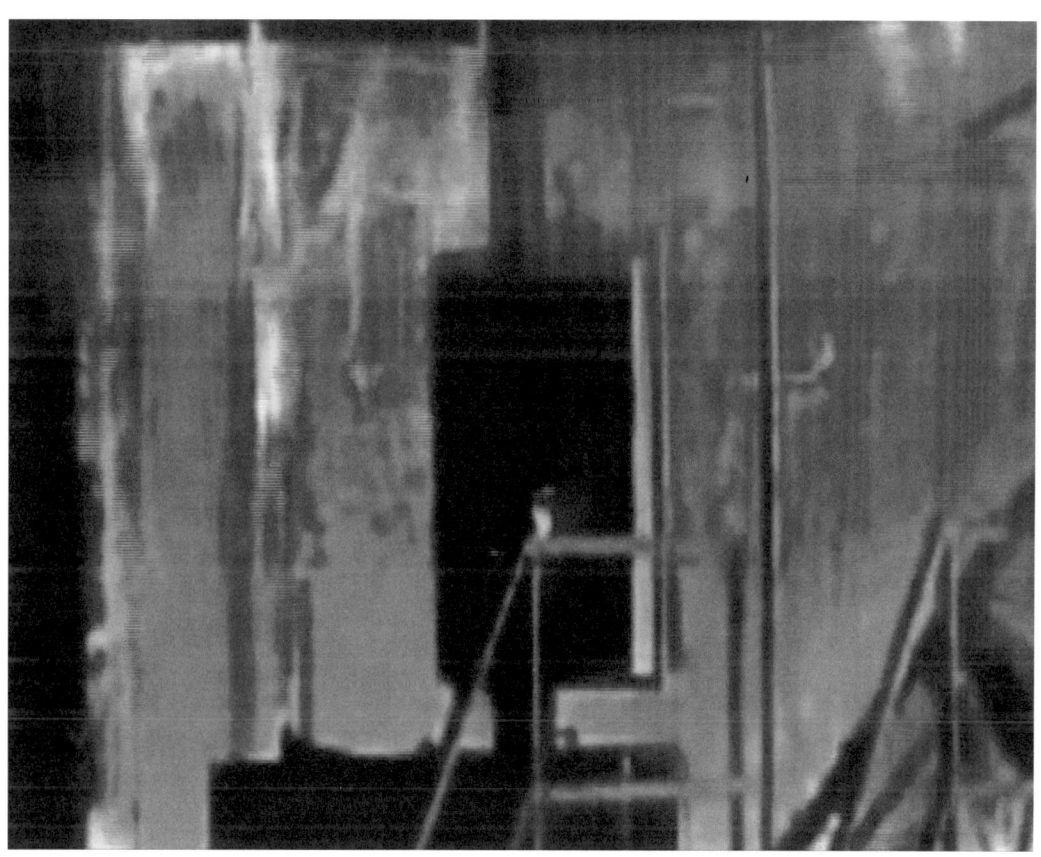

Marc Schuilenburg

The Right to *Terroir*

Place and Identity in Times of Immigration and Globalization

In order to describe a sense of connection with the local without denying dynamic physical and virtual interpersonal relationships, philosopher Marc Schuilenburg introduces the term *terroir*. Introducing *terroir* as a right makes it possible for new subjectifications to arise, with which the relationship between identity and places can be restored in this age of immigration and globalization.

The discussion about how a specific urban practice can lay claim to a distinct identity has thus far been neglected in the social sciences literature about immigration and globalization. Researchers have written plenty about the way in which immigration and globalization take place, but you could replace these terms with other general terms such as mobility. These writers also usually point out the influence of information and communication processes and the movement of people, goods and capital that this sets in motion. For example, in *Modernity at Large*, the Indian anthropologist Arjun Appadurai demonstrates how narratives and images from television, Internet and films prompt people to leave their homelands and head out in search of other destinations.[1] An important theme within that same literature is the debunking of the

1. A. Appadurai, *Modernity at Large: Cultural Dimensions of Globalization* (Minneapolis: University of Minnesota Press, 1996).

myth that the local dimension of life has disappeared because of migration and globalization. The interpretation of the local is indeed exposed to external influences, and the authority and sovereignty of national government has waned considerably, but in practice it turns out that local connections remain important for matters such as place and identity. Hence the global and the local find themselves in a permanent field of mutual tension. The mirroring of that tension, or the breaching of existing orders and the institution of new structures, is known as a process of deterritorialization and reterritorialization.

In this essay I examine the process of deterritorialization and reterritorialization on the basis of the term 'rhizomatics', which was coined by the French philosophers Gilles Deleuze and Félix Guattari. To this end I primarily explore the reterritorialization aspect: the embedding of the local by means of establishing the creation of new relationships. By introducing the concept of *terroir* I introduce a conceptual shift in Deleuze and Guattari's legacy, proposing the term as a useful alternative in discussions about the consequences of migration and globalization.[2] This touches on the demise of traditional community

2. My thanks to Mireille Hildebrandt for indicating the significance of *terroir*.

relations and the alienation of the existence of the average person. It will become apparent that *terroir* allows a deeper reading of the relationship between place and identity in the context of these mobility processes. Finally, with the 'right to *terroir*' I advocate consideration of the productive aspect of these processes and thus for new articulations of communality.

Rhizome

The current debates about migration and globalization revolve to a large degree around the tension between the global and the local, between the homogeneous and the heterogeneous, or between the universal and the personal. More than 35 years ago, in order to thematize that tension, Deleuze and Guattari introduced the term 'rhizome' in their 1975 study into the work of the author Franz Kafka.[3] A year later

3. G. Deleuze and F. Guattari, *Kafka: Pour une littérature mineure* (Paris:

they elaborated this concept further in 'Rhizome', a short essay which also appeared in an adapted form as the introduction to *Mille plateaux* (*A Thousand Plateaus*). The word 'rhizome' is a botanical term that literally means a rootstock. This rootstock is exceptional in that it grows horizontally rather than vertically and spreads its roots below ground over great distances in the form of inextricable tangles. This makes it impossible to trace back the structure of a rhizome to a single origin, core or centre. It has no beginning or end, but seems to simply start somewhere; it is always 'in the middle (*milieu*), between things, inter-being (*inter-être*), *intermezzo*,' write Deleuze and Guattari in *A Thousand Plateaus*.[4]

I have no desire to hold a philosophical disquisition about the appropriate or inappropriate use of the term here, but I do want to emphasize that Deleuze and Guattari contrast the image of a rhizome against a mind-set based on a tree structure, as encountered in Plato's two-worlds theory and Hegelian dialectics. This 'tree-thinking' is founded on a metaphysics in which the process-driven character of reality is always reduced to a single unit or a new whole. Proceeding from this, it then establishes a series of antitheses: 'subject-object', 'individual-group', 'personal-social', 'normal-abnormal' and so on. By extension, this thinking sets itself apart from the idea that reality *an sich* is never stable or static. Whitehead called this the 'fallacy of bifurcation', the attempt to subdivide reality into conceptually strict distinctions or predefined principles.[5] A major shortcoming of such an approach is that it adroitly but rather unsatisfactorily sidesteps an important problem, namely the process that precedes and shapes every form of arrangement. Hence it cannot explain how a specific structure has come about and acquired precisely this set of properties and no other. In response to this, rhizomatic thought actually operates through a multitude of intertwinings and intersections that are not predetermined. In other words this model assumes that everything 'differs' and views reality as a process that is in constant flux: its significance can only be determined in retrospect.

With the term 'rhizome', Deleuze and Guattari found a highly original image for phenomena for which there was still a shortage of adequate concepts. In the sense of migration and flows of capital, the fairly abstract concept of the rhizome has, not surprisingly, acquired a concrete and empirical translation. Well-known authors such as Manuel Castells, Saskia Sassen and David Harvey argue that these flows expand in every direction and are constantly crossing, influencing and reinforcing each other on a global scale. Another characteristic is that they mobilize and reconstitute the world, through migrants having to win their place in their new city from exist-

Éditions de Minuit, 1975); trans. D. Polan as *Kafka: Towards a Minor Literature* (Minneapolis: University of Minnesota Press, 1986).

4. G. Deleuze and F. Guattari, *Capitalisme et schizophrénie*, vol. 2 of *Mille plateaux* (Paris: Éditions de Minuit, 1980), 30; trans. B. Massumi as *A Thousand Plateaus*, vol. 2 of *Capitalism and Schizophrenia* (London/New York: Continuum, 1987).

5. A.N. Whitehead, *The Concept of Nature* (Cambridge: Cambridge University Press, 1964 [1920]).

ing inhabitants, for example. It is also typical that the greater and the stronger the links with the local, the greater the chance that the same flows will continue to exist. Deleuze and Guattari rank among the few philosophers to have pointed out the interdependence of two processes in this regard: reterritorialization (connecting) and deterritorialization (disconnecting). In a more general sense, a rhizome is a movement that deterritorializes an old structure and reterritorializes it into a new structure. Deterritorialization is about liberating certain meanings and functions from existing relationships, which in most cases means that a field of dispositions is broken open by introducing new openings and establishing different connections. Such an uncoupling can, for example, arise around a specific theme – take the transfer of work to low-wage countries like Vietnam and India, for instance. However, the momentum of decomposition always corrects itself. Deleuze and Guattari call this reterritorialization, a process that brings about a unification of a social space, a certain cohesion of place and identity among the persons present. For example, the South Central district of Los Angeles has metamorphosed fairly swiftly from an African-American neighbourhood into a typical Latino environment with all the attendant characteristics.

From Rhizome to Territory

Thinking rhizomatically opens up other perspectives for looking into the question of place and identity in an age of immigration and globalization. The meaning of these concepts has long been derived from the symbols and rituals of the nation-state. The state's values and norms were used to imbue meaning at the level of identity. In the latter decades of the twentieth century, the rhizomatic character of mobility was praised enthusiastically as a critique of this modernistic body of thought. A boundless world would be established in which one wall after another – ideological, physical, mental – would crumble. With that the idea of a global identity no longer defined by nation, family, language or religion would take root: the citizen was a world citizen and trade was world trade. Nowadays people think that matters are somewhat more complicated after all. This does not apply only at economic and political levels; it turns out that globalization bears an individual and emotional price tag as well. This makes it easy to link the idea of a world citizen with a 'McDonaldization' of our culture and thus with an increasing lack of identity and an uprooted existence. A discussion about place and identity must, in my opinion, navigate a middle course between the two positions. In a liquid world, to use Zygmunt Bauman's terminology,[6] how can the urge for community be actualized without lapsing into a naïve world citizenship on the one hand and a conservative debate about national values and norms on the other?

6. Z. Bauman, *Liquid Modernity* (Cambridge: Polity Press, 2000).

Proceeding from the process of deterritorialization and reterritoriali-

The Right to Terroir

zation, I wish to limit myself here to a discussion of actual places and more especially to the social context of two typical examples of the contemporary struggle for place and identity: the gated community and the *terrain vague*. What kind of communality is taking shape here? What signification is occurring in these spaces? The gated community is a continuation of a series of protected environments that enjoy access to a rich concentration of infrastructural services and amenities. This often involves a continuous spatial network of places with distinct social, cultural, physical and functional characteristics, such as residential domains, offices, VIP lounges, private jets, SUVs, hotels and golf courses. Examples of gated communities, where wealthy sections of the population fence themselves off from poorer city quarters, are to be found in Asian, African and Latin American cities. The densely populated city's chaos of traffic, scorching heat, criminality and noise pollution reigns outside, while inside one finds every imaginable amenity for a 'city within a city', a complex that is relatively independent of its location and immediate surroundings. The inhabitants of such complexes have 24/7 access to babysitters, support staff, a laundry service, a newspaper and magazine delivery service, clubhouses, car parks, car maintenance and shuttle-bus transportation. The physical traces that exclusion leaves behind in the process are typical: fences, barriers, moats, guarded gates and ID checks. The upshot is that groups which are less mobile – e.g. the unemployed, beggars, the homeless, drug addicts and failed asylum seekers – are perceived as a threat and denied access to the on-site facilities.[7]

7. M. Schuilenburg, 'Citizenship Revisited: Denizens and Margizens', *Peace Review on Citizenship and Social Justice*, vol. 20 (2008) no. 3, 358-365.

The term I will use for the counterpart of the gated community is *terrain vague*. This term comes from the Spanish architect and critic Ignasi de Solà-Morales and refers to a zone that still has no fixed identity, a sort of between-land or residual space.[8] The intriguing thing about this term is that the word *terrain* refers to an enclosed space, while *vague* relates to the disruption of that same space. This dual meaning builds on the idea of a Temporary Autonomous Zone (TAZ), places meant for short-term use before local authorities seize control with their regulatory mania. In Hakim Bey's inspiring 1991 essay, *The Temporary Autonomous Zone*, he demonstrates that such places have a temporary openness allowing different groups to make unrestricted and undisturbed use of them: undesirable visitors are not excluded here. Like Solà-Morales, Bey was strongly influenced by the rhizomatic thinking of Deleuze and Guattari, and in this respect he speaks of 'a temporary but actual location in time and a temporary but actual location in space.'[9] This vaguely defined place, whether a vacant, unused plot of land in the suburbs or an abandoned industrial site, has not been officially or defini-

8. I. de Solà-Morales, 'Terrain Vague', *Quaderns*, (1996) no. 212, 'Water-Land/Tierra-Agua', 34-44.

9. H. Bey, T.A.Z.: *The Temporary Autonomous Zone, Ontological Anarchy, Poetic Terrorism* (New York: Autonomedia, 1991), 109.

tively appropriated as yet and assumes a temporary elaboration. An important function of these fallow sites is that they provide space for collective activities and shelter for society's marginal groups. Familiar examples include quarters of East Berlin and the Free State of Christiania in Copenhagen, but autonomous associations or a virtual environment like the *World of Warcraft* video game can also fulfil the functions of a *terrain vague*.

It should be obvious that a gated community has little to do with what has been known as 'the public interest' since the eighteenth century. It is not an adequate response to a public problem such as a lack of safety, but primarily groups together the self-interest of its inhabitants. In addition, the *terrain vague* has much in common with a utopian-nostalgic conception of pre-modern forms of living and assumes a genuine desire for pirates' islands and free states. In any event, it is evident that what applies to the gated community also holds true for the *terrain vague*, where people lay claim to place and identity by taking destiny into their own hands. The principal effect of this – and this is the pivotal idea – is that a collective form of subjectivity evolves in these places. Living together in a zone that is demarcated from the outside world, such as a guarded urban district or a luxury housing project, can thus be traced back to a private need, but it is also defined by a community spirit and the wish to establish a collective style of living. In the case of the *terrain vague* this also involves the sharing of

interests and a process of self-organization that, however transient, results in a new collectivity emerging there. This does raise the question of which concept can be employed to make concrete the claim to such places. For this I want to introduce a new term: *terroir*. While rhizomes continue to proliferate below ground, *terroir* relates to the specific qualities of a place, in a manner akin to rocks being able to assume the colour of the earth.

From Territory to *Terroir*

Anyone who has explored the world of wine must have come across the concept of *terroir*, which refers to everything associated with the grapevine's environment. Wine lovers consider *terroir* to be the most important hallmark of a fine wine. *Terroir* has been causing plenty of furore among wine tasters in recent decades, but it is one of the most complex terms in the world of wine. Surprisingly enough, there is no adequate English translation for the concept. Sometimes 'terrain' is used, and one can find examples of its translation as 'soil', 'land' and 'ground', but each of these terms is insufficiently specific to describe all the aspects of *terroir* fully. To gain a better understanding it is useful to look at the original French term properly. In the 1694 *Dictionnaire de l'Académie Françoise, dédié au Roy* it is defined as the typical quality or specificity (*odeur, goût*) of wine that is related to the quality of a place. Etymologically, the word *terroir* is a conflation of *tioroer* and *tieroir*, which are both derived from the Latin *ter-*

ratorium, a variant of *territorium*. The Latin *terra* means 'earth' or 'land', but what is it that actually contributes to a good *terroir*?

Terroir is related first and foremost to geographical and geological factors. In that regard it concerns the region where a vineyard is situated. It more specifically concerns the soil (clay, slate, sandstone, stones, limestone, marl, and so on) on which the vines grow. For example, how quickly can the soil absorb rainwater? In this regard you could also speak of a locale's natural capital. Surprisingly enough, the properties of a soil on, for example, the west side of a vineyard can be completely different to the soil on the south side of that same vineyard. The soil's colour might be different there and that, in turn, plays an important role in the absorption of sunlight. Dark soils absorb more sunlight than lighter soils and are more suitable to grape varieties for producing red wines. *Terroir* also denotes climatological factors, namely a country's climate and the average number of hours of sunshine and rain that a parcel of land is exposed to. *Terroir* is also linked to biological factors such as the quality of the vines and the grape variety: the vines must be able to withstand drought, and white grapes require less sun than red, for example.

Human factors are also part of the equation. The craftsmanship, the whole ensemble of knowledge and expertise and passion for the work, to quote Richard Sennett,[10] plays an important part

10. R. Sennett, *The Craftsman* (New Haven/London: Yale University Press, 2008).

in the improvement of the conditions for the growth of the vines. Take, for example, the construction of terraces on steep slopes in order to gain greater solar exposure and the way the land is worked, such as the tackling of weeds and moulds. It is difficult to give a complete enumeration of human activities. The important thing is that *terroir* cannot exist without cultural and social capital, something that was already recognized by Louis XIV's military strategist, Sébastien Le Prestre de Vauban, in the seventeenth century: 'Left uncultivated, the best soil is no different to poor soil.'

There is, to conclude, a mystical aspect. People from many cultures regard wine and its consumption as a mystical symbol. 'I am the wine that I drink, and the cupbearer,' as the Persian mystic Abû Yazîd wrote in the ninth century. And in relation to *terroir* itself, the American geologist James Wilson mentions a spiritual aspect, which he describes as 'the joys, the heartbreak, the pride, the sweat, and the frustrations of its history,'[11] an aspect sometimes referred to as 'the soul of the place'.

11. J.E. Wilson, *Terroir: The Role of Geology, Climate, and Culture in the Making of French Wines* (London: Reed Consumer Books, 1998), 55.

In short, *terroir* is more than the soil alone; it points to social, mental and ecological processes – what Guattari terms an 'ecosophy' in *Chaosmose*[12] – which are always acting simultaneously and mutually affecting each other. No matter how different these

12. F. Guattari, *Chaosmose* (Paris: Galilée, 1992); trans. P. Bains and J. Pefanis as *Chaosmosis: An Ethico-Aesthetic Paradigm* (Bloomington and Indianapolis: Indiana University Press, 1995).

processes may seem on the surface, they come together in the idea that under certain circumstances a specific place acquires meaning and direction and that these circumstances can also, to a certain extent, be altered so that the whole assumes a different actualization. Let us turn once again to the tradition of wine making. Technically speaking, parcels of land that are mere dozens of metres apart can produce wines that taste totally different, so the wine from the one plot is a completely different product to that from an adjacent plot.[13] This raises the question of whether one can talk in a comparable sense about other forms of organization and identification in our everyday surroundings.

13. *Terroir* is now also used to denote the unique character of other products, such as the *terroirs* of fruit, tea, coffee, cheese and tequila. See, for example, J. Avelino et al., 'Effects of Slope Exposure, Altitude and Yield on Coffee Quality in Two Altitude Terroirs of Costa Rica, Orosi and Santa María de Dota', *Journal of the Science of Food and Agriculture*, vol. 85 (2005) no. 11, 1869-1876; H. Paxson, 'Locating Value in Artisan Cheese: Reverse Engineering Terroir for New-World Landscapes', *American Anthropologist*, vol. 112 (2010) no. 3, 444-457; S. Bowen and A.V. Zapata, 'Geographical Indications, Terroir, and Socioeconomic and Ecological Sustainability: The Case of Tequila', *Journal of Rural Studies*, vol. 25 (2009) no. 1, 108-119.

The Right to *Terroir*

However scanty the signs may be, there is reason enough to take up the characteristics of *terroir* and thus give a positive thrust to the question of place and identity in times of immigration and globalization. It requires but a small step to translate the social, mental and ecological processes of *terroir* into an urban context and apply them to the varied multitude of meaningful places and groups of people in the city who often touch one another but do not overlap. The intriguing thing about places such as a gated community or a *terrain vague* is that there is a communal 'basis', a social cohesion or interpersonal connection expressed in the values and norms that apply locally, as is the case with private residential domains where inhabitants choose to encounter like-minded people. Surprisingly, it turns out that safety and security concerns are not a reason for this. Many people are more likely to be at a loss as to how to deal with the modern city's anonymity, so the craving for 'hospitableness' fosters an environment in which social contacts and neighbourhood bonds are formed more easily.[14] A second reason for *terroir* being of interest in this context is the fact that it allows for new subjectifications, in the form of a collective signification, for example. This is evident in the temporary use of zones undergoing restructuring as places to garden and recreate, which is a fine example of a *terrain vague*. Subjectification is produced somewhere in the interaction among the social, mental and ecological processes and must then be reproduced repeatedly in order for it to survive.[15] Communality is thus the interim 'outcome' of a local group process.

14. L. Bijlsma, M. Galle and J. Tennekes, 'De herbergzame ruimte van de stadswijk', *Justitiële verkenningen*, (2010) no. 5, 90-111.

15. The project initiated by the Dutch philosopher Henk Oosterling in Rotterdam's Bloemhof neighbourhood offers a fine example of this. Since 2008, children at the Bloemhof primary school have been taking lessons in judo, gardening, cookery and philosophy. The aim is to train pupils in skills and thus teach them to experience self-confidence and self-respect. See H. Oosterling, *Woorden als daden. Rotterdam Vakmanstad/ Skillcity 2007-2009* (Rotterdam: Jap Sam Books, 2009).

To avoid any misunderstanding, *terroir* does not correspond with a notion like *Blut und Boden* – 'Blood and Soil' – which refers to the link between descent (blood) and the land that would nourish a people. The vast majority of the world population has become far too mobile for such a static – and often radically nationalistic – definition. This means that mobility does not relate to migration and globalization alone; because of tele- and automobilization, a virtual and physical increase in scale has taken place in many people's social lives. Recognizing the universal problem of mobility therefore calls for a contextualizing approach to place and identity that shifts the emphasis to the dynamic relations between objects and persons. Henri Lefebvre's classic championing of the 'right to the city' can serve as a starting point for this. The right to the city, writes Lefebvre, is 'like a cry and a demand . . . a transformed and renewed right to urban life.'[16] This right implies a claim to places rich in qualities and utilitarian value, where there is time for encounter and social intercourse without commercial motives or a profit-and-loss mentality being involved. Lefebvre formulated the right to the city in response to the urbanization occurring around him and out of a desire to organize the social, economic and political relations in the city, as well as the decisions made about them, differently. Of particular relevance here is that he wanted to append this right to the right to education, to work and to a minimum standard of living.

16. H. Lefebvre, *Writings on Cities*, trans. E. Kofman and E. Lebas (Oxford: Blackwell Publishing, 1996), 158. See also H. Lefebvre, *Le droit à la ville* (suivi de) *Espace et politique* (Paris: Éditions Anthropos, 1972).

What is now becoming especially apparent is how people can assert a right or lay claim to their actualization of *terroir*, in other words to the creation of social relationships and ways of life. In that regard several theorists refer to the production of 'the communal' (*le commun*), which is established via social connections and encounters. *Le commun* is strictly speaking what makes or produces a community, and not simply an attribute shared by all of its members. An entitlement to this is, in my opinion, made possible by translating Levebvre's argument from the 1970s into the 'right to *terroir*'.[17] Under the right to *terroir* we must then understand rights such as the 'right to community' (organizing life in small and meaningful places), the 'right to difference' (a tolerance towards practices that diverge from one another), the 'right to openness' (refraining from determining how places should look in several decades' time) and the 'right to citizenship' (linking rights and responsibilities to local practices). These rights tie in extremely well with the rhizomatic and opaque structure of migration and globalization. How one then conjoins and interlinks all these different *terroirs* is a pre-eminently practical challenge.

17. Here it should be noted that recourse to the 'right to *terroir*' will proceed according to the rules and procedures of national government. In that sense the nation-state continues to serve an important function. The influence of citizens is largely achieved via the institutional framework of the nation-state, whether this involves elections or the judiciary.

Brian Holmes

Do Containers Dream of Electric People?

The Social Form of Just-in-Time Production

Cultural critic Brian Holmes analyses the genesis of the distributional machinery of intermodal transport that circulates commodities through the global economy.

What are the implications for our way of life, both for people tied to a particular area and for migrants? Is it possible to escape capitalism's laws of motion?

Once adopted into the production process of capital, the means of labour passes through different metamorphoses, whose culmination is the machine, or rather, an automatic system of machinery, set in motion by an automaton, a moving power that moves itself; this automaton consisting of numerous mechanical and intellectual organs, so that the workers themselves are cast merely as its conscious linkages. In the machine, and even more in machinery as an automatic system, the use value, i.e. the material quality of the means of labour, is transformed into an existence adequate to fixed capital and to capital as such; and the form in which it was adopted into the production process of capital, the direct means of labour, is superseded by a form posited by capital itself and corresponding to it.

*'In no way does the machine appear as the individual worker's means of labour. Its distinguishing characteristic is not in the least, as with the means of labour, to transmit the worker's activity to the object; this activity, rather, is posited in such a way that it merely transmits the machine's work, the machine's action, on to the raw material – supervises it and guards against interruptions. Not as with the instrument, which the worker animates and makes into his organ with his skill and strength, and whose handling therefore depends on his virtuosity. Rather, it is the machine which possesses skill and strength in place of the worker, is itself the virtuoso, with a soul of its own in the mechanical laws acting through it; and it consumes coal, oil etc. (*matières instrumentales), *just as the worker consumes food, to keep up its perpetual motion.*

KARL MARX
Grundrisse der Kritik der politischen Ökonomie
(*Outlines of the Critique of Political Economy*),
orig. 1858

British sociologist John Urry has come up with an unusual idea: defining society by the ever-accelerating mobility of its members. To do this he proposes the concept of *mobility-systems*: 'Historically most societies have been characterized by one major mobility-system that is in an evolving and adaptive relationship with that society's economy, through the production and consumption of goods and services and the attraction and circulation of the labour force and consumers . . . The richer the society, the greater the range of mobility-systems that will be present, and the more complex the intersections between such systems.'[1] Urry devotes chapters of his book *Mobilities* to four infrastructural systems: pathways, trains, automobiles and airplanes. Interestingly, he suggests that these infrastructures are complemented by cultural systems serving to represent the movement of people and things, to communicate about it and to imagine its further possibilities. Yet strangely, in a book

1. J. Urry, *Mobilities* (Cambridge: Polity, 2007), 51.

that gestures towards the concept of a technological unconscious, he says next to nothing about production and distribution. What's missing from his 'mobilities paradigm' is container shipping and intermodal transport, with their associated representational, communicational and imaginary techniques. What's missing is the social form of just-in-time production.

Like Margaret Thatcher, Urry believes that in the postnational era 'there is no such thing as society'.[2] He's against what has been called the 'container theory' of the social, which relies heavily on spatially bounded categories, reinforcing methodological nationalism.[3] In *Mobilities* he refers to Foucault's concept of governmentality, observing that 'state sovereignty is exercised on territories, populations and, we may add, the movements of populations around that territory'. In contrast he insists on the increasingly transnational movement of populations, and claims that 'such a "mobile population" is immensely hard to monitor and govern'.[4]

Urry is an innovative sociologist, seeking patterns of emergent order in the vertiginous circulations of neoliberal globalism. At its best, his work reads like a kaleidoscopic register of contemporary life. However, like other complexity theorists describing the dynamics of open systems, he fails to take into account the powerful drive towards closure that inhabits all large-scale system design. Thus he ignores the determinant social form of informational capitalism – as though, entranced by mobilities that exceed the capture of the nation-state, he had fallen into the very unconsciousness that contemporary technologies impose.

How to awaken from electric dreams? In this text I will describe both the technical and the cultural dimensions of what is arguably the major mobility-system of our time: the distributional machinery of intermodal transport that circulates commodities through the global economy. The vector I will use to approach this far-flung system is an imaginary one.

Contained Mobility

Picture a video projection on the walls of a global museum (but it could also be your laptop, or an iPhone in the city). The video opens with the sound of a female voice against the background of a swelling sea. It then resolves into two contrasting scenes. On the left, the computerized view of a container port, showing ships at berth or in motion through the channel. On the right, a surveillance camera *inside* a container, where a robust-looking man in an orange shirt moves between the spartan furnishings of an improvised room (bed, desk, table lamp, maps on the corrugated wall). The scenes shift back and forth from screen to screen; the graph-

2. J. Urry, *Sociology Beyond Societies: Mobilities for the Twenty-First Century* (London: Routledge, 2000), 5.

3. U. Beck, *What Is Globalization?* (Cambridge: Polity, 2000/German ed. 1997), 23-24; J. Law, J. Urry, 'Enacting the Social' (Department of Sociology/Centre for Science Studies, Lancaster University, 2003), at www.comp.lancs.ac.uk/sociology/papers/Law-Urry-Enacting-the-Social.pdf.

4. Urry, *Mobilities*, op. cit. (note 1), 49-50.

ics change in content, granularity and focus. The man gets up, sits down, strides about, meditates, sleeps. His name is Anatol Kuis Zimmermann. A scrolling text recounts his destiny: born in 1949 of a Belarussian mother and an ethnic German father who were deported to Siberia; childhood in Brest near the Polish border; university in Minsk; marriage, children, displacement of the family after Chernobyl; liberal, pro-European political activities and attempted migration to Germany. Thus begins an odyssey of deferral, transit and legal limbo, carrying this asylum seeker through nearly every country in Europe. Life as a geography of refusal. The container, we are given to understand, is now his only home. As the off-screen voice explained at the outset, Anatol Zimmermann has 'come ashore in an offshore place, in a container world that only tolerates the translocal state of not being of this place – not of any other really – but of existing in a condition of permanent non-belonging, of juridical non-existence'. He slips into his makeshift bed as a closing text appears on the left-hand screen: 'Everything new is born illegal.'

The video by Ursula Biemann is entitled *Contained Mobility* (2004).[5] It's an extradisciplinary investigation, by which I mean a work of art that seeks knowledge of the world through a confrontation with technical operations and discourses. A crucial part of this search is the interview leading to the reconstruction of Zimmermann's itinerary. But that's classic documentary, and as such, it's not even shown. Nor is the location of the container given. What makes the work so striking, and so useful for an examination of contemporary social relations, is the juxtaposition between the existential narrative of refusal and the abstracted imagery of global transport. One feels they are mirrors of each other. As Biemann notes, the visuality of the work is based in every respect on simulation: 'None of the images of *Contained Mobility* document reality. Every image is an artificial construct: a simulated seascape, a visual rendering of digital data, a webcam set up for a staged scene. The video is a conceptual statement about a particular state of being in this world.'[6]

The question that emerges from the conceptual image is double. First, what materially constitutes 'the translocal state of not being of this place'? And second, what is the relation between this displaced mode of existence and the representational techniques of computer simulation?

Logistical Living

Let's try to answer that first question. Intermodal transport, a.k.a. containerization, is based on three pillars: rigorous standardization of the box allowing for stackability in ships and transfer by specialized cranes to truck or rail; continuous traceability

5. The video can be seen in two parts on YouTube, at http://tinyurl.com/contained-mobility. Also see http://geobodies.org/01_art_and_videos/2004_contained_mobility.

6. J.-E. Lundstrom (ed.), *Ursula Biemann: Mission Reports* (Bristol: Arnolfini Gallery, 2008), 59. The same book includes my essay, 'Extradisciplinary Investigations', also at http://eipcp.net/transversal/0106.

Stills from the video by Ursula Biemann, *Contained Mobility*, 2004.

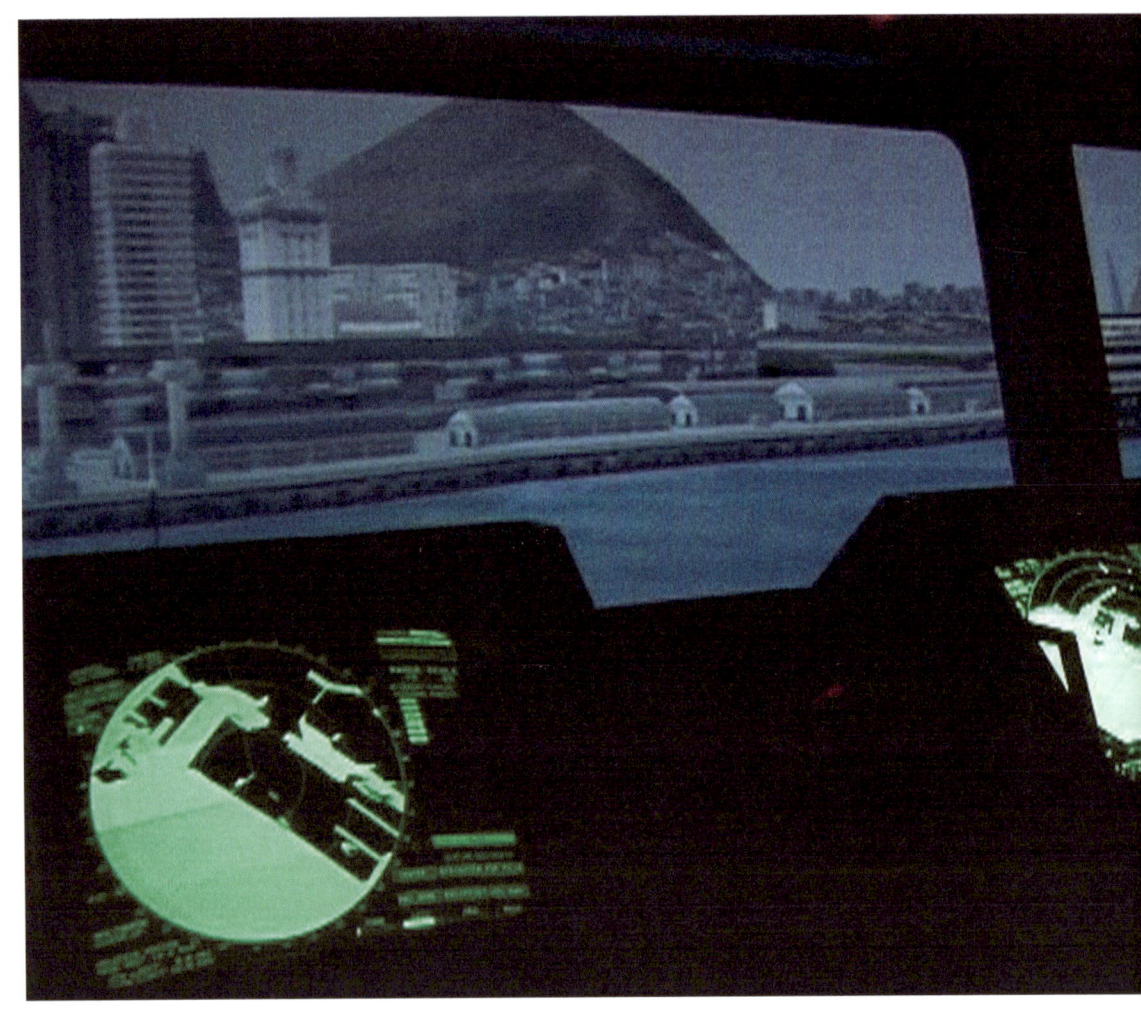

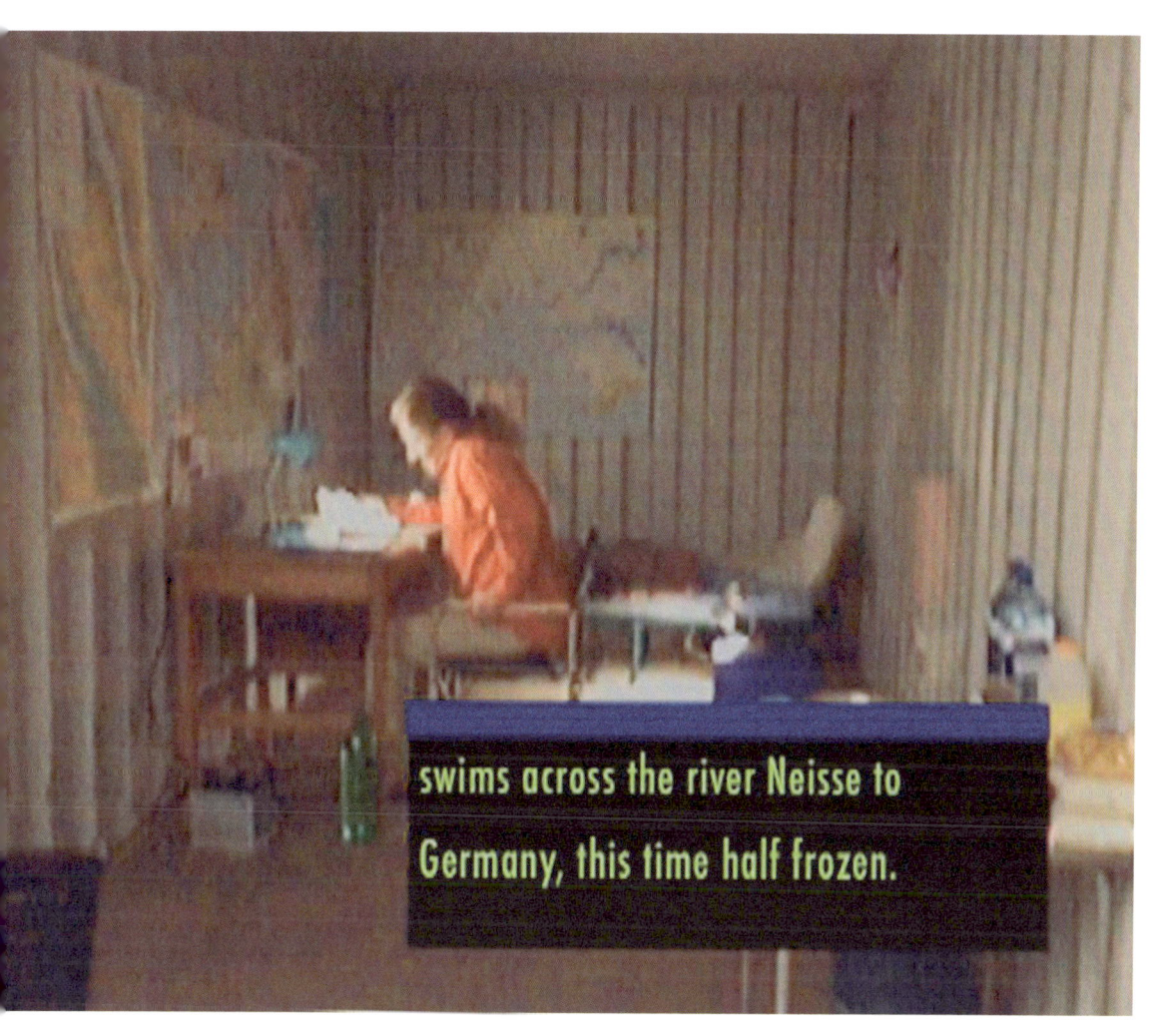

swims across the river Neisse to Germany, this time half frozen.

thanks to a machine-readable bill of lading; and finally, the ability to lock a shipment from initial departure to final destination. Locally standardized containers had been used for land and water transport since the late nineteenth century, but the onset of intermodalism dates to 26 April 1956, when Malcom McLean loaded 58 aluminium truck bodies onto a tanker named the *Ideal-X* for shipment from Newark to Houston.[7] The water-to-wheels concept offered increases in speed and security as well as big savings on labour, all of which was recognized by the US government and the military, spurring a national standardization process that was ratified by the International Standards Organization in 1970. Deregulation of the US transport industry began around the same time, as a crucial component of the emerging neoliberal order; it was completed in all branches by the early 1980s. The rationalization of the docks broke the power of the longshoremen's unions, historically the strongest and most internationalist sector of the labour movement.[8] These developments smoothed the way for an integrated intermodal system that spread rapidly across the world, slashing freight costs and making logistics the key operational discipline of a globalizing economy. Given the military origins of logistics, it's significant that the first big government contracts with

7. M. Levinson, *The Box: How the Shipping Container Made the World Smaller and the World Economy Bigger* (Princeton University Press, 2006), 1 and *passim*.

8. For a photo/text reflection on containerization's consequences for labour, see A. Sekula, *Fish Story* (Rotterdam: Witte de With/ Richer Verlag, 1995).

McLean's Sea-Land corporation were for war materiel to Vietnam. And it's equally significant that Sea-Land's wartime business became immensely profitable when McLean realized that the returning containers could be filled with the rising tide of manufactured goods from Japan.

The late 1960s saw the take-off of the Japanese economy, first in light consumer goods and then, after the oil shock of 1973, in fuel-efficient automobiles. Already the Toyota Motor Corporation had developed its system of continuous information flow between manufacturer and supplier, allowing for the delivery of custom-built parts in exact proportion to current needs without costly warehousing. The advent of containerization meant that 'just-in-time' production could be extended to an entire East Asian maritime network including the 'Four Tigers' of Hong Kong, Singapore, Taiwan and South Korea – a network that would ultimately re-centre on coastal China.[9] In the wake of Toyota's success, just-in-time or 'lean' production imposed itself on global auto-makers. It received wider attention through a best-selling industry study entitled *The Machine that Changed the World* (where 'machine' refers not to a single device but to an integrated process).[10] JIT is what made the world translo-cal. However, its

9. P.J. Katzenstein and T. Shiraishi, *Network Power: Japan and Asia* (Cornell UP, 1997); Ho-Fung Hung, 'America's Head Servant? The PRC's Dilemma in the Global Crisis', *New Left Review* 60, November-December 2009.

10. J.P. Womack, D.T. Jones and D. Roos, *The Machine that Changed the World: The Story of Lean Production* (New York: Rawson Associates, 1990).

adoption by Western corporations after 1989 turned it into something very different from the trust-based relations between manufacturer and supplier extolled by the venerable Mr Toyoda. What emerged from the open markets of neoliberalism was a vast *delivery system* commanded by retailers engaged in a vicious search for the best possible price. And that turned out to be the 'China price': the lowest number on the planet for any category of basic manufactured goods.

By 2005, Wal-Mart imported some 350,000 40-foot containers a year of manufactured goods. That's almost 30,000 tonnes *per day,* the majority from China.[11] The containers pass through the ports of Long Beach and Los Angeles before departing by rail to truck transhipment centres feeding warehouse-sized stores. Thus 'the box' spawned 'the big box' – and with it, a whole new science of supply chain management, whose effect has been to drive both prices and wages to rock-bottom levels.[12] Though big-box retailing is most common in the USA, a list of global firms operating on the Wal-Mart model now includes 'Carrefour, Aldi, Metro, Royal Ahold, Tesco, Ito-Yokado, Kingfisher, and IKEA, as well as Home Depot, Costco and Best Buy'.[13] What began as a formula for automobile production has led to a world-wide re-articulation of industry, merchandising and consumption.

Since its origins in the early 1980s, supply chain management has become the obligatory model for globalizing businessmen, who adopt just-in-time principles as a logistical ethos for corporate existence. As a technical manual explains, 'the footprint of the firm's global facilities . . . for sourcing, research and development, production, distribution and retail sales, and the effective coordination and management of all flows between them (information, physical/product, and financial flows) become the major determinants of competitive success'.[14] Marc Levinson, author of *The Box*, describes the effects such practices had on an American consumer icon as early as the mid-1990s: 'Workers in China produced her statuesque figure, using molds from the United States and other machines from Japan and Europe. Her nylon hair was Japanese, the plastic in her body from Taiwan, the pigments American, the cotton clothing from China. Barbie, simple girl though she is, had developed her very own global supply chain.'[15]

Logistics assembles the raw material of our lives. It is in this sense that everyone – not just Anatol Zimmermann – lives in a 'container world'. But crucial questions emerge, when logistics is generalized into supply chain management. How are global flows coordinated with local markets

11. E. Bonacich and J.B. Wilson, *Getting the Goods: Ports, Labor and the Logistics Revolution* (Cornell University Press, 2008), 25.

12. See the PBS documentary, *Is Wal-Mart Good for America?* (2004), available at www.pbs.org/wgbh/pages/frontline/shows/walmart.

13. M. Petrovic and G.G. Hamilton, 'Making Global Markets: Wal-Mart and Its Suppliers', in N. Lichtenstein (ed.), *Wal-Mart: The Face of 21st Century Capitalism* (New York: New Press 2006), 108.

14. Kouvelis and Su, 'The Structure of Global Supply Chains', special issue, *Foundations and Trends in Technology, Information and Operations Management* 1/4, 2005, 1-2.

15. Levinson, *The Box*, op. cit. (note 7), 264.

to make a profit in real time? And what effect do the giant distribution machines have on the stationary people who ultimately receive and consume the mobile commodities?

Real-Time Unconscious

To answer those questions we must deal with the representation of mobility-systems. At stake are the abstract models that regulate the temporal and spatial functioning of large and complex production lines. Surprisingly, it turns out that by the late 1950s the major problem of the big-box retailers – coordinating the levels of accessible stocks with the rates of flow through stores – had already been solved, theoretically at least, by a pioneer of computer simulation.

Jay Wright Forrester was a servomechanisms engineer in the Second World War, then head of a programme to build the Whirlwind, a multipurpose digital computer that was initially to be used in a flight simulator. That project morphed into the basis of the SAGE radar-defence system (for 'semi-automatic ground environment').[16] By 1956, after inventing magnetic core memory and overseeing the rise of IBM as the USA's mainframe supplier, Forrester decided that the excitement in the computer field was over, and switched to management studies. His breakthrough came two years later, when General Electric executives asked him to examine their appliance factories, which would oscillate wildly from peak demand to near inactivity, irrespective of business cycles. He immediately recognized the classic 'hunting pattern' that occurs when a servomechanism receives undamped feedback from an initial action, then overcorrects, generating more distorting feedback.

Forrester was convinced that industrial managers were unable to grasp the multiple rhythms of giant plants hooked into even larger distribution systems, and were actually *worsening* their problems instead of curing them. He designed a non-linear computer modelling program to show how policy decisions affecting the rates of flow between five interconnected categories of stocks – materials, orders, money, capital equipment and personnel – could be represented graphically in their effects over time, so as to reveal the unforeseen consequences of single interventions. The policy decisions could then be corrected via a sixth category, coordinated feedback information. This analysis laid the basis of a new managerial logic, known as system dynamics.[17]

Most histories of cybernetics never mention engineers, focusing instead on scientists and the occasional philosopher.[18] Yet Forrester is undoubtedly the single most influ-

16. For Forrester's involvement in SAGE, see P.N. Edwards, *The Closed World: Computers and the Politics of Discourse in Cold War America* (Cambridge, MA: MIT Press, 1996), chapters 2 and 3.

17. J.W. Forrester, *Industrial Dynamics* (Waltham, MA: Pegasus Communications, 1961); *Principles of Systems* (Cambridge, MA: Wright-Allen Press, 1968).

18. A notable exception is D.A. Mindell, *Between Human and Machine: Feedback, Control, and Computing before Cybernetics* (Baltimore: Johns Hopkins University Press, 2002).

From Jay W. Forrester, *Industrial Dynamics* (Cambridge, MA: MIT Press, 1985/1st edition 1961), 174.

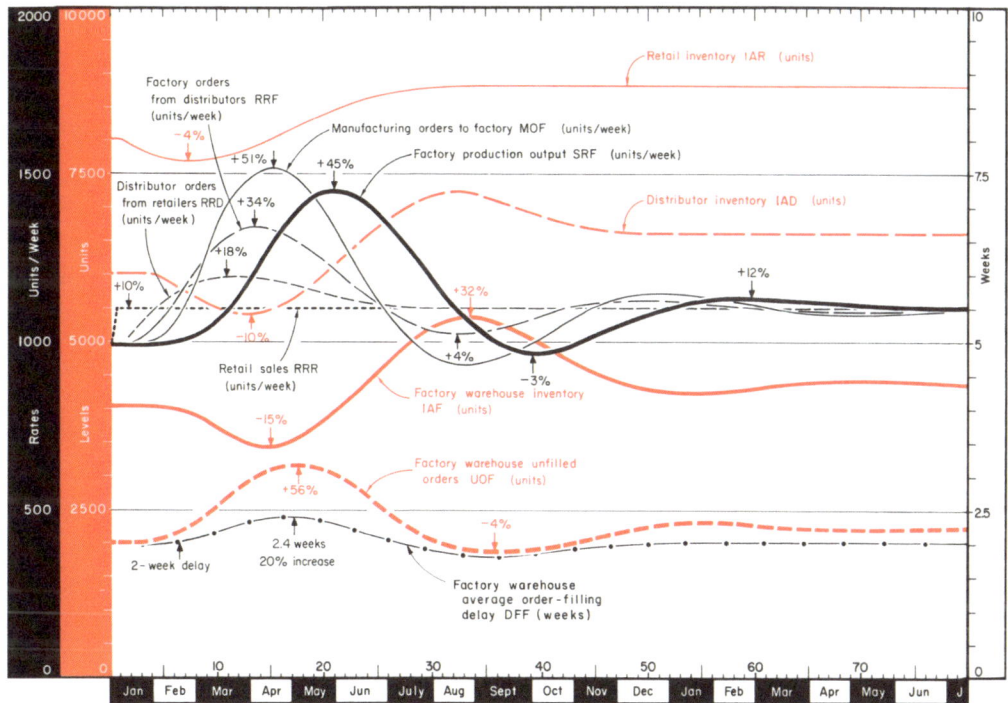

Figure 15-18 (Repeat of Figure 2-2) Response of production-distribution system to a sudden 10% increase in retail sales.

ential cybernetician, since his work has allowed the coordination of vast production, distribution and consumption processes taking place on opposite sides of the planet. It is fascinating to realize that his SAGE radar-defence program led very quickly to SABRE, or 'semi-automatic business-research environment', which is still the world's largest airline ticketing network. The ease with which we ignore the very existence of such crucial transport systems has everything to do with the technological unconscious, arising from the automation of large numbers of routine actions to which we no longer pay the slightest attention. Nigel Thrift explains this computerized repetition-compulsion: 'Through the application of a set of technologies and knowledges (the two being impossible to separate), a style of repetition has been produced which is more controlled and also more open-ended, a new kind of roving empiricism which continually ties up and undoes itself in a search for the most efficient ways to use the space and time of each moment.'[19] As the designer of semi-automatic environments including human beings in subordination to mechanical and computational devices, Forrester was at the origin of this roving technological unconscious. Yet he found that his ideas could not be understood by the corporate class he was addressing. Only in the 1980s did they start making intuitive sense to managers.[20]

19. N. Thrift, 'Remembering the Technological Unconscious', in *Knowing Capitalism* (London: Sage, 2005), 223.

20. See L. Fisher, 'The Prophet of Unintended Consequences', in *Strategy + Business* 40 (Fall 2005), 7.

There was a technical reason. In the 1960s and 1970s, Forrester's simulations could not yet run with real-time information. Instead, approximate models were created and statistical forecasting techniques were employed. From the 1980s onward, quantum leaps in data-gathering and communications technology transformed all that. With the advent of electronic data interchange (EDI), every aspect of production, transport, display and sales could be recorded, communicated, represented and analysed, so as to continuously map out the position and trajectory of each single object being handled by a world-spanning corporation.[21] The result is an 'executive information system' that gives managers centralized access to a continuously evolving set of logistical data, bringing dynamic simulation over the line into real-time representation. This provides the unprecedented ability to rationalize labour at every point along the chain, accelerating the pace and squeezing workers for higher levels of productivity. Still it's not enough for contemporary capitalism. As systems designer Paul Westerman explains, 'Aggressive retailers (like Wal-Mart) will not stop there; they will continue until all company data is available for analysis. They will build an enterprise data warehouse. They give all this information to their internal users (buyers) and external users (suppliers) to exploit and demand measurable

21. For definitions of EDI, see G. Boone and D. Kurtz, *Contemporary Business*, 13th Edition (Hoboken: Wiley, 2010), 219-20, as well as Bonacich and Wilson, *Getting the Goods*, op. cit. (note 11), esp. 5 and 35.

improvement'.[22]

22. P. Westerman, *Data Warehousing: Using the Wal-Mart Model* (San Diego: Academic Press, 2001), 26.

Such is the formula of global supply chain management, in an information-age economy where the 'push' of Fordist industrial production and state planning has been replaced by the 'pull' of giant retail conglomerates.

With enterprise data warehousing, the just-in-time machine becomes both extensively and intensively pervasive. EDI is correlated with cash-flow, marketing and financing information. Point-of-sale data is associated with individual names on credit cards, then combined with cascades of other data gleaned from the Internet, generating behaviour profiles that can be used for the fine-tuning of display and advertising strategies. The models of optimal future performance built on the analysis of past actions are then relayed upstream to govern the behaviour of workers, middle managers and suppliers, and downstream to influence consumers, creating what Westerman calls a 'unified data system' (UDS) embracing every aspect of corporate planning. The big boxes of Wal-Mart now cast a 70-terabyte information shadow. To be sure, the possibilities of UDS have not yet been fully implemented. EDI is still rare among Chinese suppliers, while surveillance operators like Google and Facebook are only beginning to codify and sell our intimate data-bodies. There is no need to exaggerate the deployment of data integration. But even less can one ignore the tremendous advances in communication between manufacturers and distributors, the increasing granularity of representation that this communication makes possible, and last but not least, the accelerating absorption of consumer imaginaries into the managed flows of the pull economy.

What appears on the horizon is a self-shaping or 'autopoetic' modelling process that can integrate hundreds of millions of individuals and billions of discrete objects and desires into a single mobility-system, where every movement is coordinated with every other in real time. The integrative capacity of this kind of autopoetic system is what defines the boundary of each corporate entity, struggling against all others to increase the market-share that it controls. Under these conditions we live in an 'open' world of universal free trade across national borders, where giant organizations strive to impose closure on mobile populations. Their computerized map becomes our intimate territory. Such a dystopian state was once the exclusive province of science fiction: Philip K. Dick novels, where androids dreamed of electric sheep. But the container, having spawned the big box, now seems destined to bring a world-spanning containment strategy into being. The electronic dream is to maintain continuous contact between a global production system and you, the consumer, whose mobility need not signify uncertainty of behaviour. According to this dream, no desire should linger free without a sale. The representational techniques that enable such a strategy have seen vast changes since the 1960s. Today they include multi-agent systems, where the decisions of autonomous actors are simulated on both the supply and the demand sides of the equation.[23]

On the basis of such simulations, multiple autopoetic systems are orchestrated into smoothly functioning machines serving unified purposes. Yet behind such sophisticated devices one can still recognize the outlines of semi-automated environments, where the individual flow-chart of every object and actor is analysed into the coordinated curves of system dynamics.[24] Like an architectural plan for a global factory in motion, those intersecting curves define the social form of just-in-time production.

23. For a definition see any of the recent business manuals, such as B. Chaibdraa and J.P. Müller (eds.), *Multiagent based Supply Chain Management* (Springer, 2006).

24. This is the thesis of H. Akkermans and N. Delaert (eds.), 'The Dynamics of Supply Chains and Networks', special issue, *System Dynamics Review* 21/3 (2005).

Escape

To tie up the threads of this argument, let's return to what started the whole thing rolling: John Urry's intriguing but radically undeveloped concept of mobility-systems. It's ironic to find Urry, in *Sociology Beyond Societies*, reflecting that his own discipline will not survive its transition to the global scale if it does not once again link its destinies to social movements.[25] Had he done exactly that with the social movement closest to his own concerns – namely, transnational migration – he might have

25. Urry, *Sociology Beyond Societies*, op. cit. (note 2), 18.

seen how the spatially bounded 'containers' that formerly defined national societies are being replaced, not by the liberal ideology of 'open systems', but instead by postliberal constructs like the big-box retailers, whose JIT distribution machines are enabled both by advanced technology and by deterritorialized state-functions (monetary regimes, transport surveillance programs, selective border controls, 'foreign trade zones' inscribed in domestic territories, etc.). The exploitation and oppression that such hybrid constructs exert on cut-price migrant labour has been made explicit by recent struggles of workers in the intermodal transport industry.[26] And the society shaped by these 'postliberal aggregates' has been theorized by a group of sociologists who take their stand with the migrants.

26. See the articles at http://www.warehouseworkersunited.org.

In a book entitled *Escape Routes: Control and Subversion in the 21st Century*, these theorists find an example of social form in the automobile industry: the recently opened BMW plant in Leipzig, designed by the architect Zaha Hadid. As they explain, 'the building enables innovative working-time models and operating times of 60 to 140 hours per week, and because of this the plant can react quickly to specific changes in the market'. What the just-in-time factory reveals is the peculiar articulation of openness and closure that defines a contemporary mobility-system: 'The BMW plant is an interactive order, neither open nor closed, but open as soon as it incorporates the actors necessary for its functioning, and closed as soon as it can protect and sustain its functionality. The plant is not maintained by its exclusivity nor by an internally generated authenticity, but rather by a fluid belonging of different independent trajectories to an effective system of production. It is an aggressive structure, opposing everything that sets limits to its own internal interests or tries to infuse it with impurity. The BMW plant reacts aggressively to the fear of viruses, it is aseptic, clean, pragmatic: Western oblivion at the highest level.'[27]

Hadid's jaggedly flowing architecture enables the material process of inclusion/exclusion in today's society, while helping the public to forget its very existence. Here again, semi-automated flows create unconsciousness, erasing histories of emancipation. For the authors of *Escape Routes*, the coercive structures of postliberal globalization took form as 'the answer to the wild insurgency and escape that emerges after the Second World War'. This insurgency reached a peak in 1968, when the nation-state's promise of rights and representation ('the double-R axiom') was challenged by excluded minority subjects. Yet the opening of borders and the relaxation of social strictures soon gave way to the new state-corporate aggregates, operating in transnational zones of exception without any requirement of legitimacy. Under these conditions, demands for class, ethnic and gender

27. Dimitris Papadopoulos, Niamh Stephenson and Vassilis Tsianos, *Escape Routes: Control and Subversion in the 21st Century* (London: Pluto, 2008), 26.

equality lose their effectiveness. The paradoxical response is a 'politics of imperceptibility', whereby migrants in their fleeting singularity become invisible to postliberal power formations. Recalling the liminal figure we encountered at the outset, the authors of *Escape Routes* might claim: 'We are all Anatol Zimmermann.'

The incongruity of the asylum seeker, abandoned in his improvised dwelling amid technological desolation, could evoke this sense of new-found freedom. As Ursula Biemann claims: 'Everything new is born illegal.' On a more troubling note, however, Biemann recounts that at one point in her interviews with Zimmermann she felt compelled to drop her documentary neutrality, offering to buy him a counterfeit Polish passport that would eventually grant him entry to the European Union: 'Anatol declined. Salvation would have meant the death of his problem, which by now was obviously not only a burden but also the condition with which he has come to identify: to march in the cracks between nations as the post-migratory subject into which he has mutated.'[28] Are we to understand the migrant's fate as double, permanently excluded from a fully satisfying life, yet irremediably attached to the mirage of inclusion? Would this be the condition of life in a container world?

28. Lundstrom, *Ursula Biemann*, op. cit. (note 6), 59

I'll close, not with an answer to those questions, but with a restatement of the enigma constituted by the social form of just-in-time production.

As we've seen, global society is filled by a rising tide of inexpensive goods, managed by increasingly automated systems and destined for consumers whose very desires are modelled by the supply chains. This is the world of the commodity, whose concrete promise of use-value is constantly belied by its abstract form as exchange-value. The conditions of exchange are such that despite the productivity gains of technology, work is still devalued to a bare minimum: the working day as the 'socially necessary labour time' required for the purchase of a minimal basket of commodities. Today it is the price of an exploited Chinese working day that exerts downward pressure on wages everywhere, throwing other workers out of a job even as it floods our lives with cheapened goods that must be thrown away almost immediately. In this sense, society really *is* defined by the ever-accelerating mobility of its members: workers, managers, consumers, all differently caught within the same compulsion to step on the pedal. The Marxist philosopher Moishe Postone points out that this dynamics of commodity production amounts to a strange destiny of 'domination by time'. His abstract statement of the problem reads like a concrete description of existence in the capitalist mobility-system: 'As a result of the general social mediation, labour time expenditure is transformed into a temporal norm that not only is abstracted from, but also stands above and determines, individual action. Just as labour is transformed from an action of individuals to the alienated general principle of the totality under which the individuals are subsumed, time expenditure is transformed from a result *of* activity into a normative measure *for* activity . . . This process, whereby a concrete, dependent variable of human activity becomes an abstract, independent variable governing this activity, is real and not illusory. It is intrinsic to the process of alienated social constitution.'[29]

Cigar-smoking billionaires still exist, of course: I saw them last night in Oliver Stone's new film, *Money Never Sleeps*. But the enigma of our era is the depersonalized principle that governs the estranging machine. Capital itself, in all its abstraction, is the electric dream. For those who do not feel at home in its translocal container world, nor free in the 'wild anomaly' of imperceptible wanderings, awakening will have to come through an as-yet unimagined social subversion of capitalism's universally represented and constantly communicated laws of motion. It's a matter of somehow altering society's unconscious rhythms. A tiger's leap just out of time?

29. M. Postone, *Time, Labor and Social Domination: A Reinterpretation of Marx's Critical Theory* (New York: Cambridge UP, 1993), 214-215. Among many commentaries I recommend Howard Slater's text on counter-cultural artistic practice as a political cure for alienation: 'Toward Agonism – Moishe Postone's *Time, Labour & Social Domination*' (2006), available at www.metamute.org/en/toward-agonism.

Allan Sekula
Noël Burch

The Forgotten Space

Last year, the documentary *The Forgotten Space* by Allan Sekula and Noël Burch was presented during the film festival in Venice. Once begun as a SKOR-initiated art project on the Betuwe route, a cargo railway running from the port of Rotterdam to the German border, the documentary shows the relation between freight shipments by sea and the growing internationalization of a worldwide industrial economy. The film is set in four seaports: Bilbao, Rotterdam, Los Angeles and Hong Kong. It examines the sea as 'the forgotten space' of our modern age, where globalization – though hidden from view – becomes visible in a most pressing way.

Below are a number of stills from *The Forgotten Space*, 2010.

Courtesy of: Doc Eye Film, WILDart Film, SKOR/Foundation for Art and the Public Domain, VPRO, CoBo, ORF, Eurimages, Media Programme.

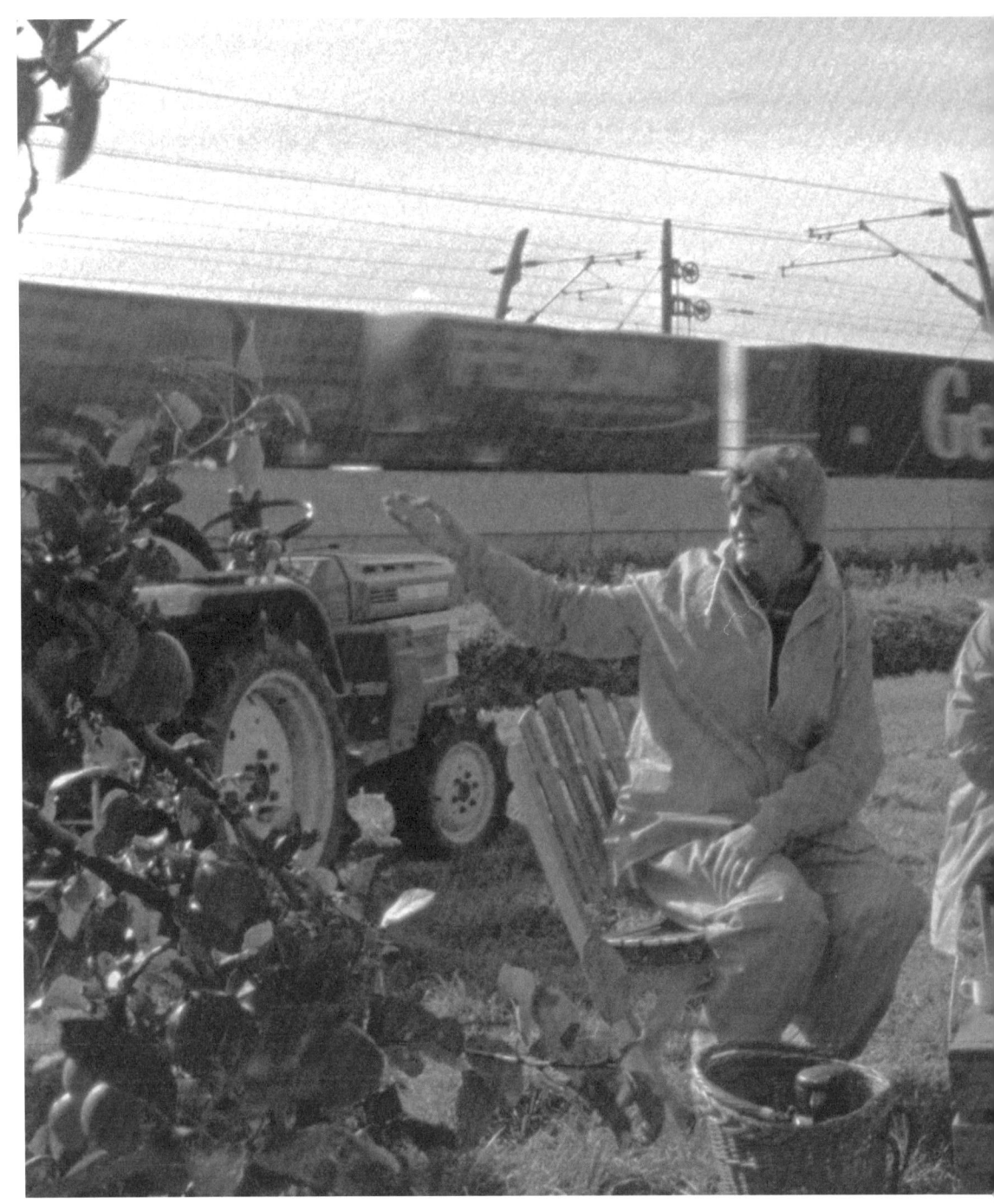

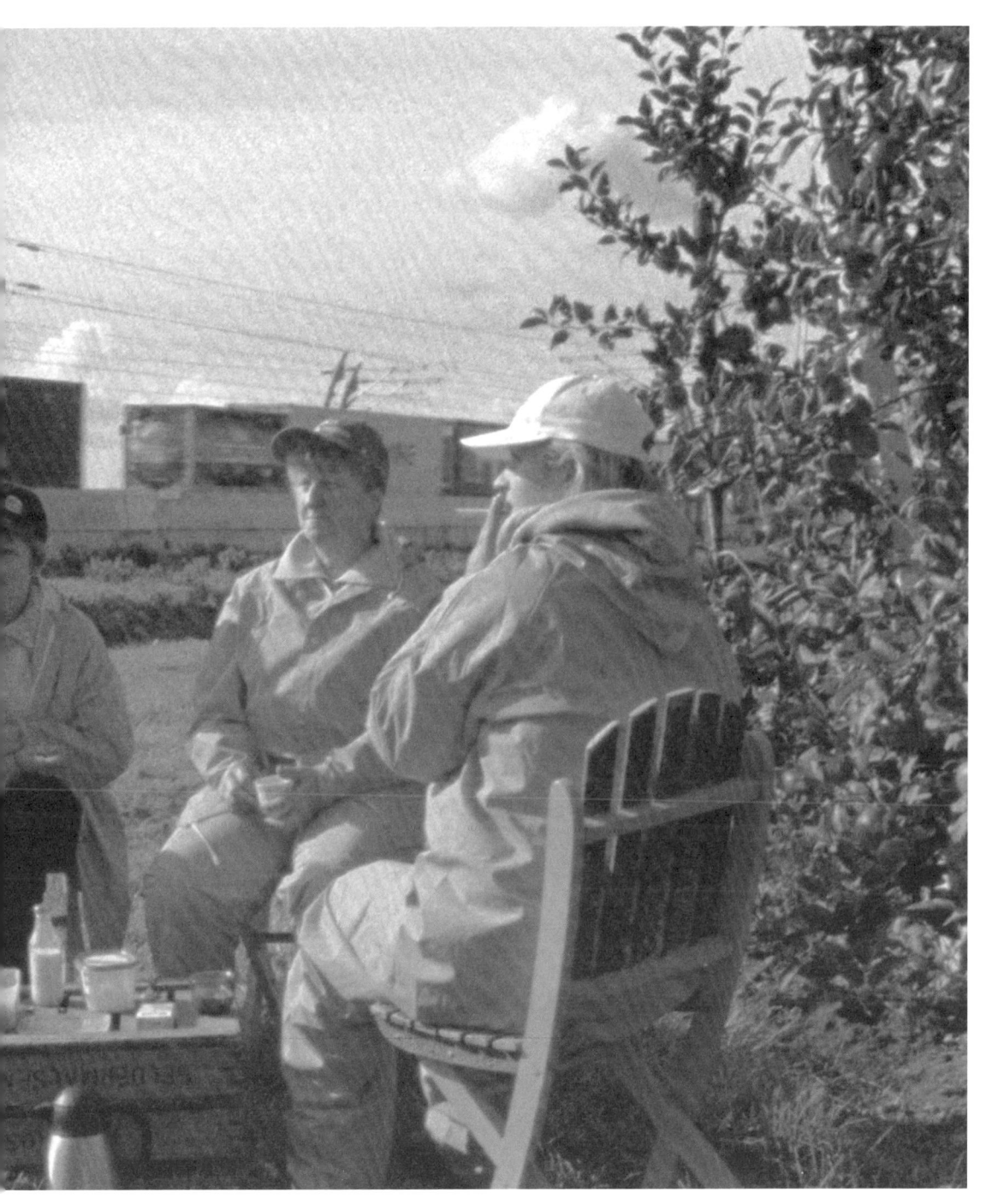

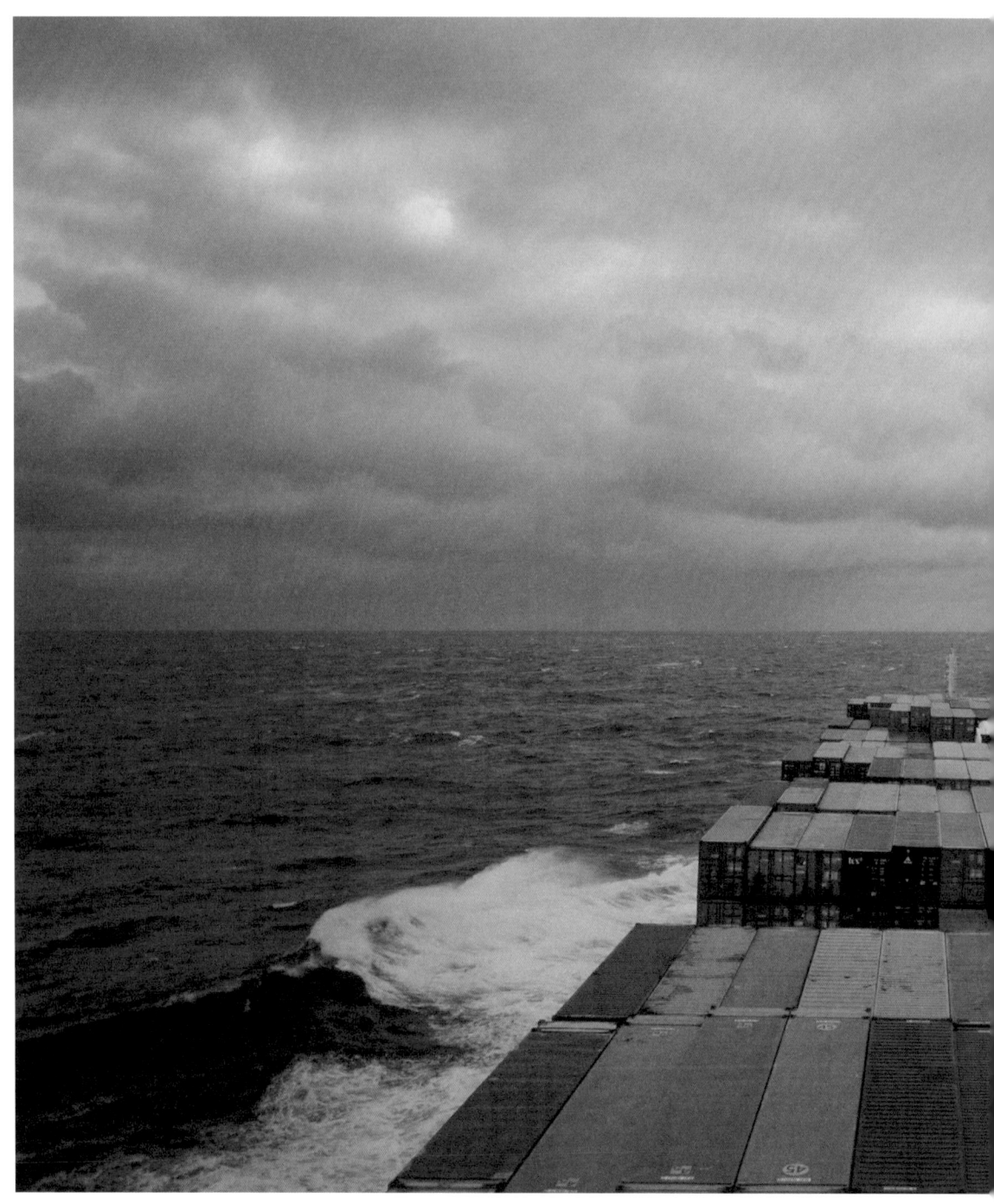

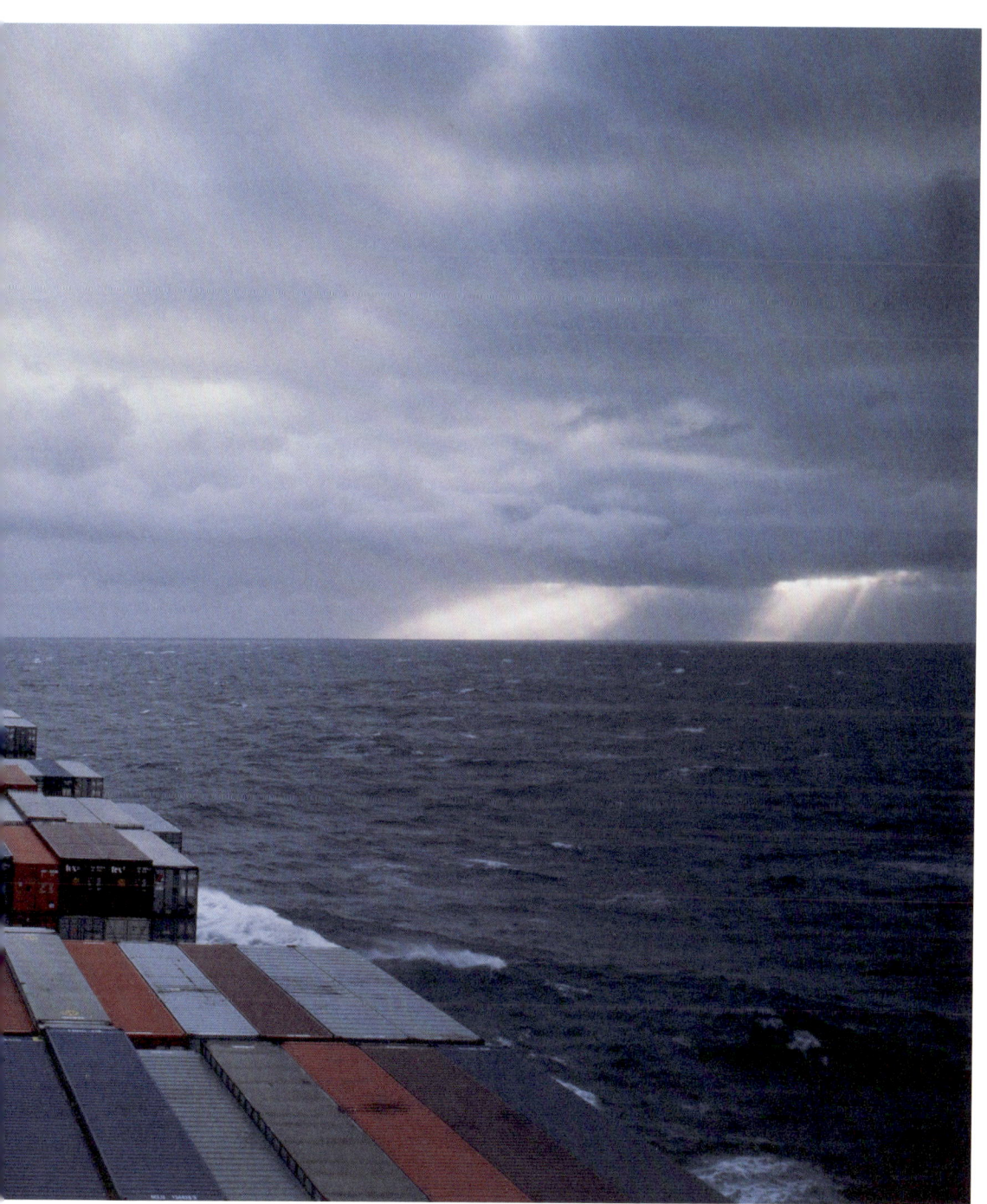

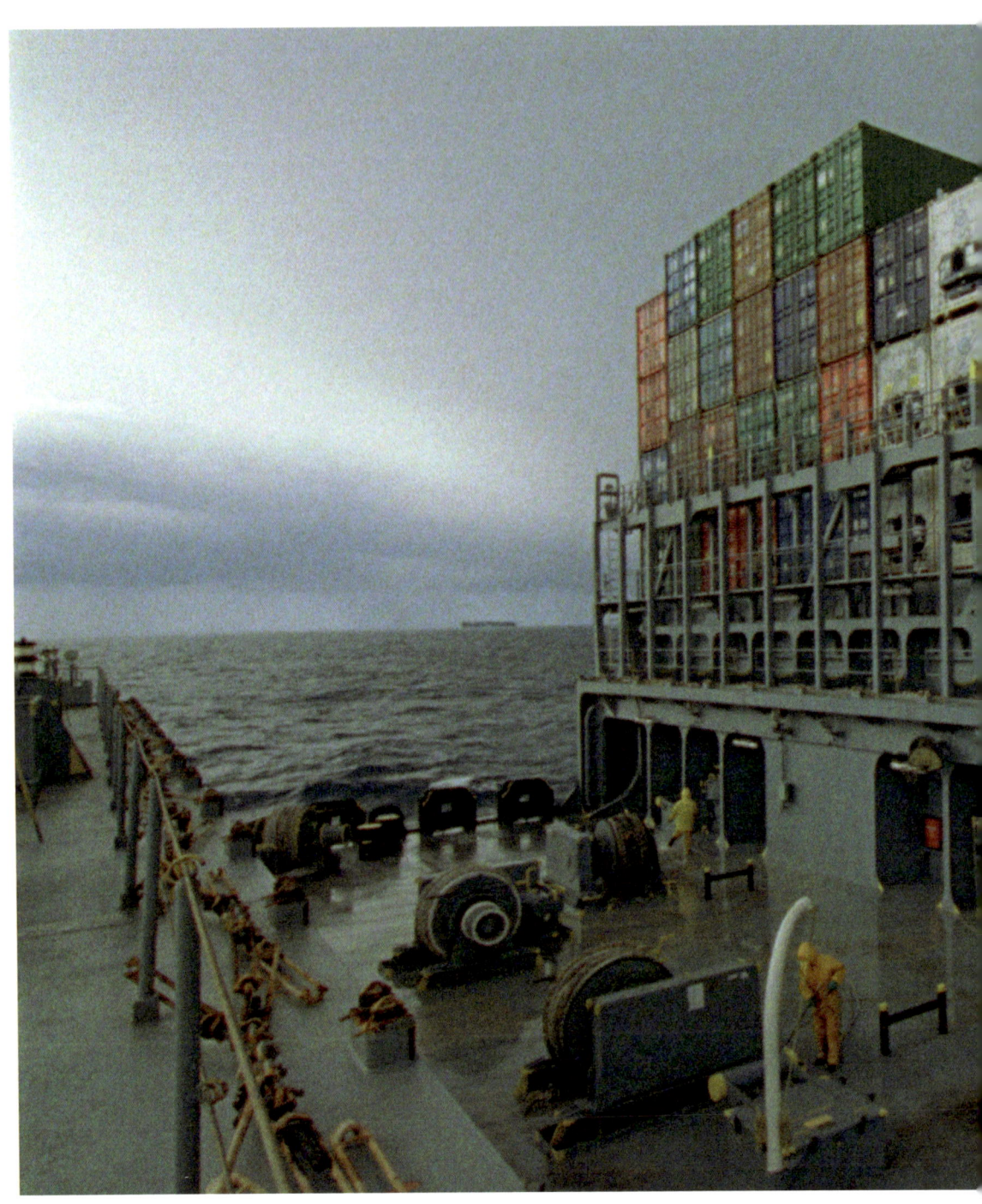

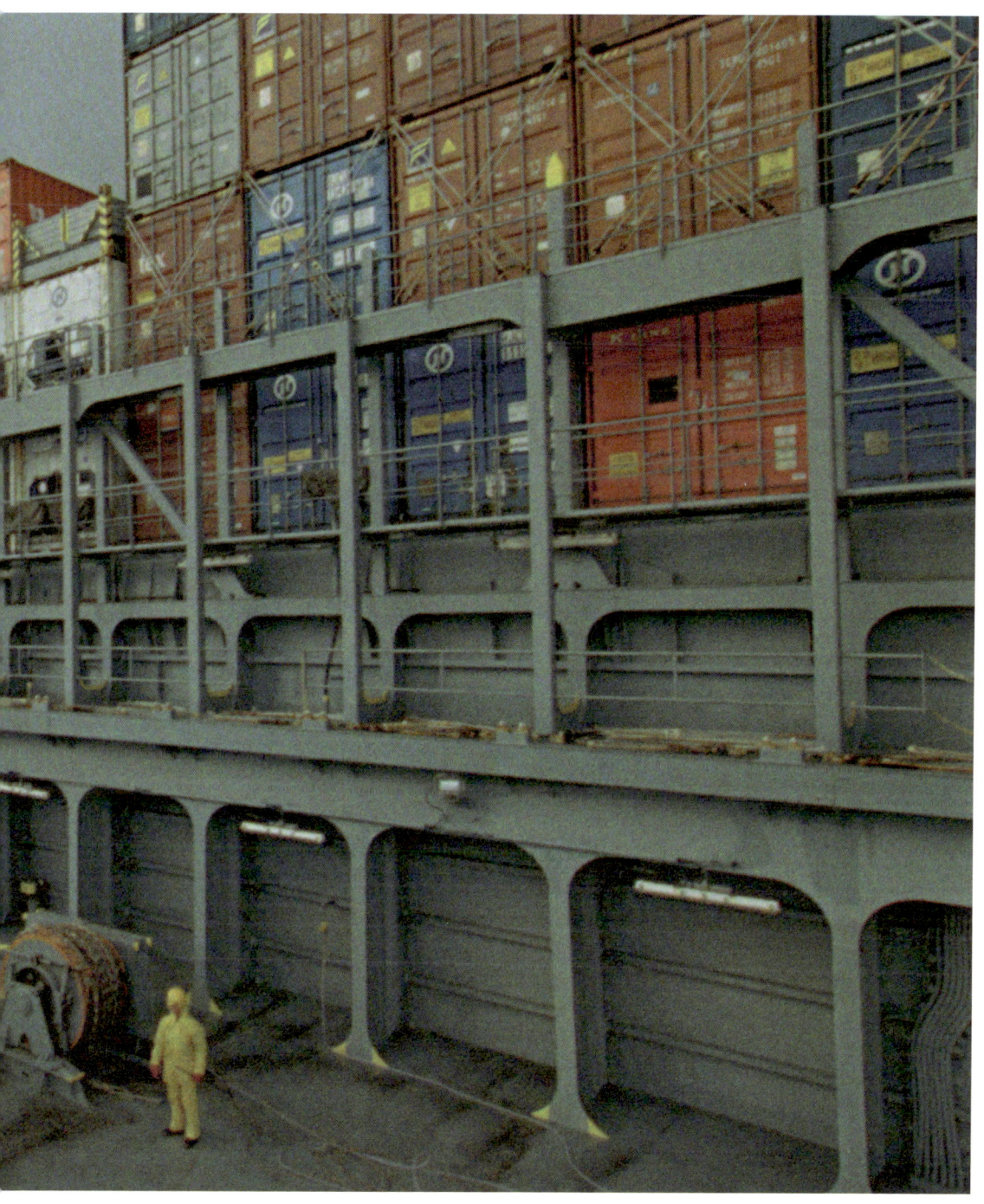

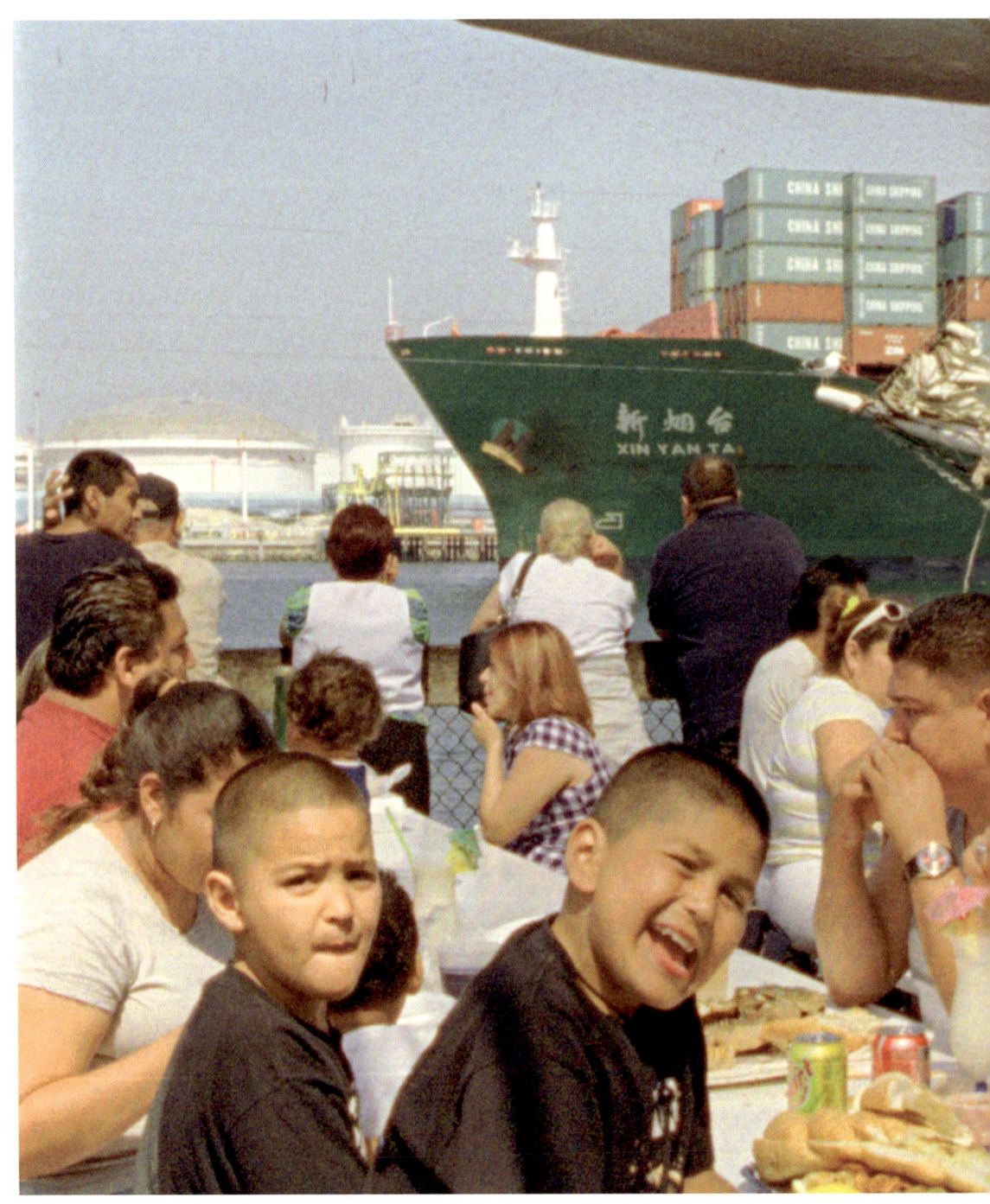

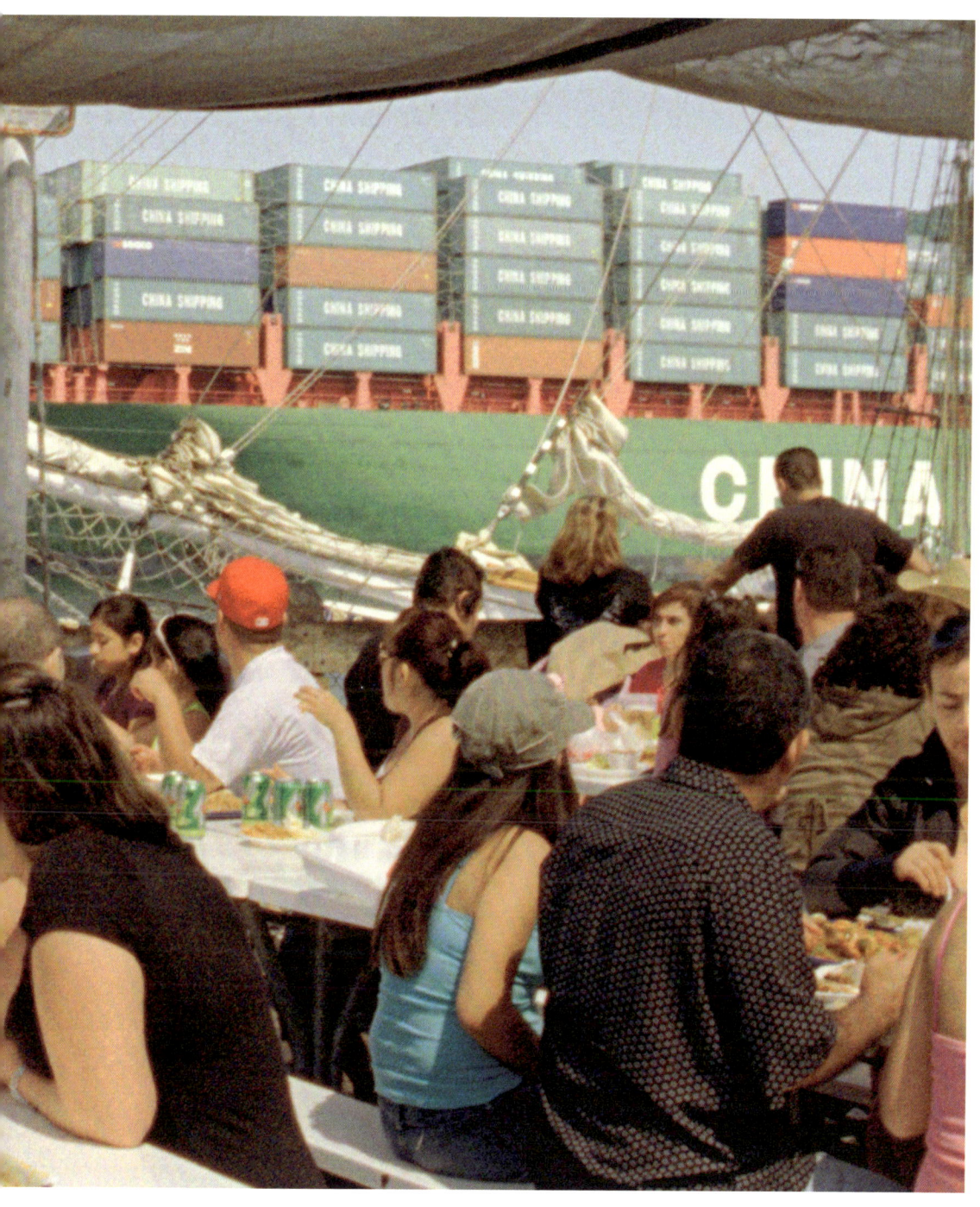

The Forgotten Space

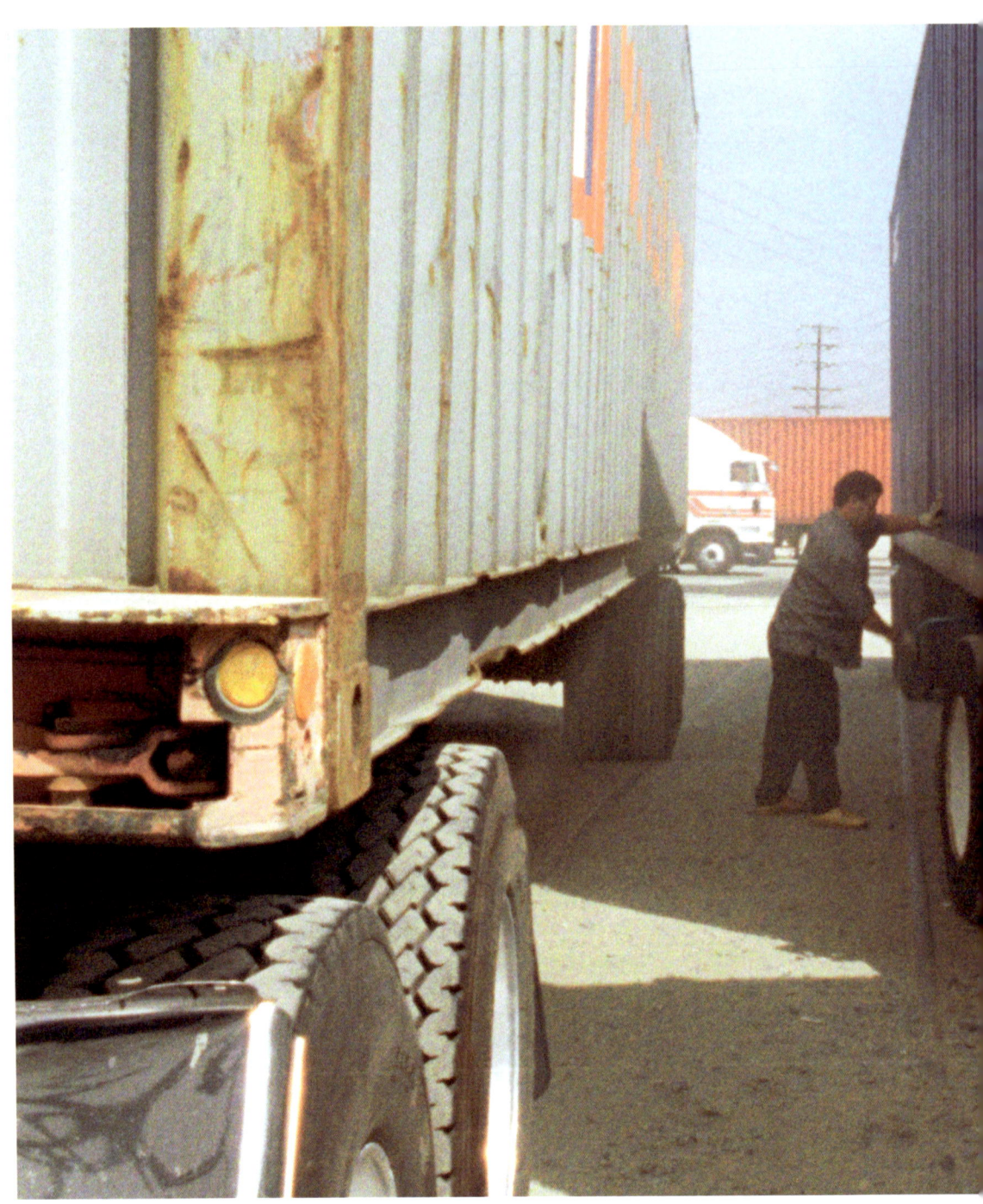

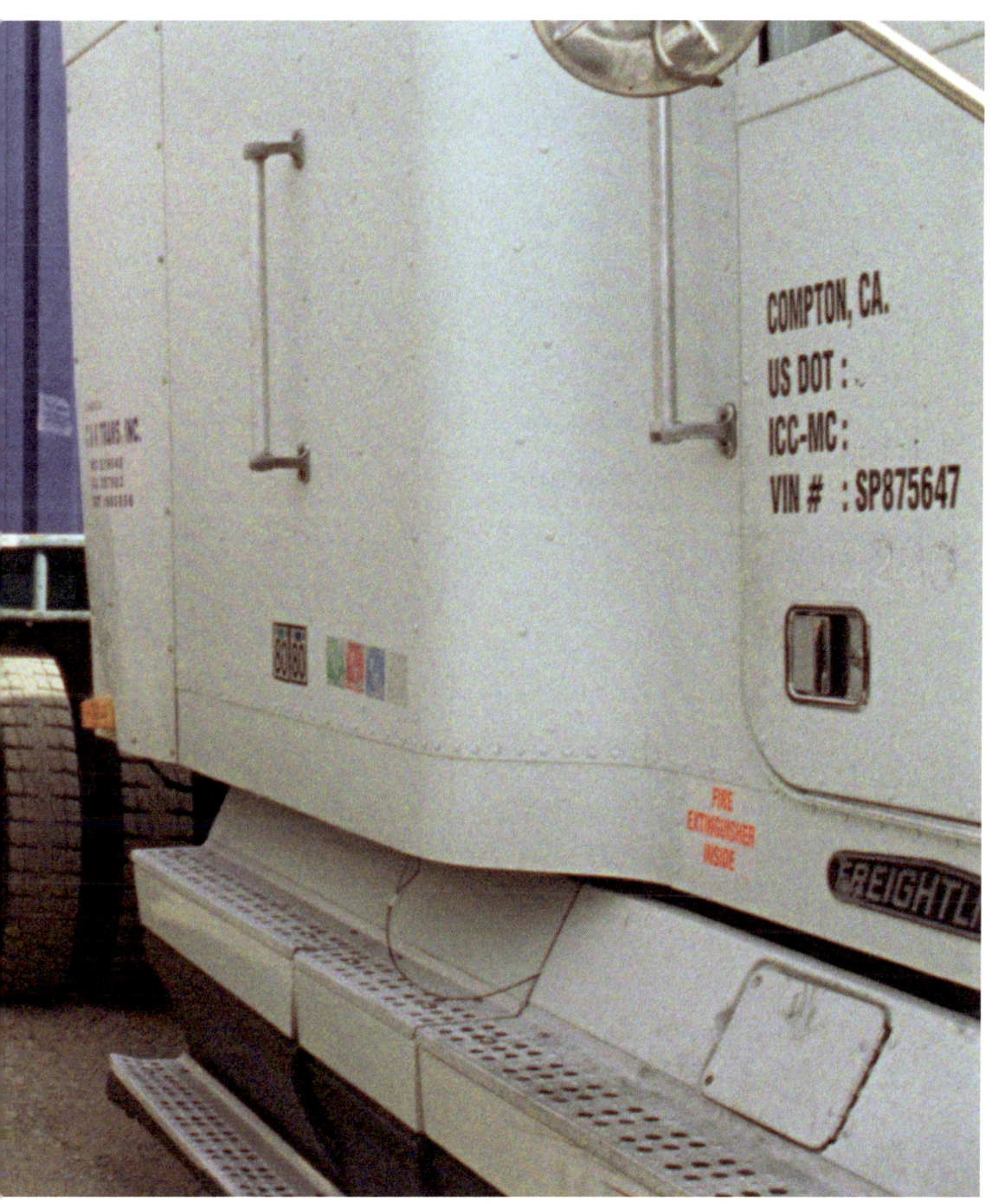

COMPTON, CA.
US DOT :
ICC-MC :
VIN # : SP875647

FIRE
EXTINGUISHER
INSIDE

FREIGHTL

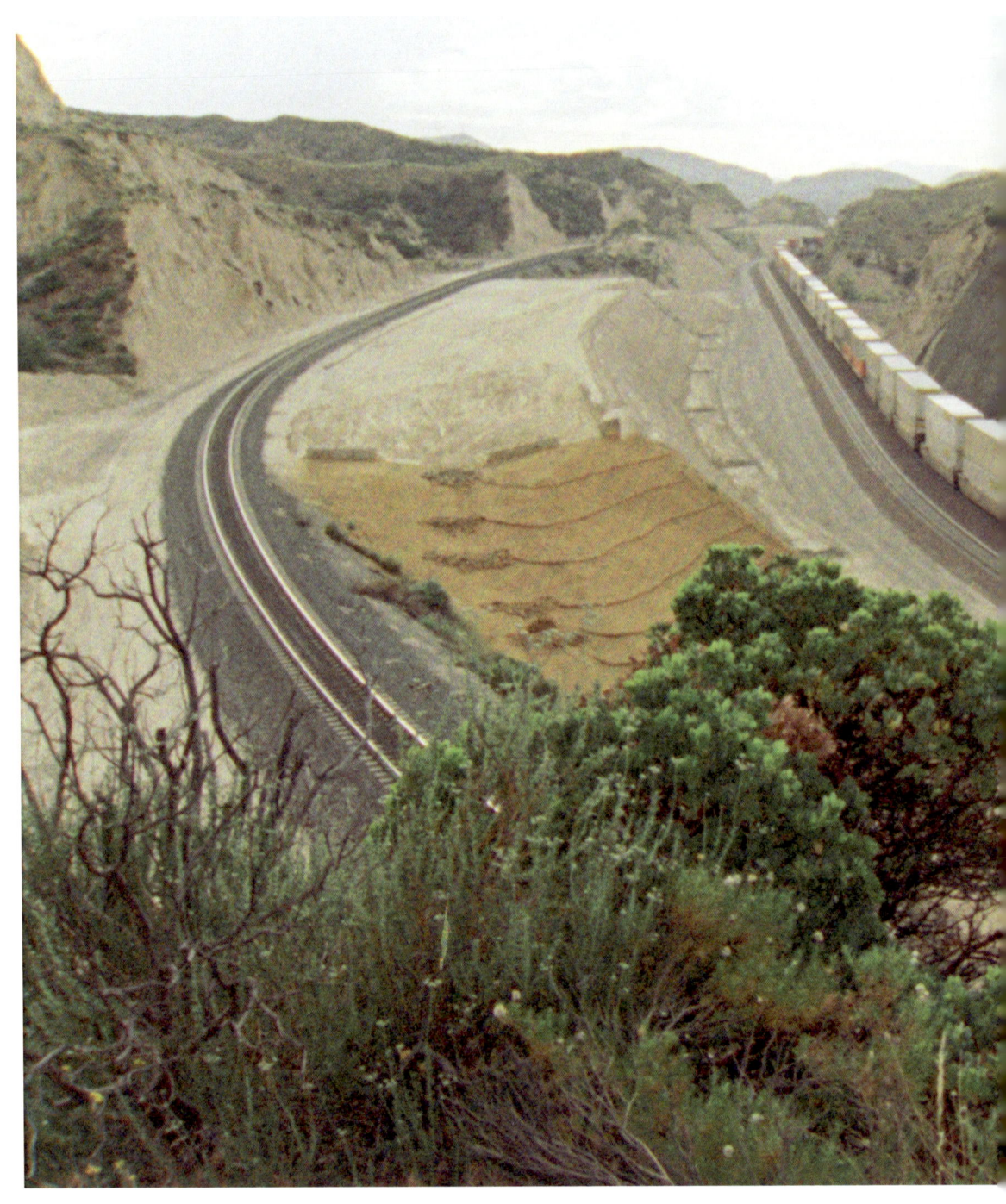

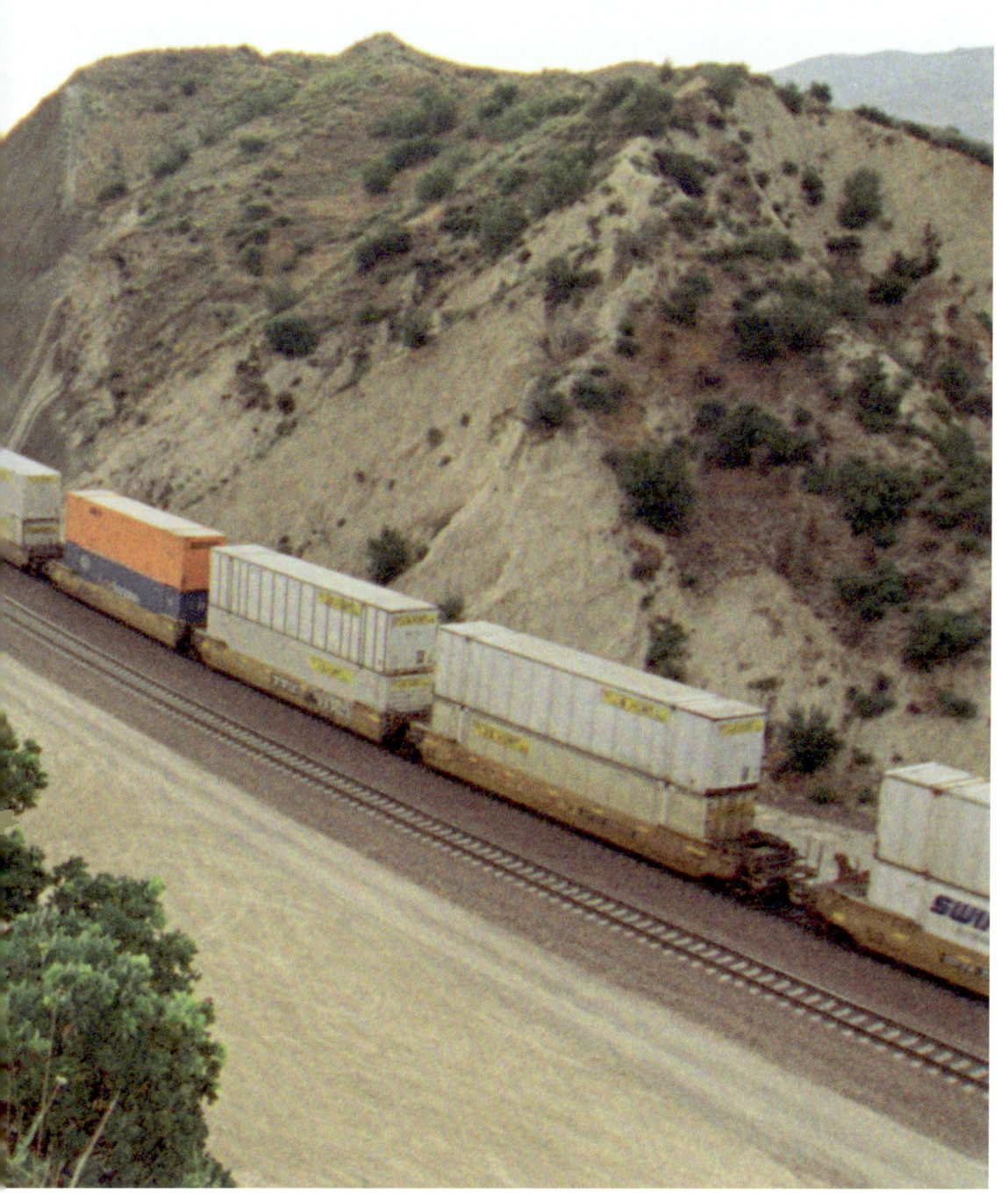

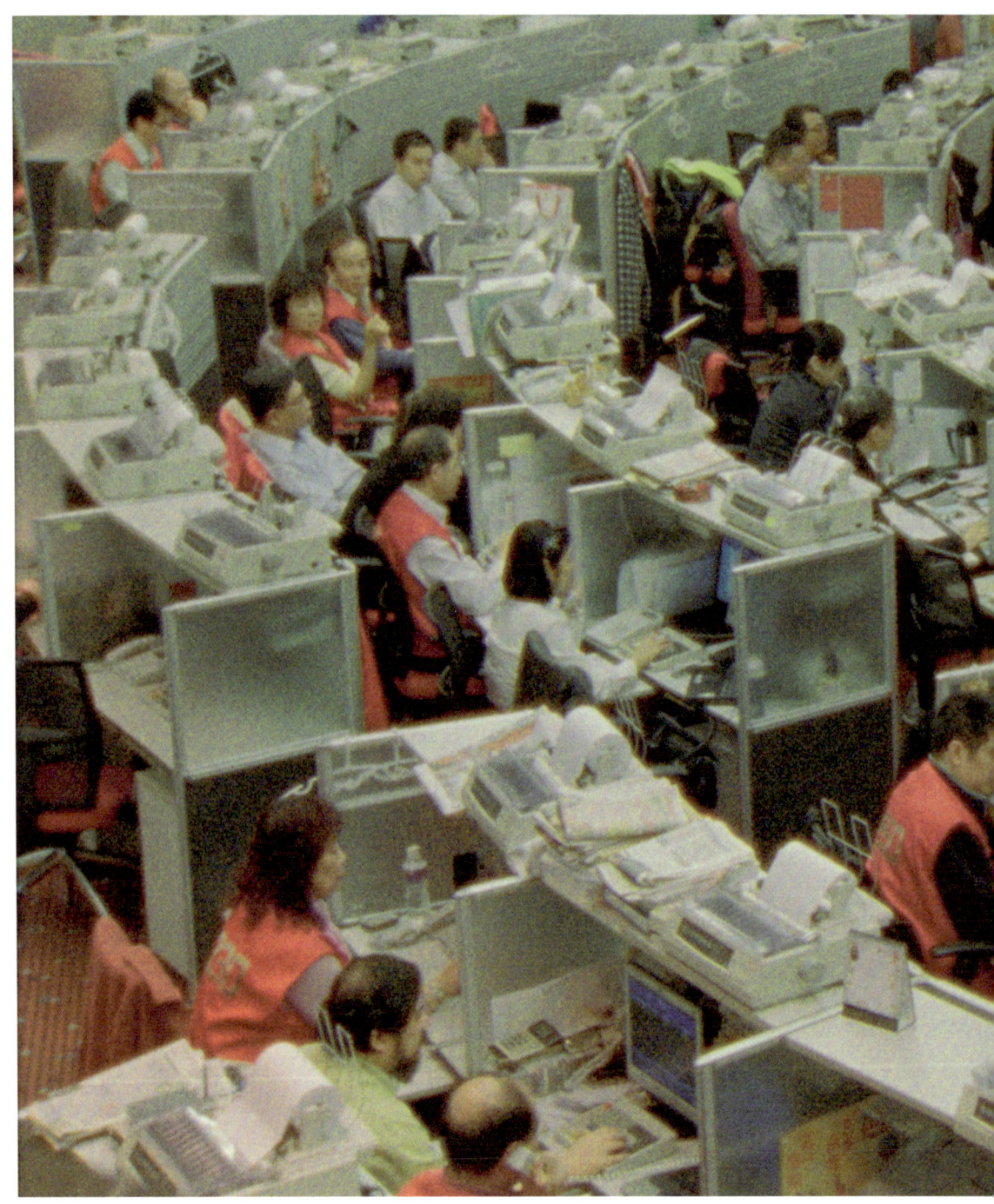

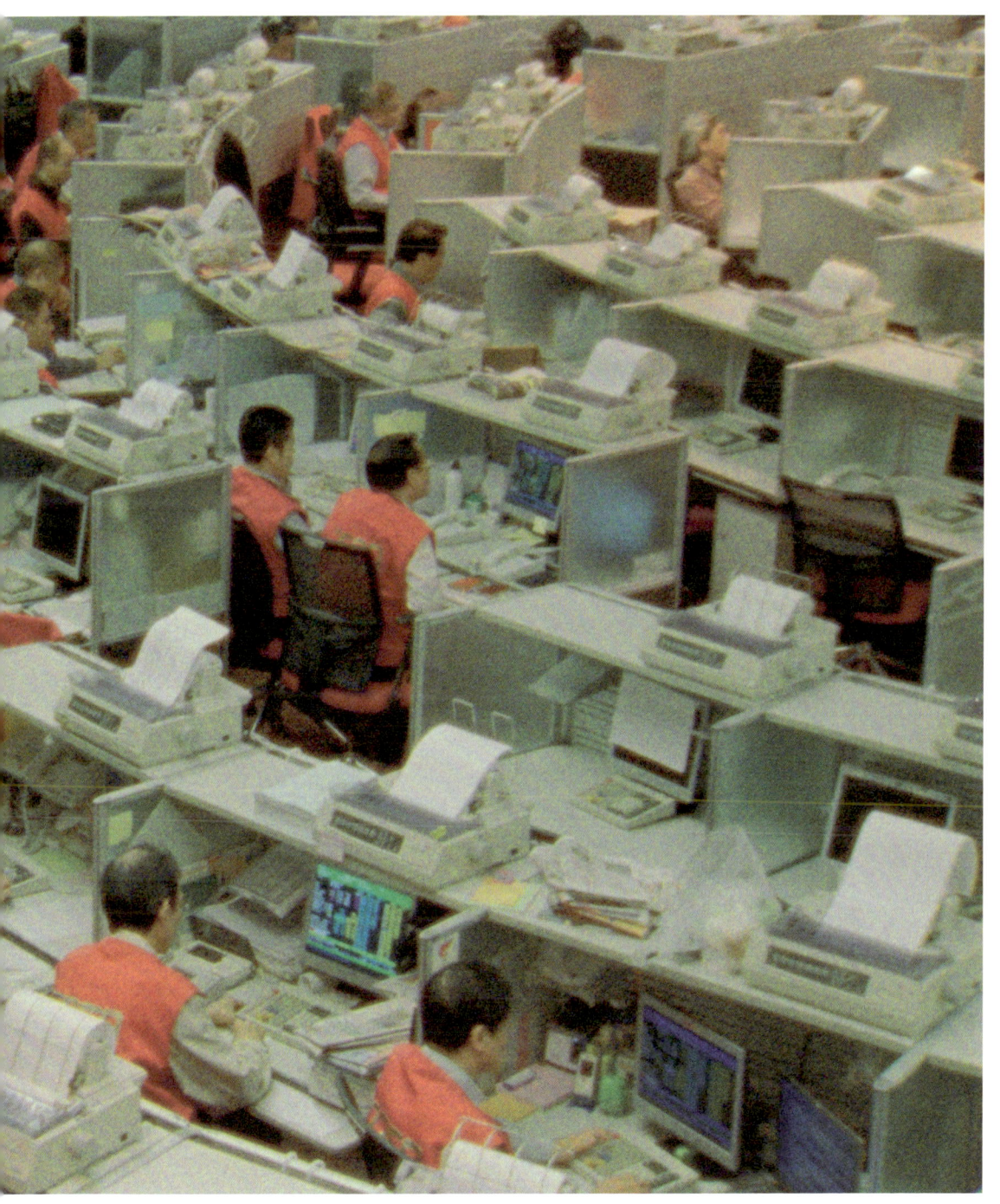

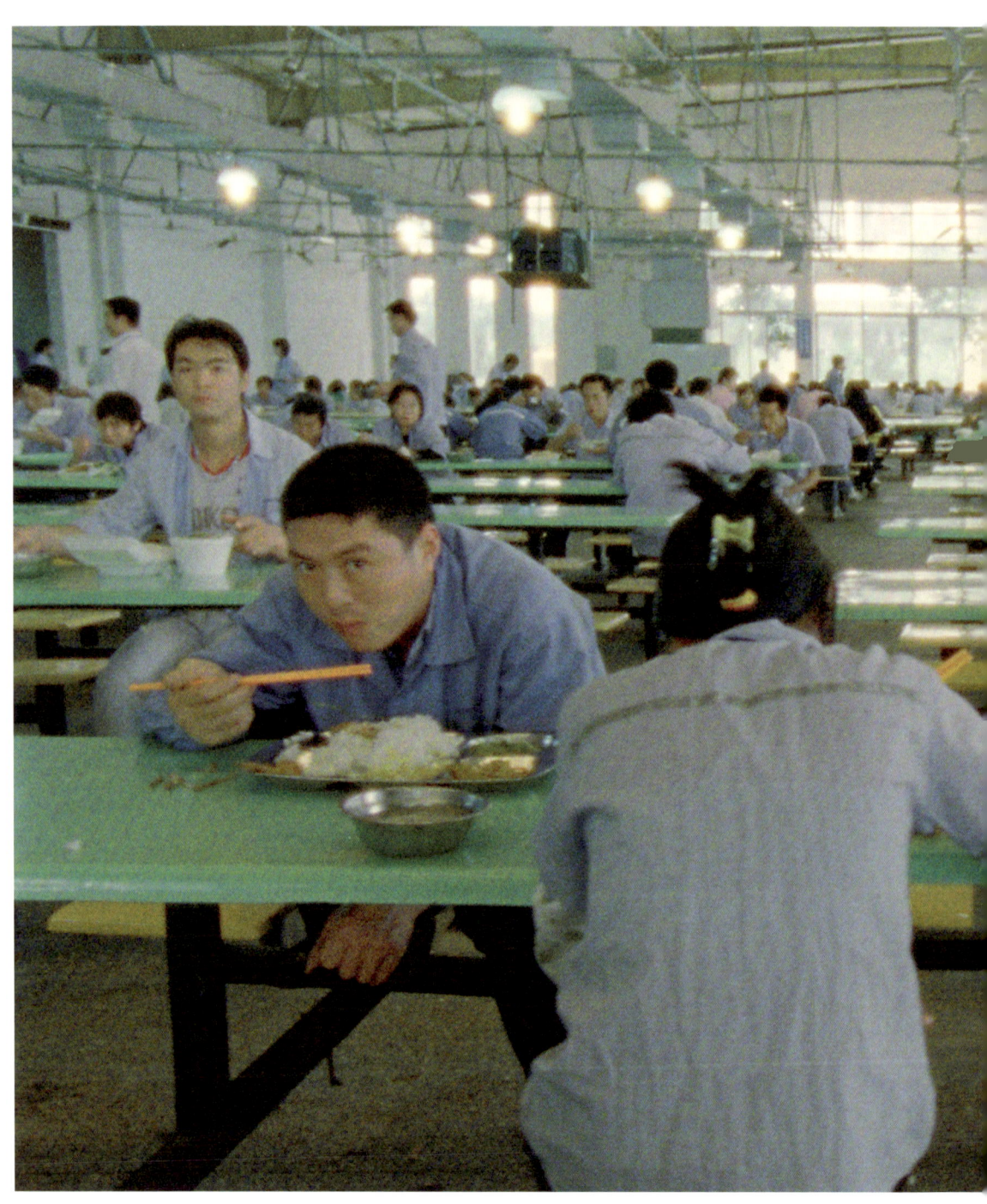

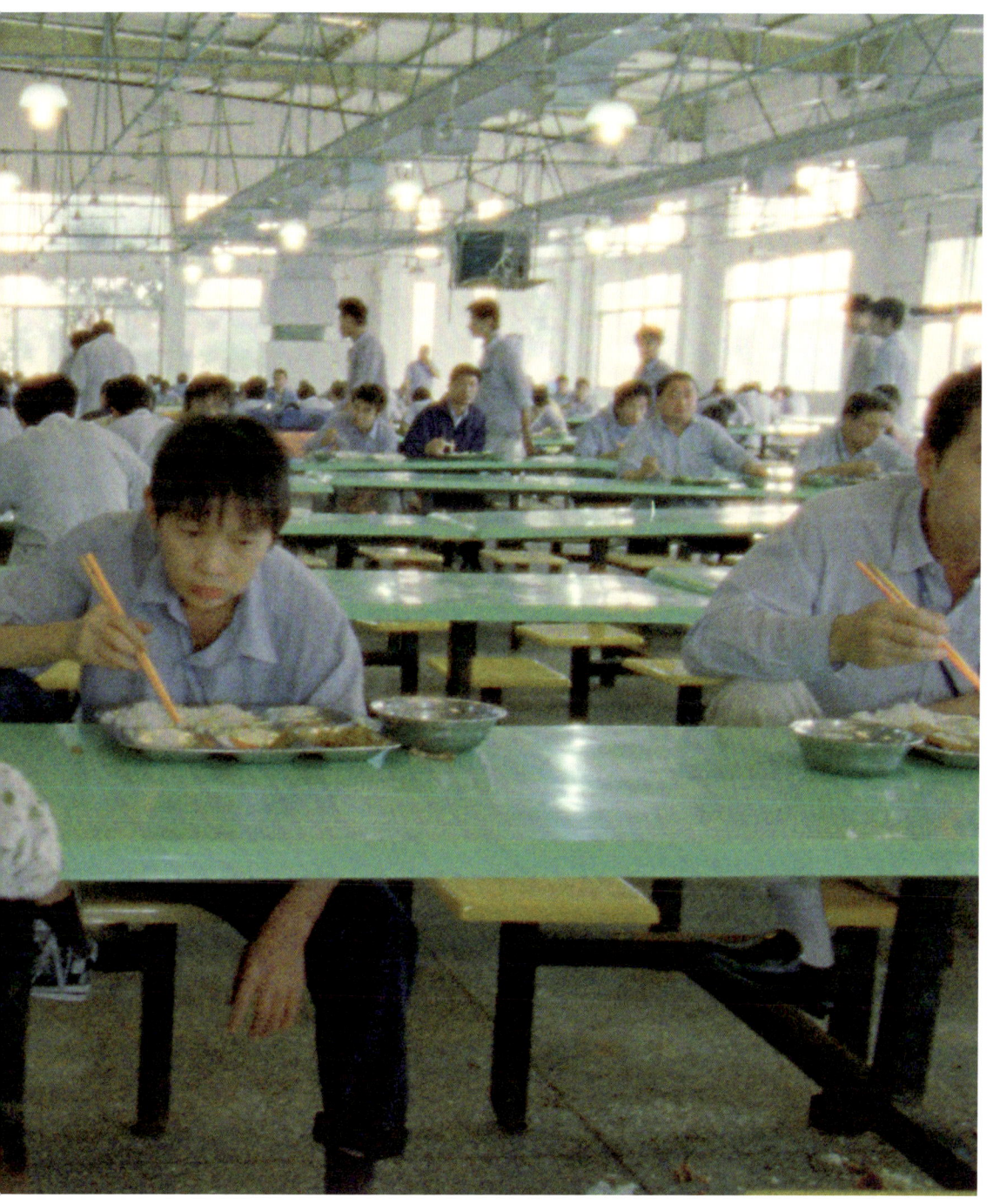

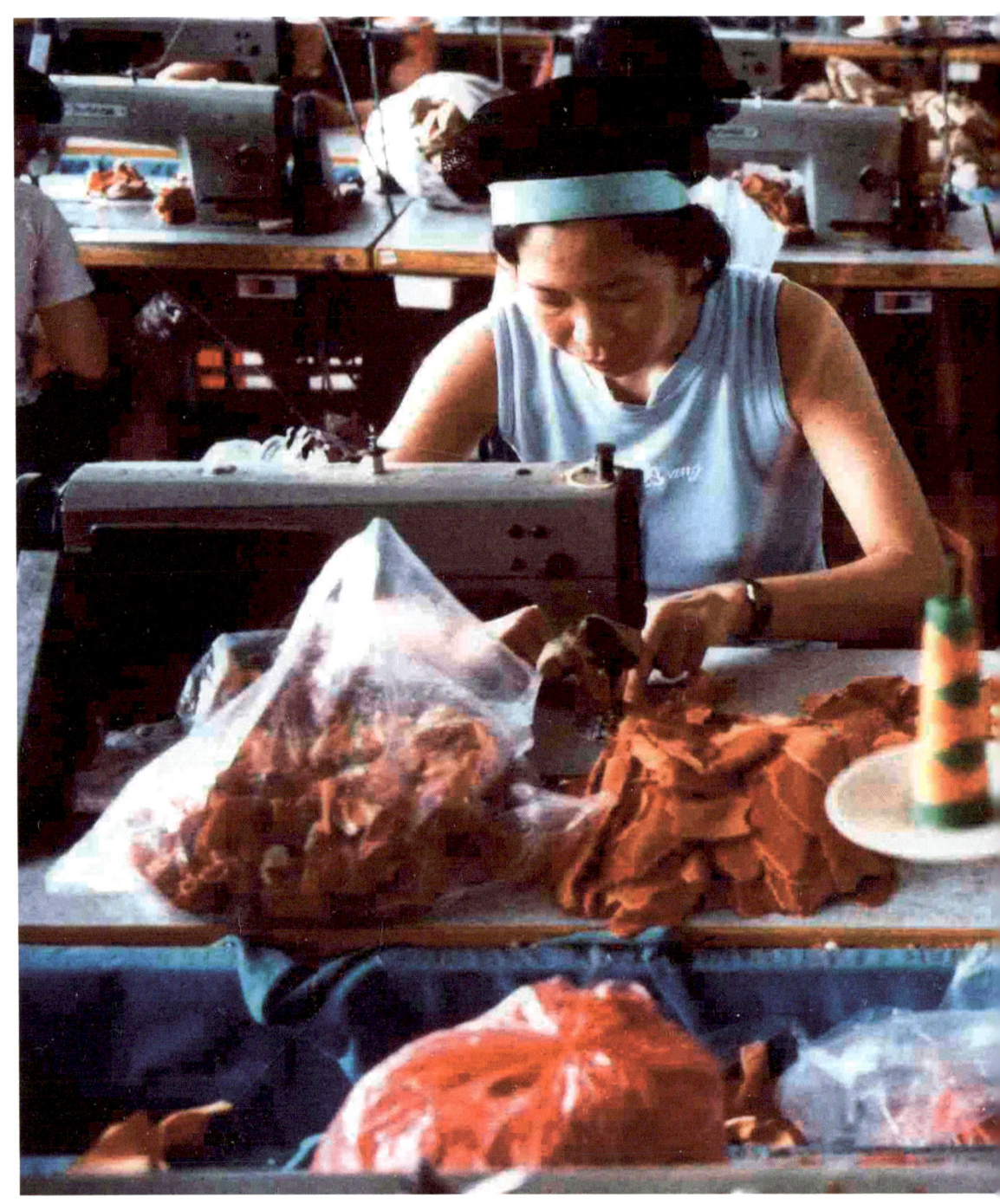

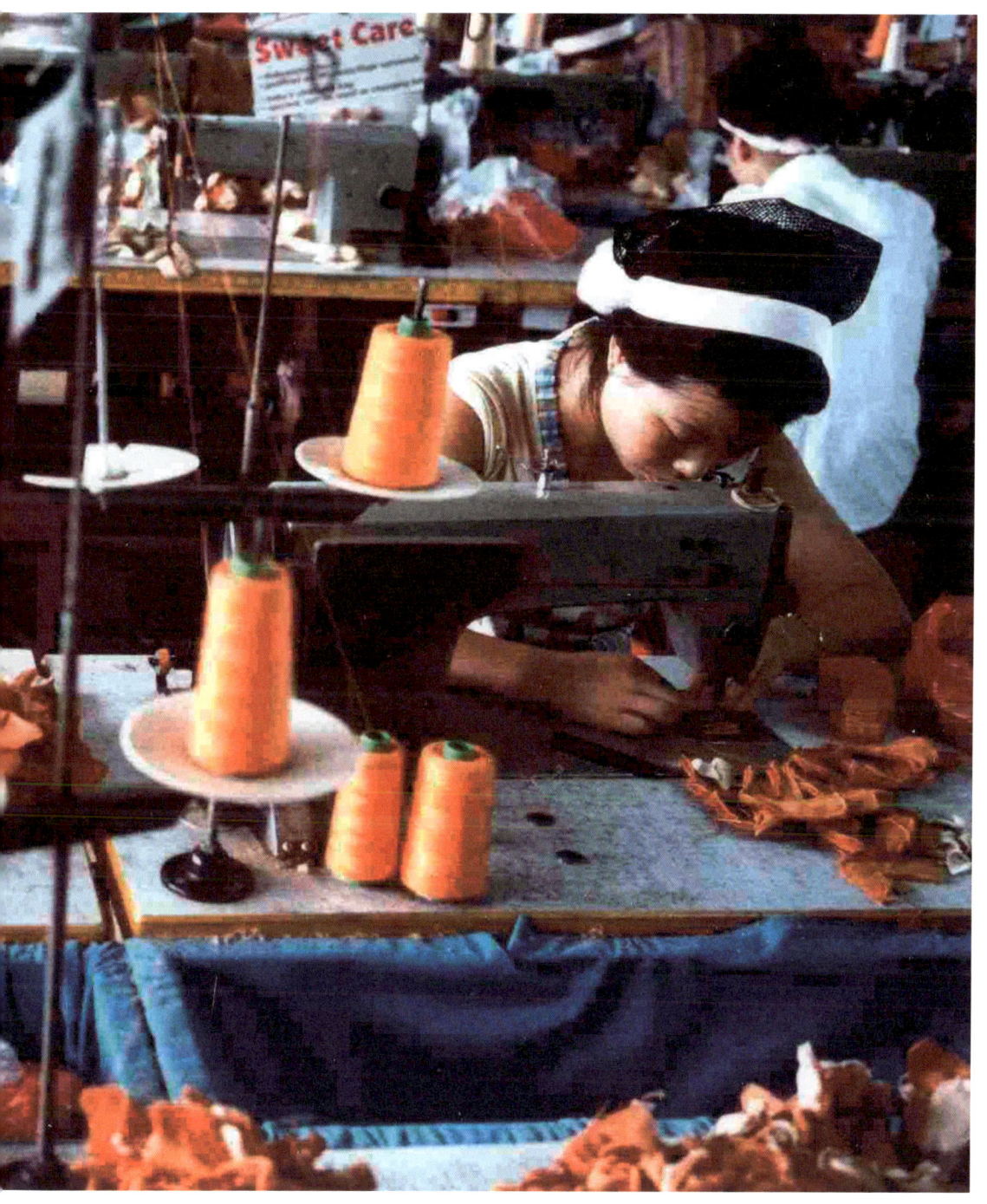

The Forgotten Space

Wim Nijenhuis

Exit City

Home Everywhere and Nowhere

Architecture historian Wim Nijenhuis charts the history of the concept of mobility and its significance for the city and its inhabitants since the Renaissance. Ultimately, the modern-day world city seems engulfed by the ethereal city-world, as the philosopher Paul Virilio argues. There's only one way out: exit!

We find . . . the exit that leads us to cities that are based on movement.

Paul Virilio

Mobility uproots. Along with the ideal of free citizenship, this experience was the foundation for the idea of human dignity. Giovanni Pico della Mirandola (1463-1494), 'comet of his time', was banished from Italy on suspicion of heresy and ultimately found sanctuary under the protection of Lorenzo de Medici in Florence. In his *Oration on the Dignity of Man* (1486) he wrote: 'Man is his own Maker.' He fashioned his idea of himself according to the rules of the *Ars Combinatoria*, that is to say through the combination and stylization of text fragments from the Christian tradition and the broad domain of Hellenic, Hebrew, Arabic and Gnostic thinking.

His complex text calls our attention to the question of whether we are still free citizens and whether we can still fashion a dignified and coherent story out of our seemingly random experiences. This essential question for any uprooted individual is once again current, now that we have definitively been cast adrift in the 'web of trajectories' of our modern-day mobility machinery.

Giovanni Pico's freedom was not autonomy, but the struggle with Fortuna, the goddess of chance. The challenge was to forge subjective coherence and some sort of capacity to act out of the random ruptures occasioned by her whims. This art (of existence) demanded an ambivalent attitude that Giovanni Pico and other great personalities of the Renaissance absorbed from Gnostic texts. *Exodus,* the Gnostic fixation on 'egress', helped them give shape to their otherworldliness: to be *in* but not to be *of* this world. To Giovanni Pico this was the gift of immobility: 'If one is the centre, one remains the gauge of oneself under all circumstances,' and he advised: do not become too entangled in the world, be nowhere with your heart and nowhere with your sinew.

Giovanni Pico undoubtedly travelled on horseback, at the time the fastest mode of transport available to man. In accordance to his otherworldliness, his departure consisted of 'distancing' and 'mounting'. He distanced himself from his home land, and the stupendous velocity of his mount abruptly cut him off from the places he passed. To depart is to withdraw. We experience the same phenomenon today in the car, the train and the airplane, all of which tear us away from our immediate surroundings.

In this context, the expression 'to mount' is evocative. Giovanni mounted his horse and we mount the train. Before we are carried off by the prostheses of mobility, we first make an upward movement. This levitation had a particular significance for Giovanni Pico, given his pronouncements on the vertical movement of the soul between the apex of mania and the nadir of melancholy. Trapped in an incomplete ascension, he floated above the ground as a hostage to his own speed. The saddle, which enabled him to spare his legs, transformed the horse into a moving seat, a hippomobile chair, which like the chair at home now provided support for the sedentary passenger during his displacement.

While the ailments of travelling by foot were avoided by the mobility of the horse, the iniquities of long periods spent sitting, such as the numbing compression of his posterior, were remedied by motility: continually shifting this way and that. This incessant motility made it possible to forget the immobility of his own body, and to forget the vast expanse of the territorial body, the mobility of the animal body was swift and violent.

Melancholy gnawed at the spirit of Giovanni Pico. His gaze was fixed on the ground, as though he were seeking, in this way, to ward off being uprooted.

The 'home' during the Renaissance was the house in the city, that is to say the house in a geopolitically defined immobile (*immeuble*: immovable property) and demarcated 'place' with a historical persistence. At the same time, its limits delineated the (military/legal) territory of a community that fabricated itself like a work of art. The techniques of the Italian *Ragione dello Stato* (reason of state) served to create a rich and powerful home for the free citizen. During the Eighty Years' War the Italian city-state became a model for the Republic of the United Netherlands, a new form of state whose geopolitical dimension remained the most significant feature of the modern nation-state that succeeded it.

The culture of the Renaissance was based on the appearance of things, the paint on the canvas, the bricks that made up a building, the perspective that presented itself. The invention of the railway initiated a culture of disappearance. With uniform speed the machine raced forth over a course that was flattened and emptied: the earth's surface reliefs vanished under bridges, tunnels, excavations and embankments; crossing gates and fences kept out man and beast; dissidents were swept away with cowcatchers. The gaze from the wagon windows averted vertigo by focusing on entities in the distance. This panoramic view eliminated the foreground, transformed the surroundings into scenery and, in the process, signalled the desertification effect of speed on a mental level.

Engine drivers compensated for the shocks and vibrations of the industrial ensemble by bouncing on their toes, and the passengers exhausted themselves in compensating with involuntary muscle contractions. From the observation of the elastic capabilities of cats and tigers was born the idea of combatting this 'fatigue' with springy material. With the introduction of spiral coils under the wagons and inside the horse-hair-upholstered seats, the industrial violence vanished beneath an almost maritime and comforting rocking.

The writer Gustave Flaubert (1821-1880) experienced the train journey as a variation on waiting. As looking out of the train window over-stimulated and bored him, he would start to weep himself stupid. Getting on dead tired shielded him from this misery by means of a healthy nap, and he correlated 'withdrawing from the surroundings' with 'departing from one's person'.

This 'retreat into apathy' became

the habit of many passengers. Their dozing testified to the fact that for them distance had disappeared in favour of the time span of the journey.

With the train began the steady liquefaction of the classical city. The former 'place' mutated into the 'web of trajectories' of the modern metropolis. The restrictive form of settlement was obsolete as a principle of security and wealth, and it was replaced by the principle of unfettered circulation. Spurred on by the railway station at its edge, a network of broad streets snaked its way across what had been the urban 'sanctuary' of the past and linked it with newer and newer suburbs under the pressure of the masses being dragged along in the flow.

Henceforth the city was a system of 'refuges, which man has reserved for his brief or permanent abode whenever he yearns to cut himself off from the great movement that propels humanity', said Ildefons Cerdà in his *General Theory of Urbanization* (1867). In Paris, great thoroughfare boulevards radiating from the train stations were laid across the existing city between 1853 and 1869. In contrast to the medieval alleyways and open places that had been stages for everyday neighbourhood life, they reflected a new idea of the city, predicated on mobility, mass, and progress. In 1848 Friedrich Engels wrote that 'the boulevards, the great arteries of Parisian life, were the stage of the first great gatherings'. Max Weber (1864-1920) observed of Rosa Luxemburg and Karl Liebknecht: 'They mobilized the street, and the street killed them.' The boulevard made the street the new

'place of politics'.

The boulevards afforded room for social mobility. The working-class girl Nana in Émile Zola's novel mingled with the bourgeoisie as a *cocotte*, and driving with her latest lover to and from the Théâtre des Variétés this *femme fatale* cast her alms, from the height of her carriage, to the local residents that stayed behind on the pavement.

In his essay 'Total Mobilization' Ernst Jünger (1895-1990) wonders why the majority of people are willing to be placated by the heightened level of activity of the modern metropolis. The secret, he says, lies in a representation of freedom that blinds people to the fatalist nature of mobilization. In practice, mobilization means the subjection of life to prescriptive demands. The useless disappears and everyone is conscripted into a great advancing 'storm assault', which also leaves its mark on the urban environment and cultural thinking.

Mobilization, Jünger says, is an act of fate, because it is the inevitable continuation of logistical warfare in peacetime. During the First World War, production capacity and logistics were challenged beyond a point of no return, which definitively transformed all societies into 'volcanic metal factories' in competition with one another.

In Total Mobilization, the Renaissance's struggle with the random withers away, and there is no room for the freedom of movement and self-determination, let alone the right to self-preservation, of the Enlightenment. Jünger's answer to the violence of Total Mobilization is *désinvolture*: nonchalance, an internally anarchist, detached and aesthetic attitude that is closer to magic, coincidence and luck than to will and desire: 'In this war . . . I had a very impersonal feeling, as though I were observing myself through binoculars. For the first time I could hear the hiss of the little projectiles, as though they were whistling past a lifeless object.'

The futurists went off in search of their freedom 'in speed'. In the charging automobile they sought the technological substitute to the *femme fatale*. Just as this vector woman whisked her lovers away from reality by beguiling their senses, so was the car the vector machine that revealed a world beyond perspective. Marinetti named his racing car Nikè, goddess of victory: the victory was over the solidity of the view of the world in favour of its generalized liquification (liquidation by liquifaction).

The motorways tamed the car. The liquid tumult of the environment was converted into a panoramic 'film' fluidly streaming by, even as the design of petrol pumps, viaducts and landscape suggested a last confinement in the unity and the measure of the national territory.

Goebbels said about the autobahn: 'Risk, but with comfort.' The driver firmly ensconced in padded clothing, resembling a moving mummy, vanished behind the windscreen into a cabin. The smoothness of the motorway, the softness of the seats, the supple suspension and the muffling of the engine noise and of the whistling wind produced a 'heightened sense of well-being', that helped one forget the 'iron roughness'

of the speeding vehicle. Gradually the enclosed cabin evolved into our 'mobile living room' of today, with as typical technological problem the quality of the 'liberated seat'.

The ultimate phase of this process was unveiled on television some time ago by a BMW advert. We see a car driving in the rain. In the front sits the driver, in the back a middle-aged gentleman. He has a reading lamp, a mobile phone, a laptop and a small television screen. Everything exudes the feel of an imperturbable interior. The gentleman pays no attention to the landscape rushing by, because he is occupied with information coming at him at a speed the car can never reach. This sedentary passenger 'inhabits' the time of the electronic information that simultaneously, at the speed of light, fixes the car in the relatively inert form of a traceable and localizable abode.

Total Mobilization brought us the 'dromocratic' (*dromos*: race and path) megalopolis, where the art of creating 'unknown soldiers of speed' out of all social categories has been perfected. Since the Second World War we have seen the city, with its set place and its set dimensions, gradually dissolve into the currents of the traffic system. First the metropolis of trajectories vanished into the commuter city, scattering pieces of the urban around the surrounding countryside. The fluid freedom of movement of the car then brought about the urban sprawl, which is now dissolving in turn into the nebular city – the fusion of urban areas – putting an end to the traditional contrast between city and country, while the relationship between centre and periphery is being upended by Edge Cities along the motorways.

'Being on one's way' is becoming a regular component of daily life. Those who surround us and give the impression of staying put will often disappear forever. Everywhere we see the disintegrating and destabilizing effects of the pulsating breath of the transport system that deports all the former inhabitants in all directions.

The majority of the people who can be found in an urban neighbourhood at any given time leave again, either because they work there but do not spend the night there, or because they spend the night there but do not work there. Where is the city dweller? Where is his neighbourhood, his refuge? Is the bus or the commuter train now where relationships are initiated? We have to learn to see the residential neighbourhood as an 'elastic range', sometimes stretched by a holiday, and the inhabitant as a 'temporary citizen', whose habitat can no longer be localized.

Fascism waged politics by addressing 'citizens sent on their way' through radio speeches. Between the mobiles on the roads and the immobiles at home, the radio established a connecting speaking space, an elastic sonosphere, in which one could be home even when one was on the go. During the Second World War, British hostesses kept the minds of bomber crews off the horrors of the moment by keeping them riveted to the familiar atmosphere of the home front with soft whispers.

In the 1960s, artists such as Wim T. Schippers and groups such as the International Situationists (1957-1972) sought to resist the elimination of street life as a result of ever-increasing automobile traffic. The 'social divorce' of the 'sluggish bodies' in the vehicles was to be countered by the *dérive*, the poetic wandering on foot with its heightened chances for encounter. The functional city was an object of revulsion, littered with useful goals and logical journeys, with as its nadir the pitifully repetitive movement pattern of working people. The *dérives* anticipated the urban nomad, unfettered and driven by his emotions, hailed as the ideal embodiment of expanding leisure time. The street was to become the space of the 'situation': 'A moment in life, concretely and deliberately constructed across the grain of the collective organization of a uniform environment and a conjunction of events.'

Electronic means of communications like television, video and the Internet put an end to the 'situation'. Because video technology, as we know it from security cameras in parking garages, can instantly present places located at any distance from the observer, it replaces the classical unity of place, shared by the observer and the observed environment, with a new and unique unity of time: real time. The direct view, dependent on the transparency of the air or the glass, is supplemented by video with an indirect view to which distance and opacity are no obstacle. At the same time, the relationship to reality changes, because the real-time presentations initiate a 'teletopological reality' in the consciousness of the observer, that is to say that not only do the places come to him thanks to electromagnetic transfer technology, but he also mentally transports himself to the places observed, without the actual distance playing any role. Topologically means that reality has acquired an elastic topography, while the prefix 'tele' alludes to the black holes created in the mental map of the observer by the loss of the unity of place. Once the static teletopological reality of the video security system is supplemented by moving cameras attached to balloons, on cars and in satellites, a global, virtual and dynamic environment will emerge, in which real time will always be the essential unifying principle.

The consequences of this can be investigated using a hybrid vehicle that will replace the view through the windscreen of the car and that could be modelled on the cockpit of a flight simulator. The traveller need no longer go anywhere to see other places; he need not even leave the house. For this fusion of dwelling and vehicle, technophilosopher Virilio introduced the term 'habitacle'. The absolutization of its interior will come at the expense of the threshold, the architectural detail that was *the* symbol of the relationship between 'home' and 'city' and the locus of the neighbourly chat in the doorway. Where is the inhabitant of the habitacle now home? His location-specific dwelling interior with the threshold at the exit will mutate, thanks to communication technology, into an abstract ethereal 'site', or better yet, an electronic anamorphosis of the threshold.

The 'politics of the polis' presumed that citizens had to leave their houses in order to take part in public affairs, but public affairs, under pressure of the habitacle, will increasingly be oriented towards those who stay home. The public space will be besieged by the public image on the display monitors. The monumental environments in the city, with their hard materials and their set dimensions, will be confronted by moving and elastic images flowing by as an organized stream, which cannot fail to make an impact on social, sexual and economic relations, which become less and less solid by the day.

In the third millennium, the nebular metropolis is being affected by the first symptoms of ex-urbanization, whereby the 'chosen place' and 'the electeddomicile' are being edged out by 'sites of departure'. After the housing debacle, which was precipitated by unsecured mortgages and the credit crisis, the real estate sector is now seeking refuge in the latest mutations of the geopolitical city gates of the past. Throughout Europe and Asia, as a result of the latest acceleration brought about by the high-speed train, we see reconstructions of railway stations and airports that simultaneously attempt to transform them into new urban centres. What is being created is the Exit City, a logistical platform dedicated to the general outsourcing of its inhabitants, for which Airport City Schiphol and the Utrecht Public Transport Terminal are still only scale models. Here 'urban potential' is synonymous with the 'potential of the sites of departure', that is to say of the number of 'passengers in circulation'. City outskirts have to become 'high-quality urban centre areas'

(Dutch Ministry of Public Housing, Spatial Planning and the Environment), 'ultimate sites of urbaneness' (Dutch Government Railways Architect), '*sites where the transport flows become one with . . . urban centres*'. In December 2010 we got a taste of the 'potential' this fusion will produce, when snow and mismanagement forced thousands of stranded passengers to spend the night on the floor, on the benches and on the quickly improvised cots of the airports and railway stations.

In comparison with the acceleration of progress, which continues to be the privileged domain of such electronic devices for instantaneous transfer as the mobile phone, transport systems have no more to offer than a gradual yet crucial expansion of transport capacity. Their focus is no longer on speed, but on the reduction of delays in the sites of transfer and transit, the 'multimodal platforms', where separate modes of transport like the car, the taxi, the (hired) bicycle, the bus, the tram, the metro, the train and even the airplane come together. The strategy is derived from the just-in-time distribution logistics of freight transport, the quantities of which have increased exponentially, to the detriment of storage in warehouses. This also explains the (network) position of all those sites along the coasts of continents where ground and air transport is being combined with maritime freight. The source of this transport revolution is undeniably at sea; it is a revolution in 'load capacity', symbolized by the container ship.

This casts a unique light on recent exercises in ex-urbanization, such as the proposal in The Hague in 2007 to house 40,000 Polish immigrants in containers, after this had become common housing practice for students in the abandoned docklands of Amsterdam. The Exit City is based on movement, but its currents are relatively 'fixed' by a fusion with the 'omnipolis', which, supported by Internet and satellite communications, can crop up anywhere in ever-changing compositions. In the omnipolis, 'time' city and interconnective domain of the global real-time community, life is not based on the 'inertia of a place' as in the polis and the classical city, but on the 'inertial effects' resulting from instantaneous, electromagnetic connections.

The first inertial effect comes from the instant traceability of anyone by means of GPS tracking, electronic ankle bracelets (to which Julian Assange was sentenced by a British court in December 2010) and implanted chips, limited for the time being to animals in the wild. We must keep in mind that as mobility increases, control over it will intensify.

A second inertial effect lies in the fact that the real-time connections of the omnipolis, through their instantaneous and ubiquitous nature, cause an effect of contraction in our mental space, which surpasses that of the globalization of capital transfer and the world economy. The inhabitants of the omnipolis will be 'planetary people' clinging to their devices, for whom the world has shrunk to an 'abstract and ethereal point in the void'.

In the global city currently under

Truck from Guatamala stopped at the Mexican border, March 1999. From: Raymond Depardon, Paul Virilio, *Native Land: Stop Eject* (Paris: Fondation Cartier pour l'art contemporain, 2008).

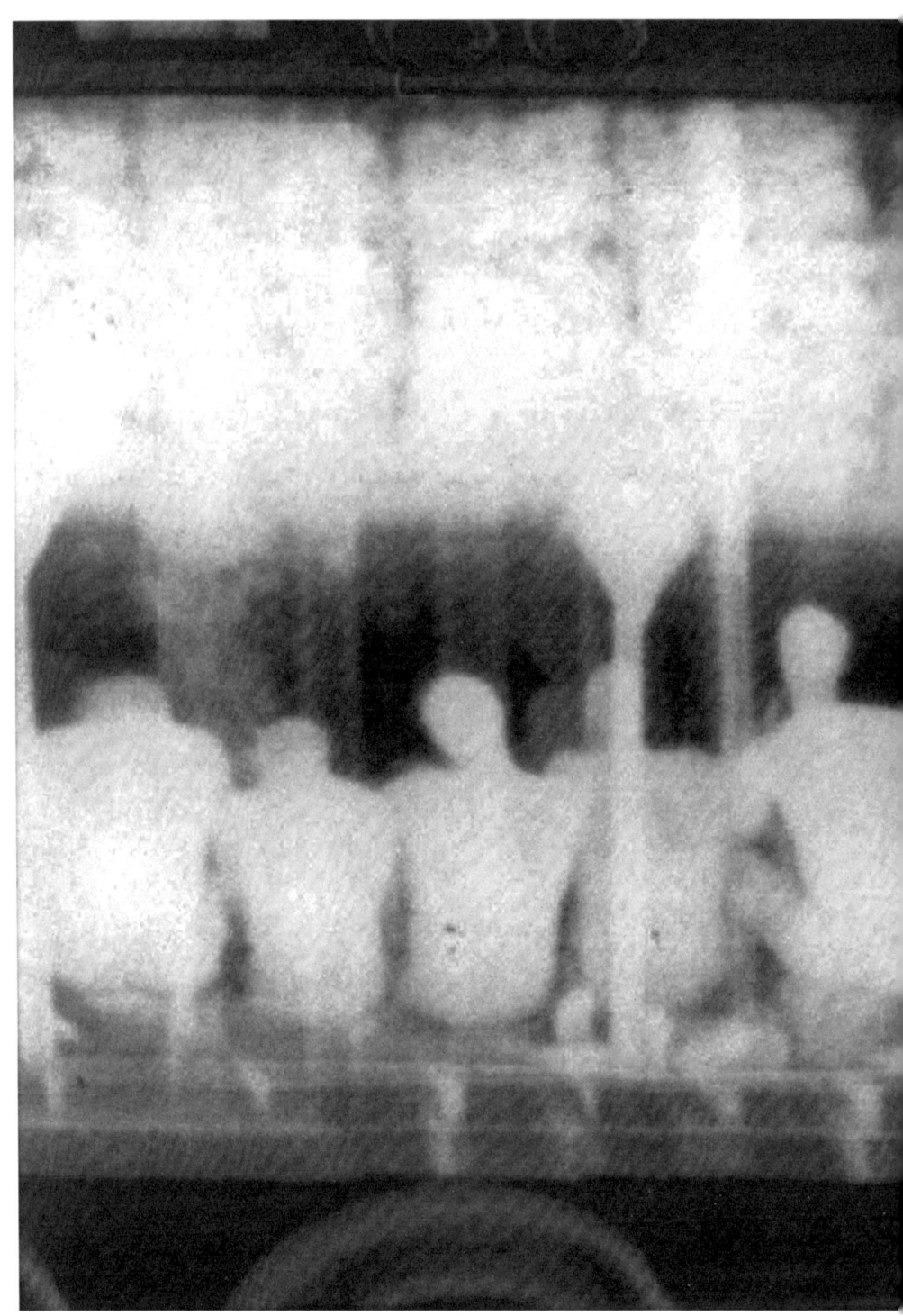

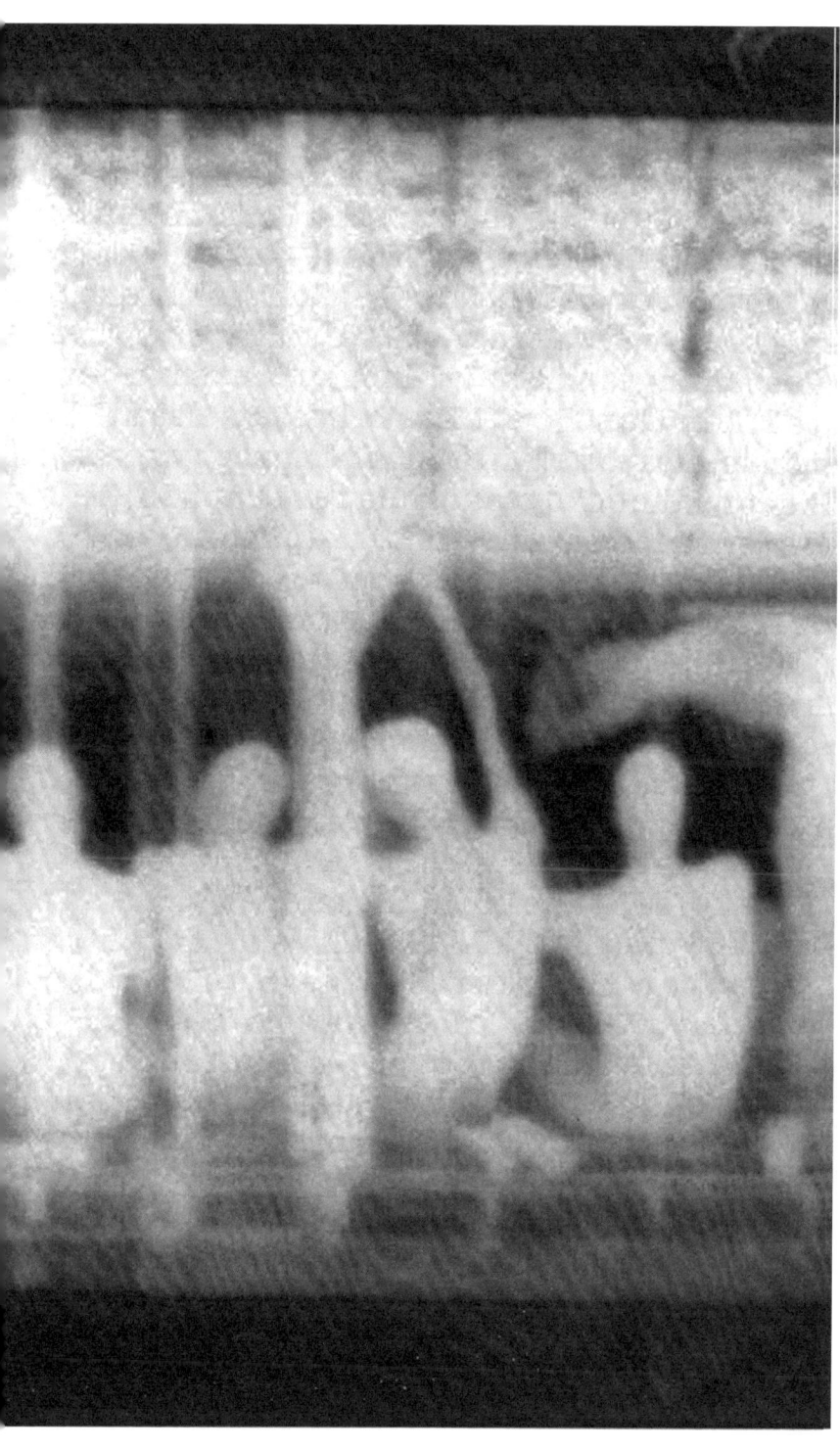

A relatively new type of vessel is the 'open top' or hatchless container ship. The advantage of the open top is that it speeds up loading and unloading times, since it is unnecessary to stop and remove the water-tight hatches that cover the holds of other types of container ships. www.transport-overzee.nl/Schepen.html

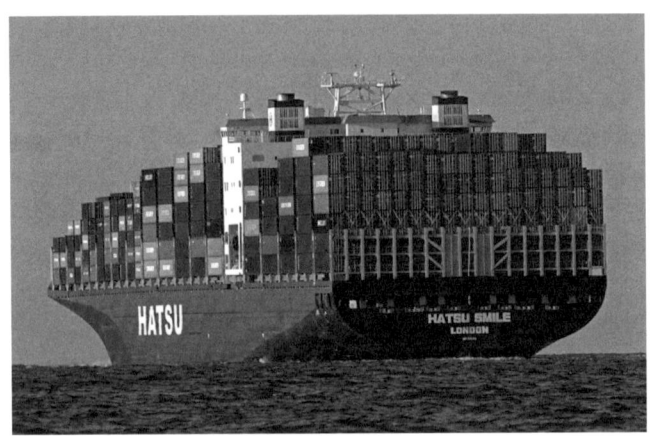

Eleven cranes simultaneously unload the largest container ship in the world, the Emma Maersk.
From the Powerpoint series *Container Ships for Big Harbours*.

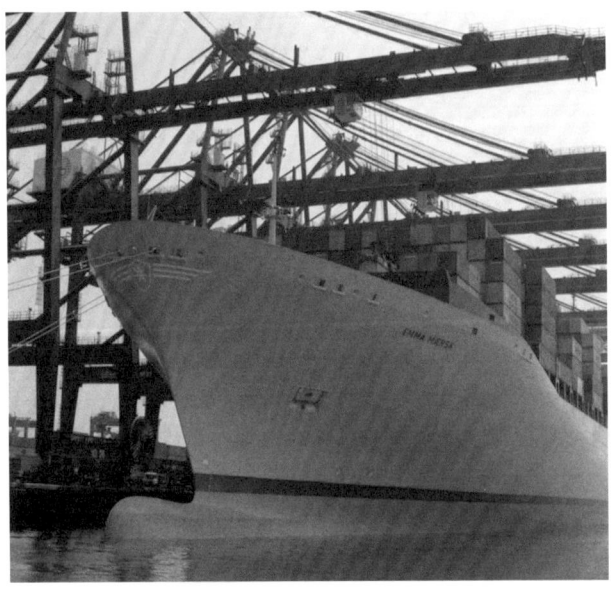

Leipzig Station, a combination of a station and a shopping mall, 1998
Photo: Matthijs van Wageningen

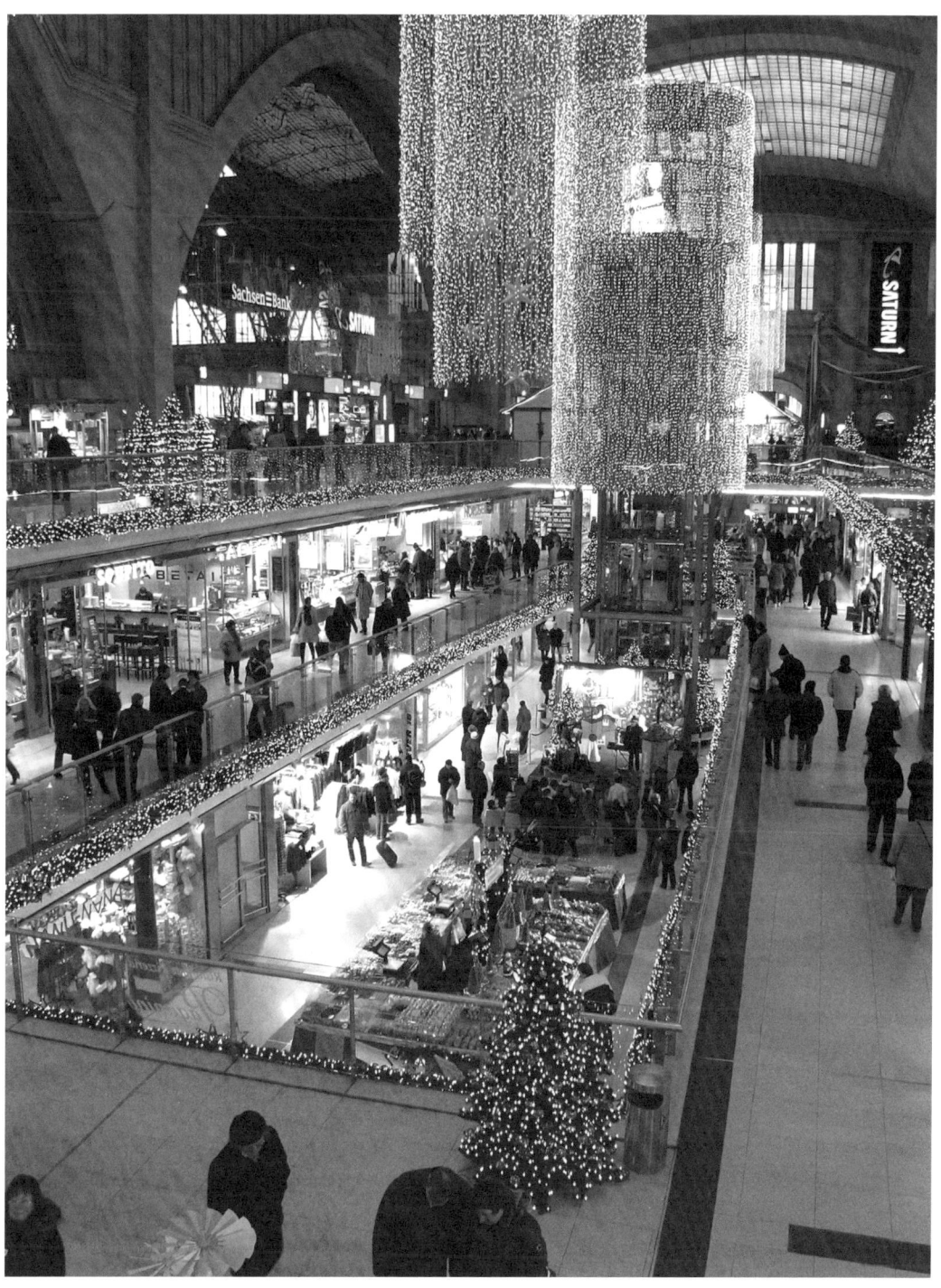

construction, geographical space, with its set distances, will take second place. The transport system, but especially the 'distanceless gaseous form' of the omnipolis, which is everywhere and nowhere, and penetrates everything, will undermine not only the boundaries and laws of a state but also the local identity of its individuals, indeed the whole idea of dwelling.

Always traceable through security cameras and GPS, and thanks to the mobile phone and the laptop, the lifts, the escalators, the stations, the display monitors and the airplanes, the dweller of the past will transform into the 'sedentary nomad' of the near future, who will be home everywhere (and nowhere).

The 'abode in the flow' or 'dwelling in traffic' that catapults the erstwhile city-dwellers in the era of globalization undermines the geopolitical foundation of the elected domicile and the meaning of the address in the city. Whereas the city in antiquity was the immobile centre of the world, with the Exit City we have dispensed with geography, for its centre consists of electromagnetic connections that know no place and distance. Today's *axis mundi* is the sacred axis of real time, spinning around itself like a whirlwind the intercontinental streams of those other nomads who are home nowhere except in the streets, the stations, the boats, the tents and the camps.

In his 2010 Spinoza lecture 'Humanism: The Human Being as Work in Progress', Richard Sennett brings up two exiles: Spinoza and Pico della Mirandola. In their personal victory over their displacement, he sees a lesson

for our world, 'filled with mobile people – economic migrants and political exiles', because the uprooted migrant could find its unity in the life story it tells. Sennett adds that modern capitalism turns 'everyone into a work migrant and many into work exiles'. Holding together the fragmentary experiences that result from displacement and job loss, and that are often sources of suffering and disorientation, Sennett says, requires the ability to take a step back: 'The social challenge people face in doing so comes from those workplaces, political regimes, religions and ethnic cultures which demand absolute immersion and total engagement.' In order to achieve distance we 'need an idea of ourselves as simultaneously engaged and detached'. This could entail a prominent role for the city as a 'material factor'. The city, to Sennett, is primarily a 'tribological training school', where by learning to deal with conflict, resistance and discomfort we can find a home base after all, as he has argued throughout his oeuvre, beginning with *Flesh and Stone: The Body and the City in Western Civilisation* (1994).

Although Sennett's thinking about distance and friction is influenced by the aesthetics of existence of Michel Foucault, with his allusion to Pico della Mirandola he places the Gnostic problem of the exodus, the egress, on the agenda. Playing with the egress makes possible a new form of critical behaviour, what Peter Sloterdijk calls 'otherworldliness' in 'Die wahre Irrlehre' ('The True Heresy', 1993). This was the quest of ancient Gnosticism, which formulated for the first time in history a dualist principle that makes possible an attitude of 'as if not': that is to say living *in* this world, without being *of* this world. 'We are not of this world and this world is not of us,' said the Cathars, who without the other world they believed in would have been effortlessly inserted into the only remaining 'world monster' and would have lost themselves in the 'endlessly twisting coils of its bowels'. For both Sennett and Sloterdijk our 'dissolution of the global imperative' will demand an attitude that is dependent on training, discursive practice and imagination.

Exile is a typically geographic phenomenon. In the free cities of the Middle Ages, the exile was someone who was condemned to reside *extra muros*, that is to say outside the city, and who could no longer come back within its legal territory. To signify banishment, the jurisdiction of the city was demarcated by banning posts. The condemned person was considered to have left the city once he or she had gone past these. This punishment was not once directed at the outsider, but at the person who had left his or her home behind in the city and whom banishment cut off from friends and family.

In *The Global City* (1991) Saskia Sassen – Sennett's wife – introduced the concept of the 'global city': a geographically diffuse network of 'specific places, the spaces, internal dynamics and social structures of which are significant'. Virilio argues that this world city, in its congregating effects, will be overtaken by the ethereal 'city-world' of interconnective and instantaneous links. In this one and only 'city-world',

everyone, thanks to the mobile phone and the laptop, will always be 'home', because here places of exile have been abolished along with distances and boundaries. In this time city without an 'outside', banishment can at most mean being put 'on hold'. (Sherry Turkle, *Alone Together*, 2011)

If in an attempt to resist the integration pressure of the labour market or of our ethnic group we seek refuge in the solid and physical world city of the future, what kind of city will that be? How can we have meaningfully practiced interaction with an environment full of cameras, detectors, body scanners and tracking devices?

Ultimately . . . as we ascend the escalators of the Exit City, the air terminals and the public transport terminals, under the watchful eye of security cameras and automatic scanners, surrounded by the streams of the public image, grab our mobile phone and proceed blindly on our way because we are concentrating more on the audiovisual pseudo-shape of the other carried over electromagnetic waves than on the flesh-and-blood people around us . . . do we not find, in the blink of an eye and without any discursive strategy whatsoever . . . the exit out of the physical world?

Bibliography

J. Armitage, 'In the Cities of the Beyond: An Interview with Paul Virilio', in *2030: Warzone Amsterdam*, *Open* no. 18 (Rotterdam, NAi Publishers, 2009), 100-111

R. v.d. Bijl (ed.), *Station Centraal. Over het samenbinden van station en stad*, Rotterdam, 010 Publishers, 2010)

I. Cerdà, *Teoría general de la urbanización y aplicación de sus principios y doctrinas a la reforma y ensanche de Barcelona* (Madrid, 1867, Barcelona: Instituto de Estudios Fiscales, 1968)
See also A. Soria y Puig (ed.), *Cerdà: The Five Bases of the General Theory of Urbanization*, with a foreword by Albert Serratosa, translated by Bernard Miller, Mary Fons i Fleming (Madrid: Electa, 1999)

L.F. Földényi, *Melancholie* (Munich: Matthes & Seitz, 1988)

G. Debord, *De spektakelmaatschappij* (Baarn: Wereldvenster, 1976). Orig. *La société du spectacle* (Paris, 1967)

S. Giedion, *Space, Time and Architecture* (Cambridge, MA: Harvard University Press, 1941)

J. Goebbels, *Kampf um Berlin* (Munich: Zentralverlag der NSDAP, 1934)

E. Jünger, 'Die totale Mobilmachung', in: *Krieg und Krieger* (Berlin: Junker und Dünnhaupt, 1930)

E. Jünger, *Oorlogsroes* (Amsterdam: de Arbeiderspers, 2002). Orig. *In Stahlgewittern* (Berlin, 1922 [1920])

R. Mulder, et al., 'Comfort', in *Forum*, vol. 38 (1995) no. 1+2

W. Nijenhuis, 'City Frontiers and Their Disappearance', in 'The Periphery', *Architectural Design Profile*, (1994) no. 108, 13-17

W. Nijenhuis, 'De auto in de tijd van de lichtsnelheid', *Rem*, October 1991, 16-21

W. Nijenhuis and W. van Winden, *De diabolische snelweg* (Rotterdam: 010 Publishers, 2007)

W. Nijenhuis, *Een wolk van duister weten. Geschriften over Stedenbouw(Geschiedenis)*, dissertation (Eindhoven, 2003)

G. Oestreich, *Geist und Gestalt des frühmodernen Staates* (Berlin: Duncker & Humblot, 1969)

Pico della Mirandola, *Rede over de menselijke waardigheid*, translated into Dutch and annotated by Michiel op de Coul, with an introduction and afterword by Jan Papy (Groningen: Historische Uitgeverij, 2008). Orig. Latin, *Conclusiones*, 1486

H-C. Puech, 'Phänomenologie der Gnosis, Collège de France, 1952-1957', in: Wolfgang Schultz, *Dokumente der Gnosis* (Berlin: Matthes & Seitz, 1986), 34-35. On the idea of egress in Gnosticism.

S. Sadler, *The Situationist City* (Cambridge, MA and London: MIT Press, 1998)

S. Sassen, *The Global City: New York, London, Tokyo* (Princeton, NJ: Princeton University Press, 1991)

W. Schivelbusch, *The Railway Journey: The Industrialization of Time and Space in the Nineteenth Century* (Berkeley, CA: The University of California Press, 1986). Orig. German, 1977

H. Schwilk, *Ernst Jünger. Leben und Werk in Bildern und Texten* [Ernst Jünger: Life and Work in Pictures and Texts] (Stuttgart: Klett-Cotta, 1988)

R. Sennett, *De mens als werk in uitvoering* (Amsterdam: Uitgeverij Boom/Stichting Internationale Spinozalens, 2010)

P. Sloterdijk, 'Die wahre Irrlehre. Über die Weltreligion der Weltlosigkeit', in: P. Sloterdijk and T.H. Macho, *Weltrevolution der Seele. Ein Lese- und Arbeitsbuch der Gnosis* (Zurich: Artemis & Winkler Verlag, 1995), 17-51

J. Tellinga and A. Mulder (ed.), *L'Europe à grande vitesse* (Rotterdam: NAi Publishers, 1996)

S. Turkle, *Alone Together: Why We Expect More from Technology and Less from Each Other* (New York: Basic Books, 2011)

P. Virilio, *The Aesthetics of Disappearance* (translated by Philip Beitchman) (New York: Semiotext(e), 1991). Orig. *L'Esthétique de la disparition* (Paris, 1980)

P. Virilio, *Pure War* (New York: Semiotext(e), 1997)

P. Virilio, *The Vision Machine* (Bloomington: Indiana University Press, 1994). Orig. *La machine de vision* (Paris, 1988)

P. Virilio, *Speed and Politics: An Essay on Dromology* (New York: Semiotext(e), 1986). Orig. *Vitesse et politique: essai de dromologie* (Paris, 1977)

P. Virilio, *The Lost Dimension* (New York: Semiotext(e), 1991). Orig. *L'espace critique* (Paris, 1984)

P. Virilio, *Het horizon negatief. Essay over dromoscopie* (Amsterdam: Uitgeverij Duizend & Een, 1989). Orig. *L'horizon négatif: essai de dromoscopie* (Paris, 1984)

P. Virilio, *Polar Inertia* (London: Sage, 1999)

P. Virilio, 'Stop eject', in: Raymond Depardon and Paul Virilio, *Native Land: Stop Eject* (catalogue) (Paris: Fondation Cartier pour l'art contemporain, 2008), 184-204

P. Virilio, 'Le littoral, la dernière frontière' (interview with Jean-Louis Violeau), *Eurozine*, 15 December 2010, www.eurozine.com/articles/2010-12-15-virilio-fr.html

E. Zola, *Nana* (Blaricum: Bigot & van Rossum B.V., 1976 [1880])

Charlotte Lebbe

The Ban-Opticon in the Schengen Area

The Ambivalent Meaning of Mobility

In the process of globalization, mobility has become characterized by ambivalence. On the one hand, we are witnessing ever greater control of the movements of migrants, and on the other, a rich elite can travel freely all over the world. The free flow of people, capital and goods within the Schengen Area has required an increasingly stricter policing of its external borders. Combined with innovative digital techniques, this has led to a shift from a system of control to a proactive system of selection and exclusion.

Globalization is generally (and certainly from the point of view of modernism) directly associated with homogenization, a process in which the world evolves into a unified whole – the global village. The speed with which goods and people travel across the globe has risen exponentially and is constantly increasing. Thanks to technological innovations, distance and time are becoming less and less relevant. Hybrid cultural expressions confirm this picture of uniformity. Millions of ideas are spread all over the world every day via the Internet. Nobody blinks an eye anymore at phenomena like 'Thai boxing girls in Amsterdam, Asian rap in London, Irish bagels, Chinese tacos and Mardi Gras Indians in the United States or Mexican schoolgirls dressed in Greek togas dancing in the style of Isadora Duncan'.[1] Political initiatives tie in with this by propagating an open border policy.

1. N.J. Pieterse, quoted in: J. Friedman, 'The Hybridization of Roots and the Abhorrence of the Bush', in: M. Featherstone, S. Lash (ed.), *Spaces of Culture* (London: Sage, 1999), 236.

Within the Schengen Area, whose territory nearly coincides with that of the European Union, internal border controls have been abolished. Here, the free movement of people, goods, capital and services is a reality.

However, the same forces that reinforce this picture of a uniform, universal world are also at the bottom of the discord and divisions on earth. 'Globalization divides as much as it unites; it divides as it unites,' writes Zygmunt Bauman in the introduction to his book *Globaliza-tion: The Human Consequences*.[2]

2. Z. Bauman, *Globalization: The Human Consequences* (Cambridge: Polity Press, 1998).

According to Bauman, the processes and technologies that lead to homogenization are the same as those that further polarize the world into an elite that travels freely around the globe and a majority that is stuck in local social circumstances in which it can no longer find protection against competition from other markets, precisely because of that time/space compression.

In our information society, 'nothing that happens in any part of the planet can stay in an intellectual "outside". No *terra nulla*, no blank spots on the mental map, no unknown, let alone unknowable lands and peoples.'[3] Everyone is aware of the contrast between Western prosperity and the poverty that exists elsewhere.

3. Z. Bauman, *Liquid Times: Living in an Age of Uncertainty* (Cambridge: Polity Press, 2007), 5.

In a world where natural boundaries are no longer a real obstacle, no one can be blamed for dreaming of a better life somewhere else. But neither do things remain in a *material* 'outside'. 'What happens in one place in the world has an influence on how other people live, hope or expect to live, elsewhere. Nothing is truly, or can remain for long, indifferent to anything else – untouched and untouching. No well-being of one place is innocent of the misery of another.'[4]

4. Ibid., 6.

The 'unity of mankind' is a dubious notion, and a 'hybrid lifestyle' seems reserved for a minority. It soon becomes clear that the open border policy is attended by a dual movement. The liberalization of commerce and finance at the international level has brought with it a fear of crime, illegal immigration and terrorism. This has led to political calls for re-establishing the power of the border. This development is a departure from the idea of the emergence of a borderless world in which flows of capital and people move freely. Globalization affects everybody; there is no going back. Yet self-assertion for an (intellectually and materially) 'open' society, to which the processes of globalization have brought us, is equally out of reach. Whereas the idea of progress used to be characterized by optimism, this has now turned to fear.

Mobility, in the sense of the freedom to move from place to place, is seen as an increasingly important value in life. But mobility also seems to be evolving into a form of unequally divided wealth. It is becoming the favoured indicator of social stratification, as Zygmunt Bauman describes in his aforementioned book, *Globalization: The Human Consequences*.[5] No longer seen as a primary right, it has become a privilege of the elite: travelling to far-off places is part of 'the good life'. Checklists of 'must-see' destinations, preferably accompanied by as much visual evidence as possible, are the distinguishing marks of a privileged group. 'Tourism is a complex industry but it has promoted a lifestyle where speed is linked with leisure and lei-sure with money. A tourist is not a "vagabond", a nomad without money.'[6]

5. Bauman, *Globalization*, op. cit. (note 2), 2.

6. D. Bigo, 'Frontier Controls in the European Union: Who is in Control?', in: D. Bigo and E. Guild (ed.) *Controlling Frontiers: Free Movement Into and Within Europe* (Aldershot: Ashgate, 2005), 87.

Mobility Regulation

Until recently, the state border was the locus for the regulation of mobility. The supervision of transnational flows of people, goods and information – and its filtering out where necessary – was one of the four basic functions of the Westphalian State vouchsafed by the border.[7] The other functions of the border were as territorial boundary of the sovereignty of the state, as an instrument for building a national identity and as a 'closed power container' for the military defence of the state.

7. The Peace of Westphalia (1648) is crucial to the concept of sovereignty. Since then, there has been no higher authority than the state.

Globalization presents a challenge for the traditional concept of boundaries. 'Before long,' says Gerald Blake, 'the world political map depicted as a mosaic of brightly coloured independent sovereign states of equal status will have become meaningless. It will need to be replaced by a map that shows the major political and economic blocks, distinguishing between the internal and the external boundaries of the block.'[8] The grouping of states into political and economic regions changes the classical notion of the national boundary. Its meaning must now be considered

8. G. Blake, 'State Limits in the Early Twenty-First Century: Observations on Form and Function', in: *Geopolitics*, vol. 5 (2000) no. 1, 1.

within a context of supranational entities such as the European Union (EU), the European Free Trade Area (EFTA), the Association of South East Asian Nations (ASEAN), the Central American Common Market (CACM), the North American Free Trade Agreement (NAFTA), the Gulf Cooperation Council (GCC), etcetera. The liberal logic underlying this regionalization has made the military significance of national boundaries within these regions increasingly inexpedient. Moreover, modern armament techniques (long-distance artillery, rockets, and so forth) have rendered obsolete the military defensive function of traditional national boundaries. As a result, borders today have more of a controlling and regulating task than a military one. According to Didier Bigo, a political scientist specialized in security, 'the priority is no longer on sanctions, but on regulation. The issue is less about condemning an individual than about deterring others, but it consists above all of managing movement and flux, of managing groups of people in advance, analysing their potential future, in order to normalize them.'[9]

9. D. Bigo, *Globalised (in) Security: the Field and the Ban-Opticon*, 2006, 41, found at www.ces.fas.harvard.edu/conferences/muslims/Bigo.pdf (last viewed on 6 January 2011).

Thus, security at the border today is increasingly focused on a new set of sociopolitically loaded concerns such as drug smuggling, trafficking in humans and weapons, terrorism and asylum requests. Even though the nature of these phenomena varies widely, they are associated with one another because of their transnational character.[10] New security methods are being developed and implemented every day. The importance of passports and identity papers, permissions to travel (invitations) and visas is increasing. The monitoring of individuals is shifting from localized, face-to-face encounters at the border to a technology of identification that can take place remotely and is kept in an electronic database.

10. W. Walters, 'The frontiers of the European Union: A Geostrategic Perspective', in: *Geopolitics*, vol. 9 (2004) no. 3, 674-698.

Panopticon

The historian Mark Poster called the electronic database for identification an 'updated cyber version of the Panopticon'.[11] The Panopticon derives its name from the eighteenth-century design for a prison by Jeremy Bentham, who also dubbed it the 'Inspection House'. The innovative aspect of this disciplinary apparatus lays in the application of new control techniques whose only principle was surveillance. This was a new type of inspection that affected the imagination more than it did the senses. 'The omniscient eye of the guard meant that instead of being physically punished ("affecting the senses"), prisoners were controlled merely by being visible ("affecting the imagination").'[12] Foucault described this design as a *disposi-*

11. M. Poster, 'Database As Discourse, Or Electronic Interpellations', in: P. Heelas and S. Lash, (ed.), *Detraditionalization* (Oxford: Blackwell, 1996). Also see: Bauman, *Globalization*, op. cit. (note 2), 50-51.

12. L. De Cauter, 'De panoramische blik', in: idem, *De Archeologie van de kick. Over moderne ervaringshonger*, 2nd edition (Nijmegen: Vantilt, 2009), 69-104.

tif, the architectural expression of a more general power mechanism (*un mécanisme de pouvoir*), in which the 'abnormals'– be they lepers, lunatics, criminals or the homeless – become the subject of control.[13] This is a power mechanism in which surveillance establishes and maintains order, but in which the principles of the cell, the dungeon – imprisonment, concealment, darkness – are inverted: of these, only imprisonment remains important, while visibility and daylight become the pivotal factors.[14]

13. The panoptic *dispositif* originated with the plague. See M. Foucault, *Surveiller et punir. Naissance de la prison* (Paris: Galimard, 1975), 197-201.

14. Ibid.

However, unlike the Panopticon, which ensures that no one can escape from the watched space, the primary function of the database is to ensure that no one enters it under false pretences. As Zygmunt Bauman says, 'the database is an instrument of selection, separation and exclusion. It keeps the globals in the sieve and washes out the locals. Certain people it admits to the exterritorial cyberspace, making them feel at home wherever they go and welcome wherever they arrive; certain others it deprives of passports and transit visas and stops from roaming the places reserved for the residents of cyberspace. But the latter effect is subsidiary and complementary to the former. Unlike the Panopticon, the database is a vehicle of mobility, not the fetters keeping people in place.'[15]

15. Bauman, *Globalization*, op. cit. (note 2), 51

With the elimination of internal borders within the Schengen Area,

perhaps the most important economic block of states today, fear of the negative effects of globalization such as terrorism, smuggling and migration has grown, and new techniques of control have been sought. Mobility regulation has been given absolute priority in order to reconcile freedom, one of the primary objectives in the European process of integration, with security. 'Compensating' measures have been implemented in order that the free movement of people, goods, capital and services not come at the expense of public order. To reduce transnational risks, the European Union has taken various measures.

The Regionalization of the Schengen Area

The primary objective of the Treaties of Rome (1957) was to eliminate the barriers that divided Europe. In the first instance, this led to the establishment of the European Economic Community, which created a common market. Within this zone, customs duties were no longer levied on mutual trade. Controls were still maintained at the internal borders, however. These were not abolished until the creation of the Schengen Area in 1985, when the Schengen Agreement was signed in the town of Schengen in Luxemburg. In this convention, Belgium, Germany (then still West Germany), France, Luxembourg and the Netherlands agreed upon the measures needed to create a transnational space in which people could move freely. In 1990, these 'compensating', or 'guiding' measures were worked out in the Schengen Implementing Convention. Shortly afterward, Greece, Italy, Portugal and Spain also signed the Schengen Implementing Convention, which came into force in 1995. Entering the Schengen Area at a later date were Austria (1995), Denmark, Finland and Sweden (all three in 1996). The UK and Ireland decided not to join. However, Norway and Iceland did become Schengen countries (1997, even though they are not part of the EU. With the Treaty of Amsterdam (which went into effect in 1999), the Schengen Acquis (or rules) became part of the EU treaties. Since the Treaty of Amsterdam, the southern boundary of the Schengen Area has coincided with that of the European Union. The treaty also implied that any member state entering the Union after this automatically becomes part of the Schengen Area as well. The countries that joined the EU in 2004 (Cyprus, Estonia, Latvia, Lithuania, Hungary, Poland, Slovenia, Slovakia, the Czech Republic and Malta) and in 2007 (Bulgaria and Romania) thus automatically became members of the Schengen Area because of the Treaty of Amsterdam. Switzerland also has joined the Schengen Area.

The Strengthening of the External Borders

The most important idea behind the creation of this 'free movement area' is to abolish controls on people and goods at the internal borders and shift them to the external borders. This is most evident at the southern border of the Schengen Area, which is mainly a maritime border. But also marking the territorial dividing line of the Schengen Area on its southern side are the Canary Islands, the cities of Ceuta and Melilla, the Isla de Alborán, Peñon de Alhecumas and the Islas Chaffarinas.[16]

16. X. Ferrer-Gallardo, 'The Spanish-Moroccan Border Complex: Processes of Geopolitical, Functional and Symbolic Rebordering', in: *Political Geography*, vol. 27 (2008) no. 3, 304.

Ceuta and Melilla are two Spanish enclaves located on the North African continent.[17] Both cities experience considerable pressure from migration, because of the fact that these enclaves are the only regions to have a land border between Africa and the Schengen Area (8 km for Ceuta, 11 km for Melilla). Africans (primarily from the Sub-Sahara) try to cross the border there every day. When Spain became part of the Schengen Area in 1991, the economic gap between these enclaves and the Moroccan hinterland steadily widened. This made the 'Schengenized' EU into a huge magnet for the African continent. Workers were attracted by its economic stability, while migrants saw the possibility, because of the abolishment of internal borders, of asking for asylum in more than one country. In order to combat smuggling and the risk of 'asylum shopping', visa policy was adjusted that year. Border controls grew increasingly strict. Moroccan cit-

17. Strictly speaking, these are not enclaves, as both Ceuta and Melilla have access to the Mediterranean. However, this is an established term when referring to the towns.

izens were no longer allowed to cross the Spanish-Moroccan border, now a Schengen border, without a visa.[18] On 19 May 1991, the first victims of 'illegal immigration' died in an attempt to cross the maritime border at the Strait of Gibraltar. 'Illegal immigration' became the new fear, and immediately the justification for implementing new security techniques as well.[19]

18. An exception was made for the inhabitants of Tetouan and Nador, who can use a day visa, by virtue of a dispensation in the Schengen Agreement.

19. Ferrer-Gallardo, 'The Spanish-Moroccan Border Complex', op. cit. (note 16), 311.

Accordingly, when the Schengen Implementing Convention came into force in 1995, a double enclosure was erected around Ceuta. The walls were outfitted with sophisticated security systems such as thermal and infrared cameras. Pepper spray and razor wire formed an extra protection against anyone attempting to scale the structures, which ranged from 3.5 to 6 m in height. Around Melilla, a triple enclosure was even built.

Later on, with financial help from the EU, the Spanish-Moroccan maritime border was also electronically protected through SIVE (*Sistema Integrado de Vigilancia Exterior*/Integrated External Surveillance System), a security system deployed along the coasts of the Iberian Peninsula and the Canary Islands. SIVE was implemented gradually, first with fixed and mobile radars along the Andalusian coast (2002) and later along the shores of the Canary Islands (2005). EU member states can also call upon RABIT (RApid Border Intervention Teams) when confronted with a sudden influx of migrants.

Migration pressure reached a high point in the autumn of 2005, when hundreds of migrants attempted to climb over the fences en masse with homemade ladders in Ceuta, and later in Melilla as well. This border crossing was planned and organized in the 'ghetto' encampments of migrants near the border in the woods of Bel Younech, Gourougou and Rostogordo. The consequences? The loss of 13 lives, increased militarization of the border and the establishment of a common policy on illegal immigration. The encampments were destroyed, the barriers around Ceuta and Melilla heightened and technologically reinforced. Detectors that can sense and record heartbeats from a distance are now also used.[20] During the two months following these events in 2005, 480 soldiers of the Spanish army were called in to reinforce the 647 police officers (331 in Ceuta, 316 in Melilla) and 1,302 members of the Guardia Civil (676 in Ceuta, 626 in Melilla) already on the scene.[21]

20. Ibid., 310-311.

21. European Commission, 18-10-2005, Technical Mission to Ceuta and Melilla on Illegal Immigration: Mission Report 7th-11th October, 2005, 7.

Collaboration between Member States

When the Schengen Area was created, the first priority was to combat organized and transnational crime. The 'compensating measures' implemented after the abolition of internal border controls involved not only strengthening external borders, but also improving collaboration between member states. One of the organizations assigned to this task was Frontex, an EU agency set up to carry out border inspections and additionally charged with making risk analyses. Frontex also sought methods of exchanging data between member states and countries outside the EU. An advanced database, the Schengen Information System (SIS), was also created. This enables national authorities (responsible for border, customs and police controls within the Schengen countries) to exchange data on certain categories of people and goods.

The Schengen system is based on the assumption that admission through one of the external borders of the Schengen Area implies admission to every Schengen country. A resident of a country outside the Schengen Area cannot gain admittance (even when in possession of a short-term visa) if he or she is deemed a potential security risk for one of the member states. When a person or object is registered in the database, it can mean that the person or object is sought by a Schengen country or that admission to the Schengen Area must be denied. A registration can refer to missing persons or undesirable foreigners, but also to false identity papers or stolen vehicles. Currently there are some 31 million registrations in the SIS database, referring to over 25 million identity papers, almost 4 million vehicles and 1 million people. [22]

22. M. Besters, 'De schaduwzijden van het Schengen Informatiesysteem', in: G. Munnichs, M. Schuijff and M. Besters (eds.), *Databases. Over ICT beloftes, informatiehonger en digitale autonomie* (The Hague: Rathenau Institute, 2010), 76.

The SIS is a 'hit/no-hit' system. If a person being checked at the border is registered in the system, the system generates a hit. This can lead to that person's arrest or to the confiscation of goods.[23] In 2008, the SIS generated over 120,000 hits.[24]

23. Ibid., 78.
24. Ibid.

The political and judicial authorities of the member states decide whether a person should be registered in the SIS. The information held by the member states in national networks (N-SIS) is linked up to a central system in Strasbourg (C-SIS). This allows any member state to share data with the others. Within the Schengen member states, there are more than half a million terminals with access to the SIS. National SIRENE agencies (Supplementary Information REquest at the National Entry) form the human interface of the system and check the information put into the database.

By the time the Scandinavian countries joined in 1996, the technological capacity of the Schengen Information System had become inadequate. A decision was made to develop a second generation, SIS II, which in addition to integrating new member states in the database also integrates extra applications, such as the coupling of registrations (for example, between criminals and terrorist suspects) with the Visa Information System (VIS), which keeps a record of all persons who apply for a visa.

When it turned out that SIS II would not be ready in time, SIS+1 was developed as a temporary solution in order to grant membership to the Scandinavian countries. Since the Treaty of Amsterdam, the need for SIS II has grown even greater, certainly in view of the Eastern expansion of the EU in 2004 and 2007. However, its completion was once again postponed, and a second temporary solution, an expansion of SIS+1 called SISone4all, was adopted and is still being used.

The laborious expansion of the SIS is the reason some member states of the EU have still not yet been completely integrated within the Schengen Area, seeing as the SIS is also used in the membership procedure for candidate member states, which must comply with the visa policy. First the SIS is implemented. Only when results show that a potential member state is fully capable of carrying out the required external border control measures can the internal borders be abolished. Satisfactory results are thus a prerequisite for membership.

Profiling System

Didier Bigo, like Zygmunt Bauman, sees the SIS as a profiling apparatus. According to Bigo, 'the main focus of the system is to ensure that persons who are or might be considered unwanted by any participating state are not permitted into the territory. Thus the rules focus on who must be excluded and provide little guidance on who should be admitted.'[25]

25. Bigo, 'Frontier Controls in the European Union', op. cit. (note 6), 46.

The system was originally set up to combat forms of transnational crime and to search for missing persons more easily. But instead of fighting organized crime, the SIS functions as a database that maintains dossiers on individuals in order to prevent illegal immigrants from returning to the EU. Over the last several years, immigration has been given priority, and a uniform visa system has been one result. Around the turn of the millennium, police authorities were still denying that the Schengen system was set up in order to provide a policing body for immigration, but that time is past. In the words of Bigo, 'it is hardly even contested by police authorities in question that Schengen institutes an immigration police, that this is its priority . . . and that there is no focus on the relation between crime and disappeared persons.[26]

26. Bigo, Globalised (in) Security, op. cit. (note 9), 40.

By building a uniform visa system into the (not yet operational) SIS II and coupling data on criminals and terrorist suspects with migrants, not only has Schengen extended its sphere of influence far beyond the EU and can the system increasingly operate from a distance, but the SIS has also ceased to be a neutral profiling apparatus. After all, such a coupling confirms the mistrust of migrants. 'The profile of the guilty changes; it no longer derives from a supposed criminality, but from a supposed undesirability,' says Bigo.[27]

27. Ibid., 21.

According to Bigo, a culture of control holds sway in the EU. But here too, double standards apply, for not everyone is subject to the same degree of control. Using databases of information from police records and mixing them with records from the public sphere (social security, taxes, and so forth) and the private domain (insurance, credit bureaus, supermarkets), it becomes possible to categorize people and ultimately determine who should be checked further. This is a proactive approach, a risk management logic. Who represents a possible risk and who does not, who is dangerous and who is not, is determined beforehand. Mobility is not for everyone. Databases determine who has a right to it and who does not.

This proactive stance forms the legitimization for the policy of a liberal EU that considers freedom of movement essential to its existence yet maintains strong external borders and monitors people. A proactive policy targets an action even before a law has been breached. Gathering and filtering information makes it possible to anticipate the behaviour of possibly dangerous individuals or groups. This is not about committing a crime, but about an indication that connects a potential crime with an individual or group. In order to normalize a majority and filter out a minority, the super vision and control of their movements must be given priority. The justification for monitoring migrants is weak in itself, but not in light of the fight against terrorism. Lumping transnational threats together provides support for the logic of 'acting before it is too late' – a logic that is very much alive in the public discourse.

A Ban-Opticon

Moreover, the control of societal risks should not be viewed purely as a police responsibility. An entire spectrum of risk management systems should be considered: not just special architectural facilities such as asylum centres and detention zones in airports, the adoption of emergency decrees, administrative measures such as the regularization of undocumented migrants and mutual agreements among governments concerning transport costs for deportation, etcetera, but also the role of public discourse.

This surveillance *dispositif*, a term of Foucault's whereby architecture is part of a more general power mechanism, is a strategic project, but also a means of understanding the broader workings of society.[28] Because of its proactive strategy, which consists of controlling a selected group, it cannot be described as a Panopticon, however. Surveillance no longer depends on immobilizing institutions or on the omniscient gaze of a guard. In the words of Bigo, 'this diagram is not a panopticon transposed to a global level, it is what we call – in combining the term "ban" of Jean-Luc Nancy, as refigured by Giorgio Agamben, and the "opticon", as used by Foucault – a Ban-opticon.'[29]

The term 'ban', according to Agamben, refers

28. As a 'machine' that uses different institutional, material and administrative mechanisms and representations to establish and maintain power in a particular place.

29. Bigo, *Globalised (in) Security*, op. cit. (note 9), 34.

both to exclusion from society and the sovereign's power to suspend the law.[30] Bigo gives it a broader interpretation, however: he connects the notion with a general form of policy he calls 'the management of unease', which is developed through routines and technology by professional politicians, the police, judges and the constitutional state. The 'ban' is a way of excluding and normalizing, of using computer databases to create profiles and subsequently determine who is allowed to move freely and who is not. The objective is to determine beforehand who forms a possible threat to Europe and who does not. The labelling of certain people as 'illegal', 'criminal', 'terrorist' and so forth can thus easily proceed, with the argument that it is better not to wait 'until it is too late'. The Ban-opticon lets us realize that controlling a particular group of people's mobility, and thus not everyone's, has unarguably become the leading trend in the age of globalization.

30. G. Agamben, *Homo Sacer: Sovereign Power and Bare Life* (Stanford, CA.: Stanford University Press, 1998).

Border near Melilla, separating Spain from Morocco.
Photo: EFE/Laureano Valladolid, 2006

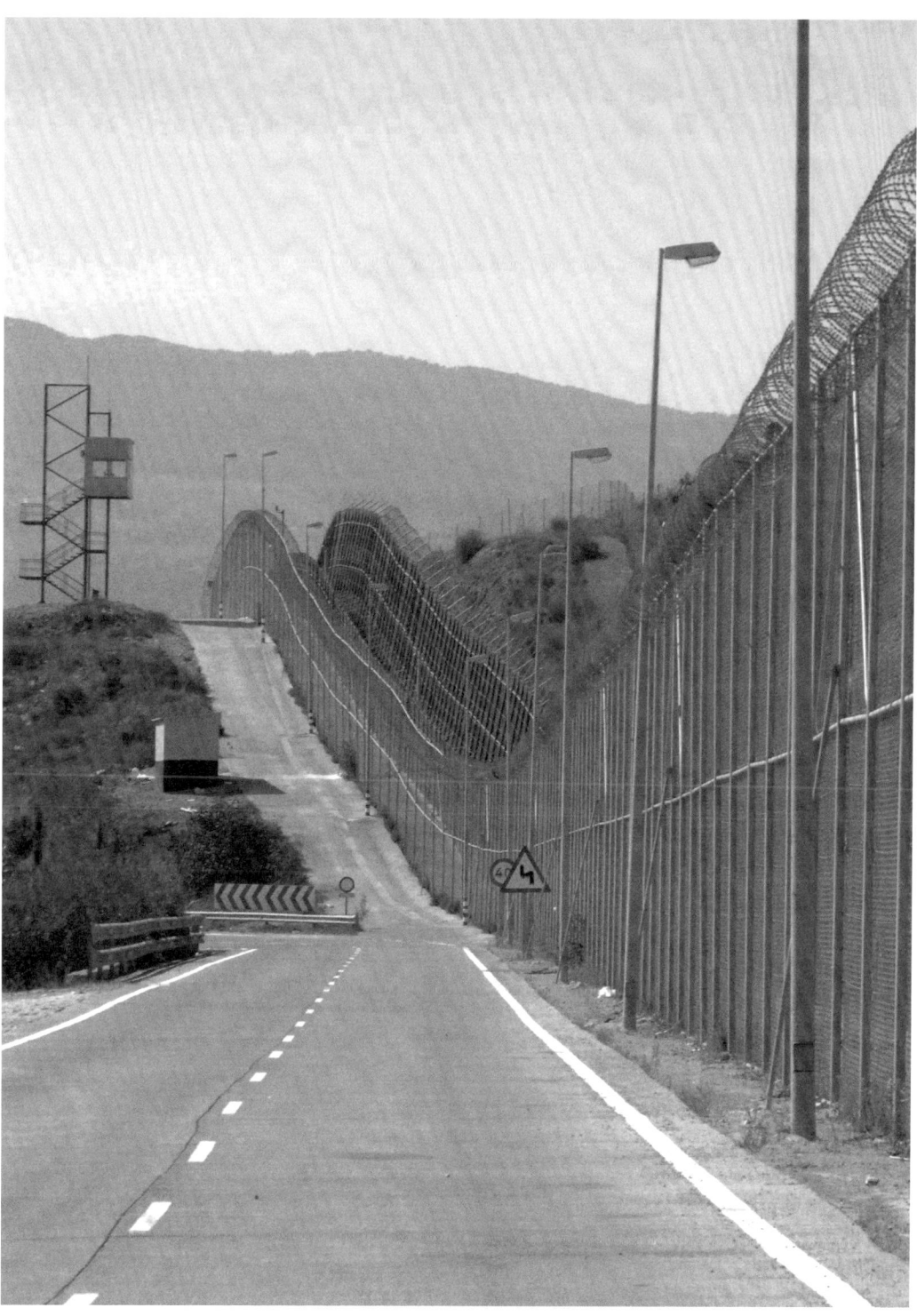

Merijn Oudenampsen
Miguel Robles-Durán

Mobility, Crisis, Utopia
An Interview with David Harvey

Space is not a given, but is continuously produced, reproduced and reconfigured. Taking up where the French urban theorist Henri Lefebvre left off, the Marxist geographer David Harvey has focused on the development and incorporation of a spatial analysis in Marxist theory. He has emerged as one of the foremost intellectual commentators on the global financial crisis, portrayed in his recent book *the Enigma of Capital* (2010) as an instance of those same structural contradictions Karl Marx forewarned us about.

In 1873, Jules Verne's novel *Around the World in Eighty Days* appeared, in which Phileas Fogg, an English nobleman, accepts a bet to circumvent the globe. The novel, a portrait of British Empire at its peak, was a celebration of the cult of mobility and modern transportation.[1] The world was now within arm's reach – at least for those who were rich enough to afford it. Fourteen years earlier, writing a series of sketches and annotations that are now known as the *Grundrisse*, Karl Marx described this quest for mobility as the structural drive within capitalism towards 'the annihilation of space with time': 'While capital must on one side strive to tear down every spatial barrier to intercourse, i.e. to exchange, and conquer the whole world for its market, it strives on the other side to annihilate this space with time, i.e. to reduce to a minimum the time spent in motion from one place to another. The more developed the capital, therefore, the more extensive the market over which it circulates, which forms the spatial orbit of its circulation, the more does it strive for an even greater extension of the market and for greater annihilation of space by time.'[2]

1. A similar theme is present in the other works of Jules Verne, broadly esteemed as one of the first science-fiction writers. He wrote on space travel in *De la terre à la lune* (*From the Earth to the Moon*, 1865) and on underwater exploration in *Vingt mille lieues sous les mers* (*Twenty Thousand Miles Under the Sea*, 1869) long before these became technical realities.

2. Karl Marx, *Grundrisse: Foundations of the Critique of Political Economy* (Harmondsworth: Penguin Books, 1993 [1859]), 538-539.

    Written in an earlier phase of what is now commonly called globalization, what stands out is how little Marx's observations on the spatial dynamics of capitalism have seemed to age, in a time that is characterized by the ever-greater expansion of global markets and the ever-growing pace and volume of transported goods, people and financial capital. According to Harvey, laws of competition drive corporations and states to seek advantage through superior command over space and time as much as through technological innovation. As a consequence, the 'collective psyche' of capitalist societies is taken up by the conquest of space and time, a mobility fetish arises, for much of the same reasons that a fetish belief in technological progress takes hold: both are essential for capitalist innovation and growth. Accordingly, the celebration of hyper-mobility, represented by publications such as Thomas Friedman's *The Earth is Flat* (2005), or by Rem Koolhaas's eulogy of the kinetic elite in *S,M,L,XL* (1993), has been a structural and persistent trope of capitalist modernity over the past 150 years.

    In contrast to the celebratory nature of the dominant view of mobility in society, Harvey sketches a more complicated and contradictory picture. His central concern, which he reflects upon in his work *The Limits to Capital* (1999), is the barriers that exist towards ever-greater capital accumulation. Where to reinvest the profit accumulated throughout previous economic cycles? One of the strategies for resolving this problem has been the spatial fix, the geographical expansion and restructuring of the economy, which has been an integral part of the last phase of globalization. In the history of economic

Mobility, Crisis, Utopia

crises, and through the deployment of the spatial fix, there is a persistent tension between capital that is invested in the built environment for longer periods of time – 'fixed capital' – and the competitive drive towards ever-greater expansion and mobility that renders existing infrastructure obsolete. Starting out from the building boom in nineteenth-century Paris under Haussmann, to the post-war redevelopment of American suburbia, to the real estate boom in China and the redundancy of entire newly built cities, capitalism is always on the lookout for anther 'fix', the frantic and irrational nature of which becomes only startlingly clear when overproduction ensues and value evaporates.

Though in the short term the financial crisis seems to have been largely contained and averted, in the long run the unending appetite for compound growth is bound to encounter its limits, ecological or otherwise. The brunt of Harvey's work has been focused on the description and analysis of what is, but another significant part of his work has been the speculative exploration of what could be. In *Spaces of Hope* (2000), Harvey advanced some of these utopian explorations, and in the *Enigma of Capital* Harvey is cautiously continuing on that path: 'While nothing is certain, it could be that where we are now is only the beginning of a long shake out in which the question of grand and far reaching alternatives will gradually bubble up to the surface.'[3]

What Harvey anticipates in his utopia at the end of *Spaces of Hope* – in the years after capitalism's final crisis – is the slow self-assembly of relational political bodies outside the conceived boundaries of a state. Granting that new technology would make a much more horizontally organized society technically feasible, Harvey aims for a politics beyond the oldest schism of the left: that between the anarchist and the Marxist tradition exemplified by the furious polemics between Marx and Bakunin over the course of the Paris Commune in 1871. Harvey's utopian agenda is to construct a dynamic set of intense interrelations that allow their co-evolution into an ecological totality of political will.

Granting that we don't fall into common determinisms, the 'new' will come when we begin to conceive movement as an uneven totality, radically reassembled by the interplays between daily life, social relations, production, technologies, imaginations and our relation to nature.[4]

3. David Harvey, *The Enigma of Capital* (New York: Oxford University Press, 2010), 225.

4. In a short essay titled 'On the Deep Relevance of a Certain Footnote in Marx's Capital', first published in the journal *Human Geography* (vol. 1, no. 2, 2008), Harvey addresses sociospatial development in terms of six relational criteria derived from footnote 4 in Chapter 15 of *Capital* vol.1. These points are: 1. The relation to nature, 2. The technological mixes envisaged, 3. The forms of production to be implanted in the city, 4. The predominant forms of social relations, 5. The qualities of daily life, 6. The mental conceptions of the world.

M. OUDENAMPSEN & M. ROBLES-DURÁN *Paul Virilio in*
Speed and Politics (1977/1986) talks about the arrival
of a class division of speed. Mobility is stratified, between
what Rem Koolhaas has called the 'kinetic elite', and those
banlieusards *and ghetto dwellers that rarely exit their*
neighbourhood. In your work you talk about a competitive
necessity for capitalists to achieve a superior command over
space and time, how in your view is mobility structured?

D. HARVEY It is really difficult to generalize about this because
the motivations for migrating are usually multiple, it's an overde-
termined kind of problem. Don't forget the difference between
cross-border mobility and internal mobility; it is very significant. You have had these mass movements internal to China,
hundreds of millions of people come off the land and have gone
into the cities. That's a migratory stream that has of course been
encouraged. There is a certain degree of push and there is a certain degree of pull. You have a phenomenon like that, you then
look at the consequences for mobility in the formation of the
European Union, all of a sudden people from Poland are serv-
icing the hotels around Heathrow and Lithuanians were in
the Irish pub when Ireland was still humming along. But now,
quite a lot of people have gone back because of the crisis. So
there are a lot of flows around that occur for very different reasons. Concomitant with that, among the lower classes there is
of course the question of remittances; the flows of remittances
around the world are huge. They have diminished somewhat in
the last couple of years but there are certain villages you can go
to in Mexico or Ecuador, frankly they just live off remittances.
One of the problems with that is that people are just using the
remittances to live. The hope would be that the money that is
sent back would provide the resources for some kind of autonomous development. As far as I know, studies suggest that this
does not happen very often.

In the upper class you have this tremendous reassign-
ment because of people continuously moving around. What
you typically get are these ghetto-like structures in places like
Manhattan, where the transnational bourgeoisie can park
itself for two or three years before it moves onto Shanghai or
somewhere else . . . You have a completely different pattern
of mobility there, coupled also with something else. I mentioned earlier the importance of the cost of social reproduction.

To train a doctor in this country is extremely expensive. Most people who get into that area, when they finally get a job they usually have about a half a million dollars in debts. You can hire somebody who comes fully qualified and well trained from India without any of those debts. Hospitals are under the gun right now so they are increasingly looking for a labour source that does not have those overhead costs attached to it. That labour source can depress the wages so that the American who's got half a million in debt finds that he cannot get enough money unless he goes into private consultancy, something that a doctor with a social conscience would not want to do, but finds himself forced to do as a result of migration. The consequences are manifold and if you look at it, the USA since the 1970s in particular has been underinvesting in education because it can get educated people from elsewhere. In fact it is a dispossession of resources from the rest of the world. This is not beneficial in aggregate at all. You have to look at it in strata, at the same time you look at the *banlieues* in Paris and you see populations that are effectively trapped in space and ghettoized. You have to be very careful about making any kind of simple generalizations.

MO & MRD *In your work you write that crises are never resolved within our economic system, they are merely moved around. One way this is being done is from the books of the banks towards the books of the governments. But you write about a specifically spatial element to the resolution of crises: the spatial fix, the expansion of capitalism towards as yet underdeveloped areas and a form of 'creative destruction' of non-viable infrastructures in developed economies. Is there a spatial fix at work in the present context?*

DH The spatial fix as it unfolded in countries like the USA or the UK during the 1980s and the 1990s was more about cannibalizing the abandoned de-industrialized world, it was not about extending outwards so much as it was rebuilding internally: loft conversions, waterfronts, etcetera. At present, the aging infrastructure of the USA requires massive renewal. Obama wants to do these things, but of course that is all being rejected by the Republican right wing because to go that path would be to go a bit Keynesian. To some degree their logic is that if they can keep the economy in its current state of very high unemployment, but with very high profit rates for capital, they'll stand a very

Erenhot was built in the middle of the desert of Inner Mongolia and half of it is empty, the other half is unfinished.

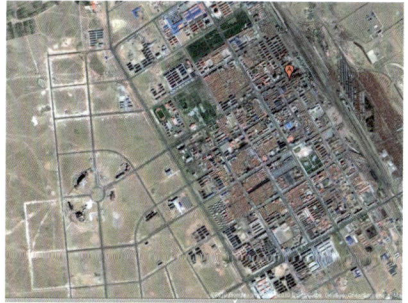
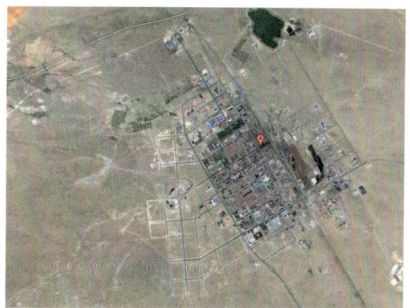

Is that a hotel in Erenhot?

China's most famous ghost city: Ordos.

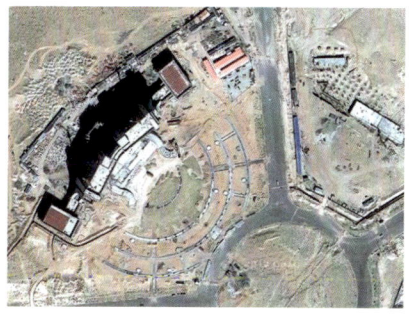
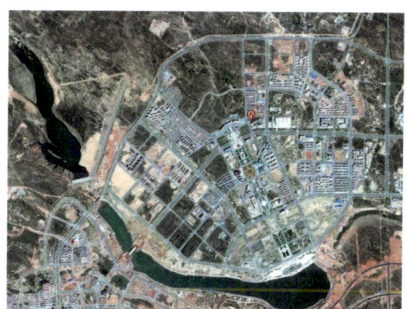

No cars in Ordos, except for approximately 100 clustered around the government headquarters.

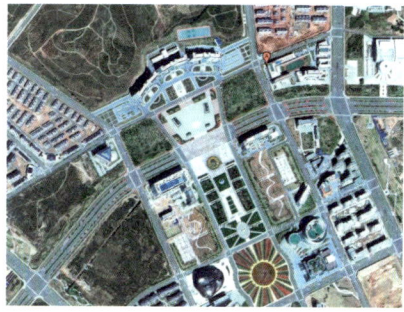
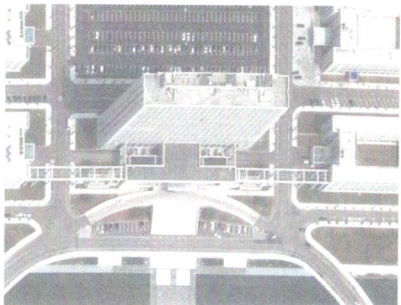

Ordos has an avant-garde art museum that is totally empty.

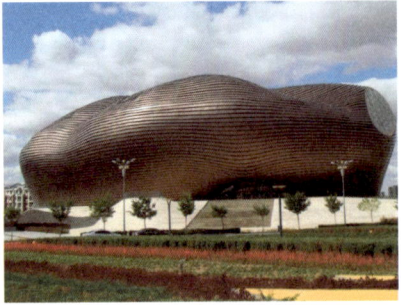

China's biggest ghost city: Zhengzhou New District.

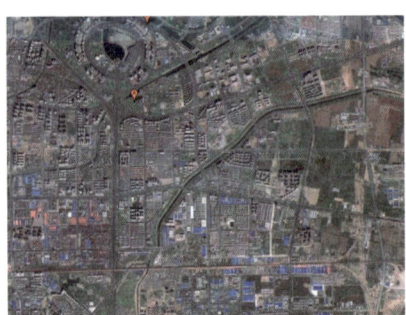

Like Ordos, Zhengzhou New District has glamorous public buildings.

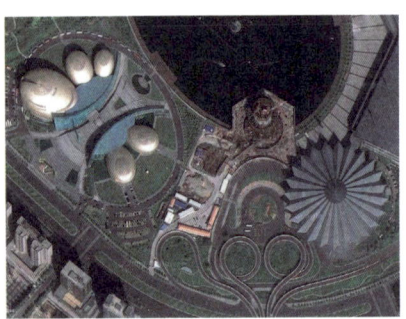

This 19-billion-dollar development project in Zhengzhou New District is packed with blocks of empty houses.

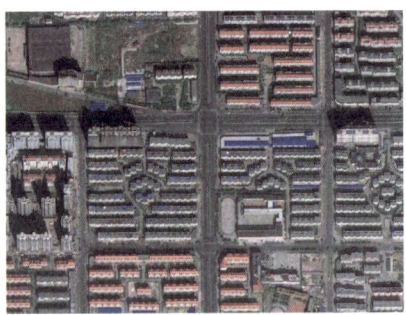

Zhengzhou New District's empty residential towers.

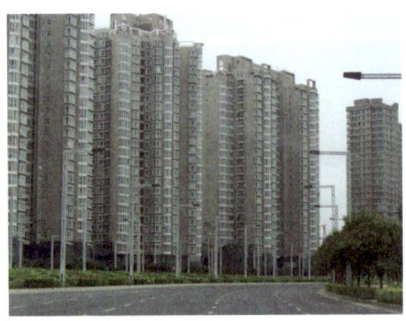

Kangbashi is a new city with a capacity for 300,000 people that houses 30,000.

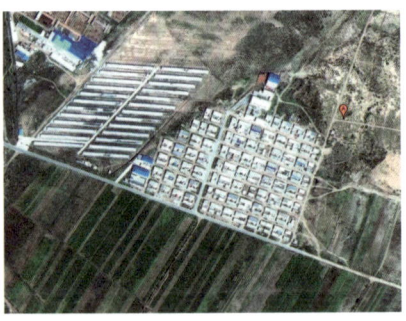

The orange area is a giant development to the north-east of Xinyang.

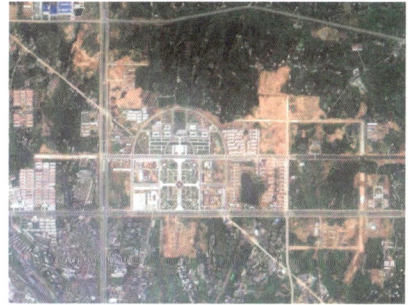 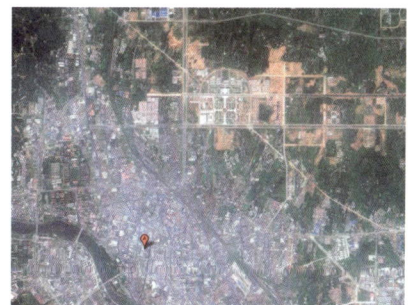

Zhengdong New District Wetland Park; the people are added with Photoshop.

The mostly empty city of Bayannaoer boasts a beautiful town hall and a water treatment facility sponsored by the World Bank.

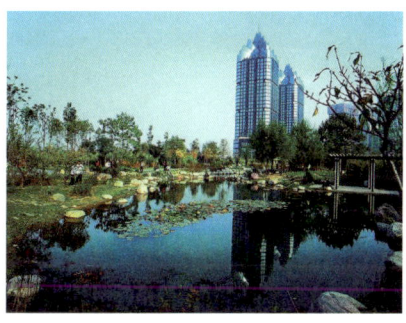 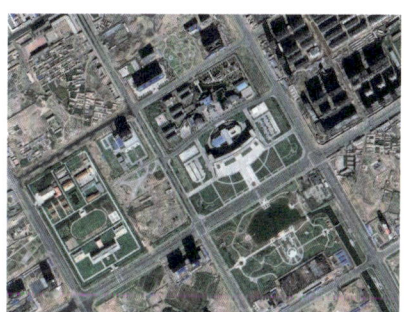

The ghost city of Dantu has been mostly empty for over a decade.

In most areas of Dantu, there are no cars, no signs of life.

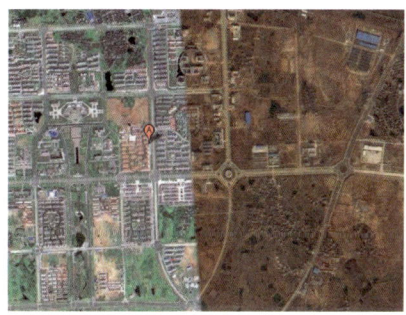 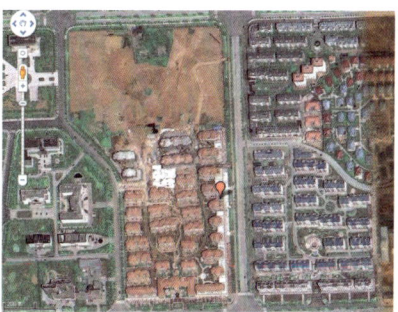

good chance of destroying Obama in the next elections. The Republicans are rejecting Obama's plan for high-speed rail, they rejected his 55 billion dollar infrastructure plan. They are rejecting any kind of spatial reconfiguration. In which case, where is surplus capital going to go? Well, where it has been going all along, it is going to the emerging economies. In fact, one of the worries right now, one of the reasons why you have a strong revival of emerging economies, is that you have a capital outflow. There is a strong capital inflow to fund the US debt, but there is a strong outflow of investment capital.

MO & MRD *When the financial crisis occurred, we heard many apocalyptic predictions, aired by commentators and intellectuals, especially those on the left, about the imminent collapse of capitalism and the ideological implosion of neoliberalism. Reading the newspapers now, you get the feeling the system is back on track. Where are we now, what are the mutations that are taking place as a consequence of the financial crisis?*

DH I think that the crisis, such as it is, is technically over, for a year and a half now. Formally, in this country it was supposedly over in June 2009. China went into a dip and came out of it almost within a year. There is not an economic rationale behind the present crisis, but there is a huge political rationale. This political rationale has been there in two forms, all along. For the first, we can go back to events like the Mexican debt crisis of 1982, where they bailed out the banks and then passed on the cheque to the people. Now is a time of passing on cheques, in other words we are still firmly in the neoliberal trajectory. The second element concerns the USA in particular, but you can see elements of it in the UK and Europe as well. In the 1980s, Ronald Reagan ran up the debt in a huge way, through an arms race with the Soviet Union and also through a huge tax cut to the rich. His budget director at one point said: our rationale was that if we would run up the debt, then you could use that debt situation to go after all of the social programmes you didn't like. And he said: that was our strategy. Now what did Bush junior do? He came in and cut taxes on the rich just as Reagan had done. He fought two wars of choice, running up a huge debt on the wars. The third thing he did was to allow a Medicare drug subscription benefit, which was a huge subsidy to the pharmaceutical industries. During those years, Dick Cheney kept on saying: Reagan taught us that deficits don't matter. So now the point has been reached where the deficit situation can be used to go after all the social programmes. So the crisis – in brackets – is being extended. People are focusing on unemployment, but now the crisis is not about unemployment at all, it is about the debt that is being used to externalize the cost of social reproduction.

MO & MRD *There seems to be a contradiction here. A new wave of austerity measures is being implemented, there seems to be a reinvigoration of the neoliberal agenda, with the Big Society ideas as presented by the UK conservatives as the clearest example. But you yourself in the* Enigma of Capital *state that the most logical reaction from the side of capital would be a Keynesian response, to increase effective demand, because this is where you traced the origins of the crisis in the first place. The opposite is happening. Recently George Soros also questioned the cutbacks in the UK as counterproductive, likely to plunge the UK into a crisis. Could you elaborate on this contradiction?*

DH First of all, there is a Keynesian project in motion. That is of course in China, but also in Latin America where the rate of growth in countries like Brazil and Argentina is 8 per cent right now. China is using Keynesian tactics to come out of the recession: vast infrastructural investment projects, building new cities, allowing wages to rise. There is one half of global capital that is a big Keynesian, then there's our half, the USA and Europe, which is going the other direction. The right question here is whose interest this serves. Corporations right now are making higher rates of profit than they have made for a very long time. They are doing extremely well. In part because widespread unemployment allows them to introduce what is called a two-tier labour system, in which people who are employed are under one kind of contract, and people who are being newly brought in are under another kind of contract, with almost no benefits. So the rate of profit for singular capitalists right now, is as high as it has ever been. In other words, you don't have enough of a fraction of capital right now that thinks like Soros, and who promote the politics you would need from the standpoint of stabilizing capitalism in general. What business is constituted of is like the Koch brothers, who have always hated any kind of government regulation of the environment, any kind of interference that forces them to internalize any cost of social reproduction. Then there are other factions: finance capital is very happy right now; they don't want to see any kind of change. When Marx talks about this in the chapter on the working day, he writes that in competition with each other, individual capitalists pursue a politics of *après moi le déluge*.

MO & MRD *What do you make of the relation between new communication technologies and the uprising in the Arab world? In Western media reports on the events, Facebook and Twitter become the signifiers of modernity and Western freedoms, while at the same time Western governments are highly ambivalent towards developments in Egypt, and the policies of Facebook and Twitter are far from controversial themselves. To what extent do you perceive technology acting as a fetish belief and to what extent does it offer real possibilities of challenging power?*

DH I am very suspicious of this overemphasis on Facebook and Twitter. Even if I accept that the youth movement there, which was a very important part and may have triggered the uprising, certainly used that as a tool. I do not think it is any different to what happened when the telephone came around or the radio. In other words, all sides can use it, and there is no inherent political quality to it.

If you looked at the pictures of the people on the square, listened to the interviews, they were not middle-class youth, there were some but a lot of them were ordinary folks. And there has been quite a history throughout North Africa in general, of riots and uprisings around the cost of food. I bet a lot of the people came out because of the cost of food and they came out not because of Twitter, and they were not so much concerned about abstract freedoms, they were concerned about the monopoly pricing that is going on and there not being enough food to eat. There has been a lot of industrial unrest in Egypt since 2002 or 2003, strikes are illegal in Egypt, or they were under Mubarak, and there have been strikes. Working people have been very discontented. Maybe the students triggered it, but it would not have gone anywhere if there wouldn't have been other sources of discontent that were ready to blow, which came in and were very much a part of it. There was a very interesting comment from a reporter on MSNBC, Richard Angle. He went to live in Egypt 15 years ago, for four years he lived in a very poor area of Cairo, and learnt the language. He was asked what he saw as one of the triggers. And he said: 15 years ago, when I was with all of these people they were very poor, but they got by and they felt that somehow that was their life. Now they are hit with the fact that somebody has built a huge mansion just across the street. They suddenly see the signs of immense wealth. And they are as poor as they ever were, if not poorer: services are non-existent or declining. The reporter said the social inequality has become so much more blatant and in your face. He said for a lot of people this has sowed their discontent. There is a theory of discontent that talks about relative deprivation. If there is absolute deprivation, if everybody is deprived, you do not get a revolution. When there is relative depravation you are much more likely to get huge discontent. He was very explicit about it: he talked to people that said: How come I am still so poor while they have become so rich? A class antagonism which has now become explicit, the same can be said of the workers struggles of the last ten years. All those elements are a part of what is happening there. You have to look at all those things before you tell me it was entirely due to Facebook or Twitter.

MO & MRD *In your book* Spaces of Hope *you speculated on a possible scenario of a transition from capitalism. With the benefit of hindsight would you change your utopian speculation on the future?*

DH I set a scenario for the transition, I could write another scenario now, and the interesting question would be how much I would change it. As part of that, I'm starting to think more coherently as to what it means to be anti-capitalist, and what capitalism could get displaced by. One of the things I did was to take the first four chapters of Volume II of *Capital* and look at the definition of capital that comes out of these four chapters. Marx says it is not money, because money can only do as money does, help you buy and sell, and besides, there is lots of money going around that has nothing to do with capital. The other thing about money is that money is the only stage in the circulation process where you can clearly see whether you have made a profit or not. Therefore there is a fetish belief that money is capital. Marx is very strong in his language; he says you are deluded if you think money is capital. Then he asks: is the buying and selling of labour power a definition of capital? No the exchange of labour for money has been going on all along. In fact that is a precondition, as is money for the rise of capitalism. He goes on and says: Can we look at it in terms of commodification? The answer is no, commodity exchange has been around for a long time. And then he talks about production: it is not even production, you know production can occur in all kinds of ways. You realize that the definition of capital that he is giving is that of a social relation between capital and labour, which permits the production of surplus value. Which then goes back to those passages in the *Grundrisse*, where he says that production dominates over all else, but it is the production of surplus value, not just physical production. If you want to be an anti-capitalist, you are committed to the abolition of that class relation between labour and capital, and the production of surplus value. That would be the core of the anti-capitalist agenda. What do you replace it with? Nowhere in *Capital*, this is really interesting going through it, nowhere does Marx ever say the state should do it. He says it is the association of labourers. In effect he is coming down on the side of worker control, autonomy of workers collectively deciding on the course to follow. You then look at the big history of all of this. That idea is all around and we see it also in the contemporary factory occupations. One of the good things of taking that as the core of what the socialist project is about is that if you would take polls in the country to ask if that is a good idea, you would probably get a 70 per cent approval rating. Look at the popular response when the people of Windows Republic in Chicago sat down and took over their factory, everybody said, yeah! You get a tremendous popular response that you would not get if the state took over. This is the core of what we should be doing. That comes out several times in *Capital*, is what its imaginary is. Which ironically is not too far from where Proudhon was. Marx could be paranoid about some people and he got a bit paranoid, he went overboard to discredit everything that Proudhon said. For that reason he probably got very nervous about articulating this notion of the associated labourers too much, because it would probably get muddled up with Proudhon. Again that line gets to notions such as mutual aid and the anarchist tradition. It is much easier to integrate it in that tradition than it is to argue for state control of the means of production.

Solidarity rally outside Bank of America in Chicago with the UE workers of Republic Windows and Doors on 10 December 2008. Photo: Carrie Sloan

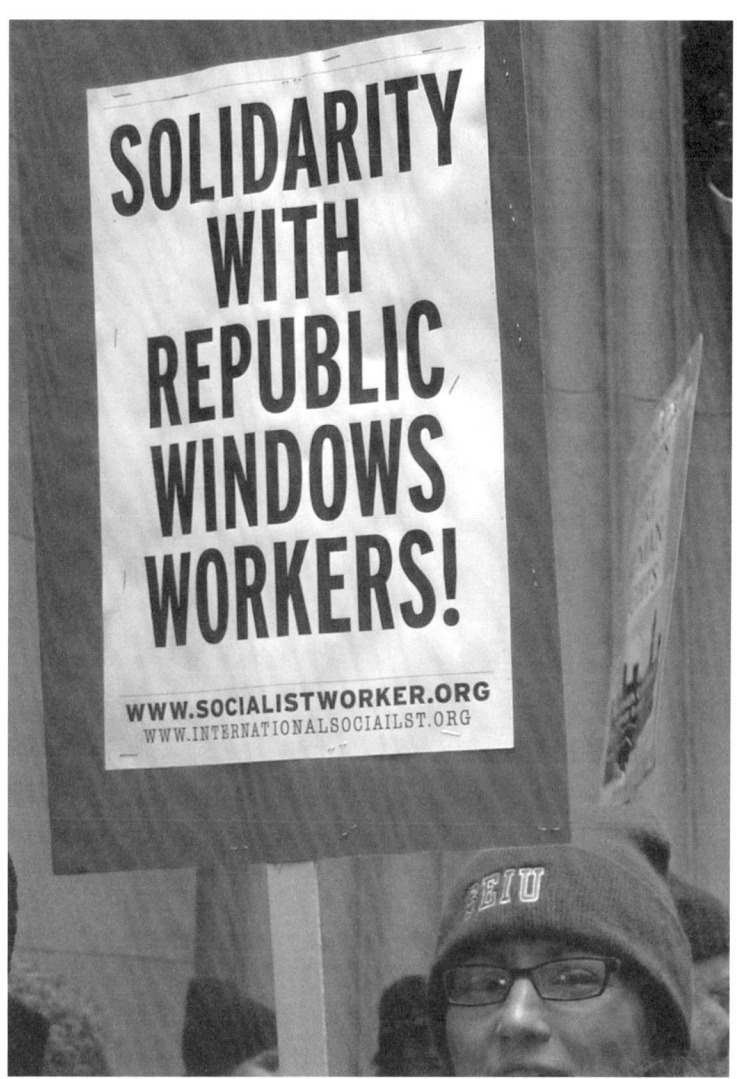

column

JOSS HANDS

SOCIAL MEDIA AND THE MOBILIZATION OF THE MASSES

'The city was a fused group' – so says Jean-Paul Sartre, speaking of Paris during the 1789 storming of the Bastille. What Sartre apprehends in his analysis of this revolutionary moment is the necessary interdependency of space, time, movement and will. His concept of the fused group brings these elements together in a way that recognizes the capacity to transform the given into something altogether new. In the moment of fusion Sartre sees a transformation from an isolated seriality, in which each person is a lonely powerless unit, into a collective entity – a being together in the most powerful sense of the term, a mutual recognition of that which he understands as most human, freedom.

If ever such a moment has been witnessed in recent history, the revolution sparked by the 25 January movement in Egypt must surely be a candidate – producing a rupture with a seriality of domination so profound there was not time to name it, to figure out what it meant – it was an event in the truest sense of the term. But it was not an event born of an inevitable historical progression or natural catastrophe, but of the force of combined will. The question that presents itself is: How did this will come to exist and how was it so forcefully imposed?

One must recognize that this was in the first instance a moment of negativity – a reaction against a despised regime – a condemnation that propagated solidarity. This is important in the process of 'fusion', which is a reaction against, and overcoming of, the inert weight of the given world. But this is not enough in itself and the danger of new containment and new forms of isolation always appear on the horizon. Here the capacity to think together, to recombine and to move – to splice space into the becoming of time – is primary, which means to act: to mobilize.

It is the role of social media in the recent waves of mobilization that has caught the imagination of the West, no doubt in some measure because of our firsthand familiarity with the most widely known web platforms, 'Facebook' and 'Twitter', and their increasing centrality in everyday social life, but not without further justifications.

While global communication networks expanded in the 1990s, in the context of a burgeoning information economy the key question for activists was always: Can this network support resistance? The answer is that spread of Capital over the globe has been matched by the interconnection of civil society, piggybacking on the global infrastructure to quietly build networks of mutual recognition within and across borders, as well as between struggles. This was first seen in the global response to the rebellion of the Zapatistas in Mexico, it was used by the World Social Forum to interlink movements from around the world. This is not to say these networks are the cause of resistance movements, but they do provide the capacity, the space and opportunity to coordinate horizontally beyond the constraints of immediacy. The Internet's distributed and scale-free topology, in combination with mobile Internet-enabled devices, enables the organization of action on the fly and a meshing of the space of the 'real' and the 'virtual', thus opening up a new front for activism.

On Tahrir Square this dynamic was most clearly apparent, 'Tahrir square is on fire, every inch of cement is covered with people chanting "Leave" "Invalid" Mubarak' tweeted Gsquare86, AKA, Gigi Ibrahim on 10 February. For several days it was to Tahrir Square that all eyes turned and bodies flowed, the usual patterns of media coverage, with its attempts to manage space and time with a familiar narrative arc and a unified perspective, was disrupted by the very jaggedness of the unfolding of the events. 24-hour news channels took the square's CCTV feed, tapping into fragments of the

voices from social media, trying hopelessly to capture the velocity of movement. Such disruption was a manifestation of a constituent power no longer subject to such standard forms; it was what Henri Lefebvre has described as an appropriation of space. But in the network age space is not merely three-dimensional, in relation to a linear time, but rather manifold, what Manuel Castells calls a 'space of flows' and interlaced with a 'timeless time' which multiplies the capacity for fusion, not into a single entity as Sartre defined it, but a coordinated multitude. The square was transformed into a space of resistance; of chanting in unison, tweeting, messaging – and all the while Al Jazeera, CNN and the rest fed back images in real time. This feedback loop, weaving place, space, voice and image into a mosaic, meant the moment was witnessed, shared and shaped like few before it. So it is that the concept of the fused group, while only a rough tool to hand, does open up this mobilization to imagination as one of recombination and fusion, not just of the Egyptian people, but of the peoples of the region and the world.

References

Manuel Castells, *The Rise of the Network Society* (Oxford: Blackwell, 1997)
Henri Lefebvre, *The Production of Space* (Oxford: Blackwell, 1991)
Jean Paul Sartre, *The Critique of Dialectical Reason Vol. 1* (London: Verso, 1976), 358

Cairo, 8 February 2011. Anti-Mubarak protesters continue to occupy
Tahrir square. Photo: John Moore, Getty Images

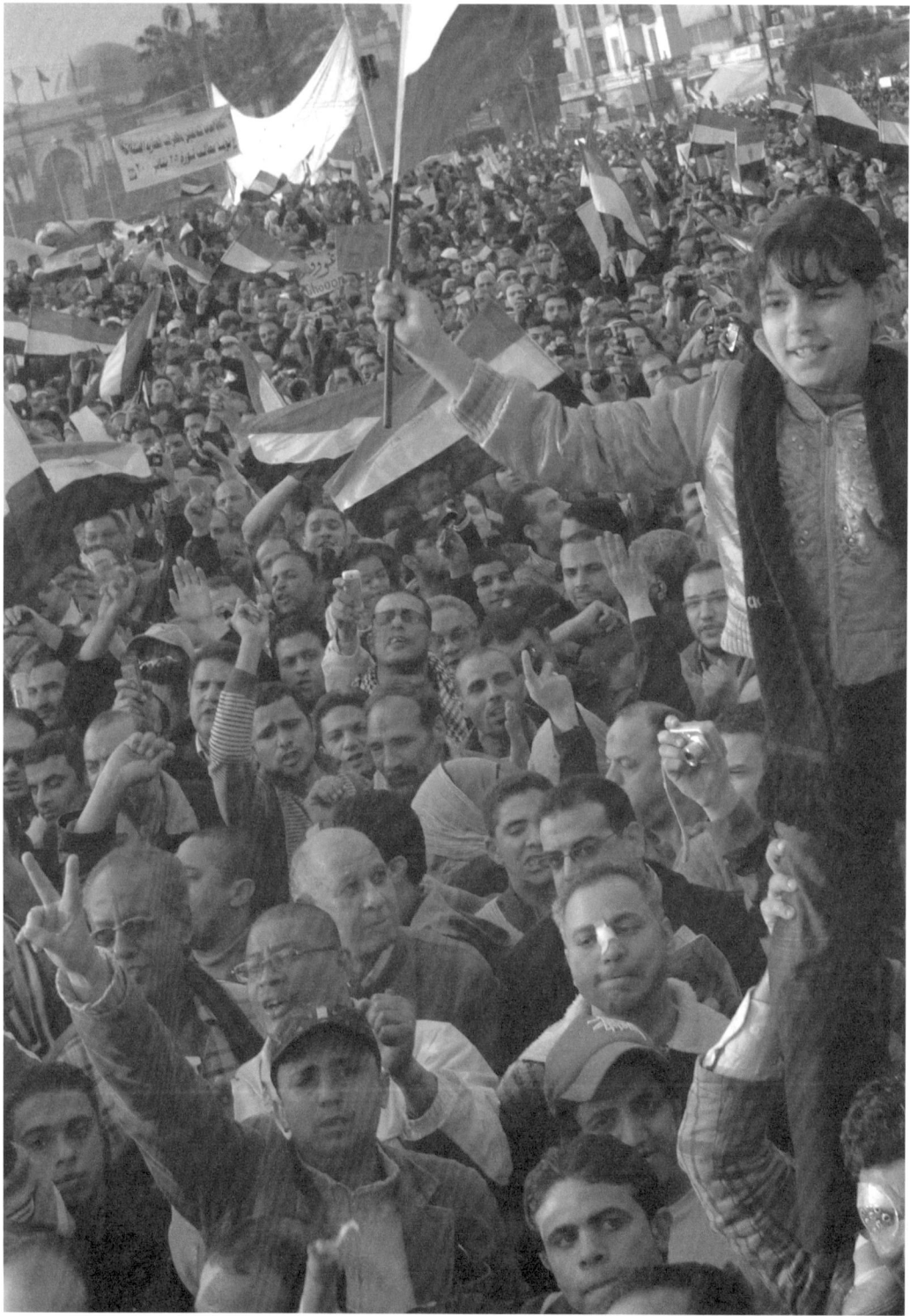

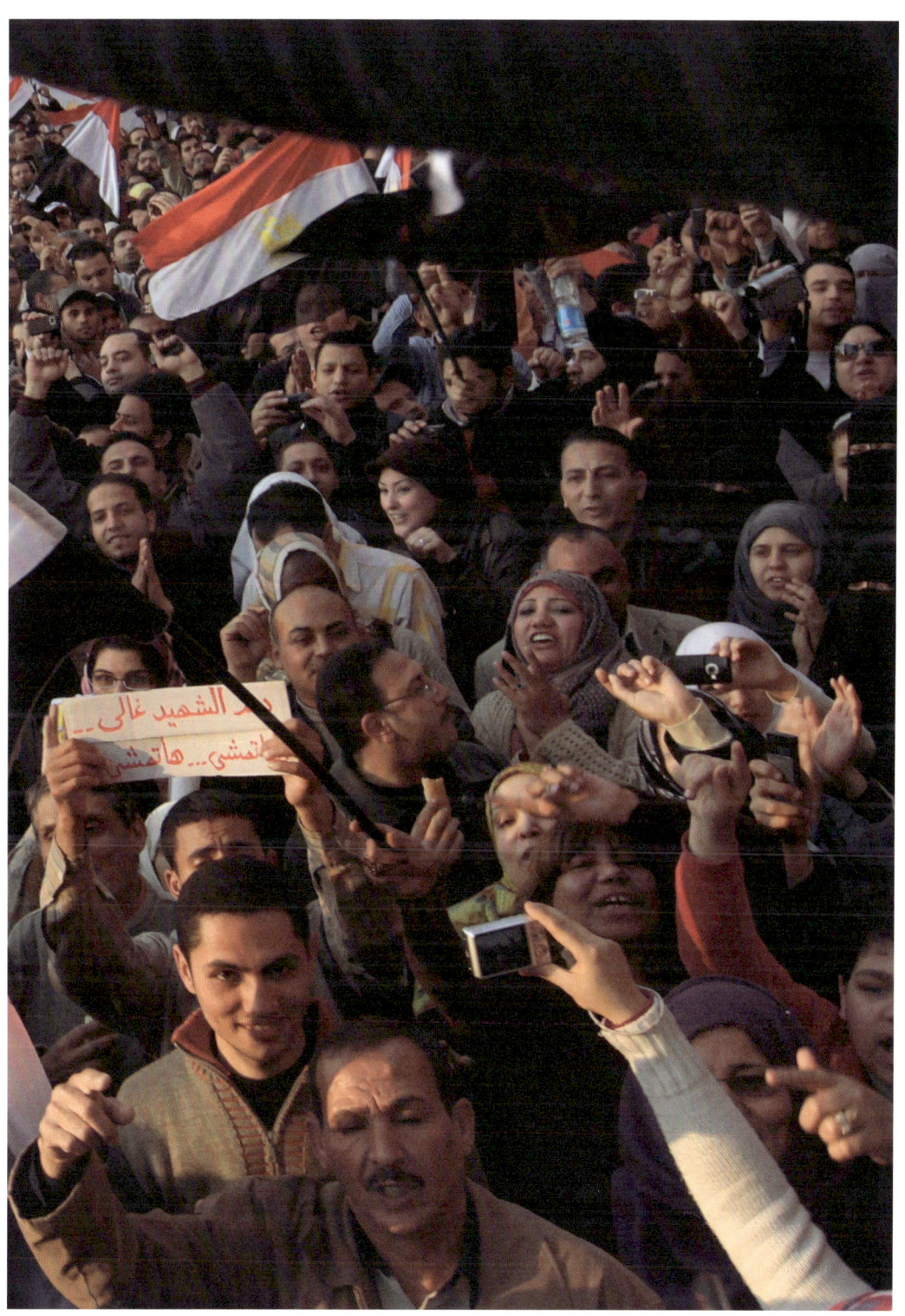

Florian
Schneider

Towards a Theory of Borders

According to Florian Schneider, researcher at the Jan van Eyck Academy in Maastricht, the world's current border policy is based on the outdated liberal ideology of the nation-state. He advocates the development of a new border regime in which the key concept is 'transnationality'.

A border is always a matter of imagination. It appears as a feigned condition that is supposed to limit mobility for certain people and in a certain situation. Allegedly, a border marks a distinction: it may be visible to some and not to others. It may be considered artless or genuine when viewed from one perspective, but critical or bogus from another.

What seems like a truism at first glance is precisely what makes it so difficult to talk about borders, let alone act on them. In order not to be rendered useless, a border needs to refuse any attempt to abstract from its latent ambiguity in practical terms.

Borders are ambigrams: illusionary images that depict two mutually exclusive motives. This becomes evident, for instance, at specific locations around the Mediterranean Sea, where the two different mobility regimes of luxury tourism and clandestine migration overlap and holiday resorts are situated next to detention camps without disturbing each other's presence at all.

It comes as no surprise that the inherently uncertain meaning of borders has turned out to be both the subject matter and the structuring device of great narratives and mythologies of migration: from the parting of the Red Sea that saved the lives of the Hebrews and destroyed the army of the Egyptians to *Star Trek*, which was originally pitched as a 'Wagon Train to the Stars', across a new frontier of outer space; from the Underground Railroad, a secret network of safe houses and clandestine routes that helped slaves escape to the free states in the North of the USA and to Canada, to the metaphorical belittlement of the EU border regime as 'Fortress Europe'.

To leave one's country behind, to flee from persecution, to seek happiness or at least a better life somewhere else – if not sanctified or bureaucratically approved beforehand, the crossing of a border implies, in the first place, a collision with or at least the change of a regime of mobility that in very specific terms constitutes a certain notion of freedom of movement.

Rather than enclosure, rather than confinement to a country or any other disciplinary regime, the postmodern border regime is characterized by a deregulation of mobility that increasingly becomes subject to ad-hoc management: temporarily granted in real time, it can be revoked as quickly as it was accorded – without any need for further mediation. It is enforced by a system of control that is no longer limited to specific checkpoints or focus areas: it is in place virtually everywhere.

Borders fold and shift inward or outward, they are advanced into third states and expanded into the hinterland. Controls are no longer limited to the margins of a nation-state; they cover the traffic junctions of inner cities and supra-regional traffic routes to the same extent as they are extended into semi-public or private spheres.

There is a ubiquity of control. The drawing up of border-lines is becoming virtual, and its repressive character can hardly be generalized any more: it could happen here as well as there, for this reason or another, and with a series of different consequences.

Outdated Ideology

Yet the discourse on borders is still ruled by the predominance of a somewhat outdated kind of liberal ideology, which operates through patterns of inclusion and exclusion. Regardless of the intention, whether used in favour of migrants or at the service of xenophobic resentment, the dichotomies of inclusion and exclusion trace back to the core concept of the modern nation-state as the unique reference point: the idea of a homogenized and unified people as collective agency and the resulting need for a high degree of cohesion through identity.

In the last instance, any understanding of borders as a device that regulates inclusion or exclusion affirms a sieve principle that is supposed to act as a filter. It reduces the complexities of migratory movements to a single plot that switches between the alternate binaries of 'in' or 'out'. The more it feeds the fiction of the nation state, the less it is capable of grasping the paradoxical but increasingly relevant realities of transnational mobility and immobility.

The illusion of a governmentality able to restrict freedom of movement on a global scale, the belief, as naïve as it is popular, that politics could reduce migration to 'zero-migration', makes claims to be considered as a matter of course. In reality, it lacks any empirical basis, and is mere propaganda that has been spreading only most recently.

It has come with apocalyptic scenarios of a massive influx of so-called illegal immigrants into Europe and North America, it has been accompanied by the fable that misery and poverty are causing movements of people at a scale hitherto unseen, and it has generated a number of related mythologies, such as the notorious 'brain drain', unproductive money remittances, or failed integration, just to name a few of the most popular rumours.

The fact is that borders are beyond control.[1] But if it cannot prevent what it promises to hold off, what then is the function of the border? Obviously, the criminalization of migration creates the conditions for the over-exploitation of a migrant labour force in the informal markets of late capitalism.

And those who cross the border without the necessary paperwork may experience the passage from one regime of mobility into another as the nullification of any remaining subjectivity. It is an extreme process of desubjectification – often characterized by living in ways that are almost unliveable.

As soon as the border is crossed, engineers turn into cleaners, academics into sex workers, professors into casual farm labourers or domestic workers. Pushed beyond the conditions and limits of what is often described as 'human', their experiences become a sort of negative freedom.

Scandalization

Mainstream media regularly provide footage that illustrates what is supposed to be going on out there at the border: reckless fortune seekers trying to make it across the borders against overwhelming odds. It is a scandal in the truest sense of the word:[2] in order to enter countries like Spain, Italy or Greece, people are climbing fences, squeezing into overcrowded boats, hiding under trucks or trains.

Not only does the border justify itself by a scandal, it is performed

1. In 2001, the EU Commissioner for Justice and Home Affairs, António Vitorino, acknowledged that Europe had lost its battle against clandestine migration. 'Europe must avoid repeating the zero-immigration mistakes of the past,' he said, concluding with surprising precision, 'restrictive laws have done nothing to halt the flow of clandestine migrants.' On the contrary, 'the ability to control migration has shrunk as the desire to do so has increased. Borders are largely beyond control and little can be done to really cut down on immigration,' as the economist Jagdish N. Bhagwati argued in 2003.

2. Scandal derives from the Latin *scandere*, to climb. But there is yet another, no less compelling, etymological perspective: the border as *skandalon*, which is the Ancient Greek word for a stumbling block.

through a scandal. The grammar of its performativity consists of scandalization: a continuous loop of images and imaginaries that are widely publicized in order to produce allegations of wrong-doing or disgrace. In that respect, the postmodern border regime appears as a global soap opera that reiterates what everybody seems to know anyway. Its looping plot is based solely on the implicitness of unwritten laws that regulate that which is permitted to some and not to others.

There is no point in exposing this scheme, since any further critique on a practical level risks increasing the efficiency of its performance. Scandalization transforms an otherwise ignorable event in order to solicit a moral outrage whose purpose is nothing but the reaffirmation of the border – a border that may otherwise be invisible, disputed or disbelieved.

As the product of a mixture of both real and imaginary incidents, it suppresses any distinction between certain degrees of documentary value and what needs to be considered fiction. The result of this blend is a single-purpose device: the scandal affirms that the border is still there, still true.

Its conceptual homogenization of real and unreal, documentary and fictitious elements reaffirms a collective identity thrown into crisis by the fading power of nation-states. In perfectly postmodern fashion, it makes it possible to enjoy and cooperate with a regime that relies on frail and ineffectual facts on the ground, as long as they provide the illusion of a border that can be controlled. Then one can even worry about its excesses and moderately criticize its violent character.

Victimization

But the other side of the coin is no less irritating. The scandalization of the border comes with concurrent strategies of victimization. First of all the criminalized migrants are deprived of any agency and turned into victims. At the mercy of human traffickers, kidnapped and abducted, they are reduced to human beings that merit only sympathy.

Left-wing and human-rights activism often falls into the same trap when it reduces migration to misery and calamity and understands it as a logical result of the movements of capital, as its unsavoury aftereffect or appendix.

Even contemporary right-wing populism can be conceived as a set of mirroring strategies that compound the victimization of migrants. In the aftermath of multiculturalism, right-wing populism mobilizes the desire of a non-migrant, anti-urban mentality to become a minority itself: it inverts the patterns of victimization. It reverse-engineers virtues that were formerly known as progressive. It recycles and reads against the grain the ideology of inclusion and exclusion, the morals of participation.

Condemning right-wing populism as racist or xenophobic is missing the crucial point: white, male, middle-class or heterosexual subjectivities that have usually been identified as perpetrators and that are gradually losing their privileged positions suddenly manage to seize the opportunity to frame themselves as victims, as an endangered species, or as a native population that will soon be overrun by heinous invaders.

As far as it addresses a certain need to treat the fading certitude of Western supremacy in the sunset years of its world domination, both the scandalization of borders and the subsequent victimization of migrants may turn out to be quite a successful therapy for the collective psyche. But its pain-relieving and alleviating effect is only temporary, and there is not even any great imperative to unmask it.

Instead there is an urgent need for a theory of borders that rejects the permanent temptation to remain descriptive and illustrative, to act in an ultimately affirmative sense and to provide a decoration of the border by indulging in recurrent tropes of charity and compassion, nostalgia and resentment.

As soon as the border becomes actual and concrete, every sign is subjected to a wide range of possible interpretations due to ever-changing perspectives. The imaginary character of the border is not only constituted by the deficiencies of laws and a lack of interpretive authority: first and foremost it manifests itself in an indiscernibility of real and unreal, an undecidability of true and false.

The phenomena of borders result from the experiences that the distinctions between these terms keep changing round. The constant exchange of meaning renders any form of independent, let alone subversive, thinking almost impossible.

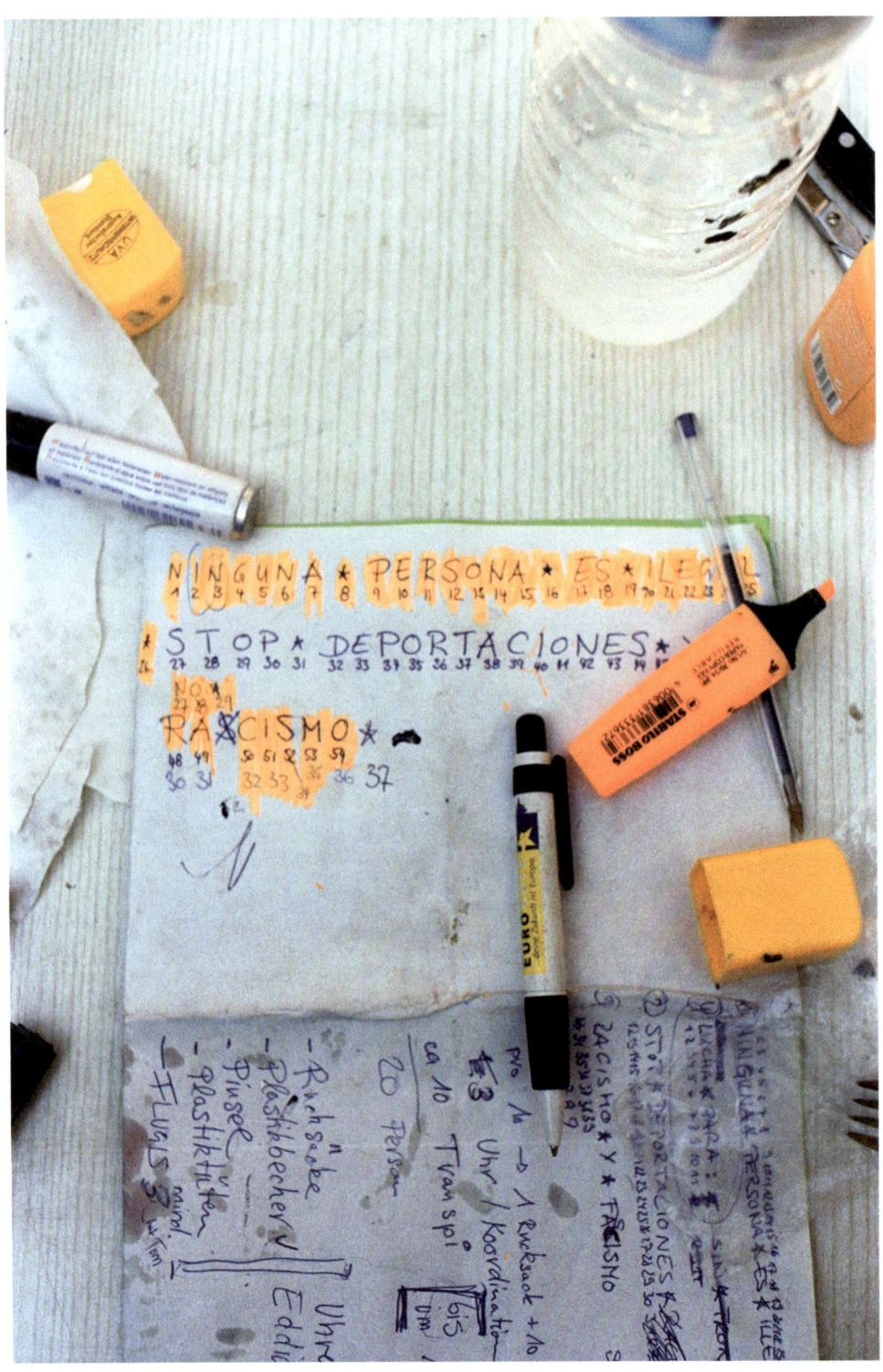

Naked Against Borders: Activists stripping on the beach of
Tarifa. Photo Armin Smailovic

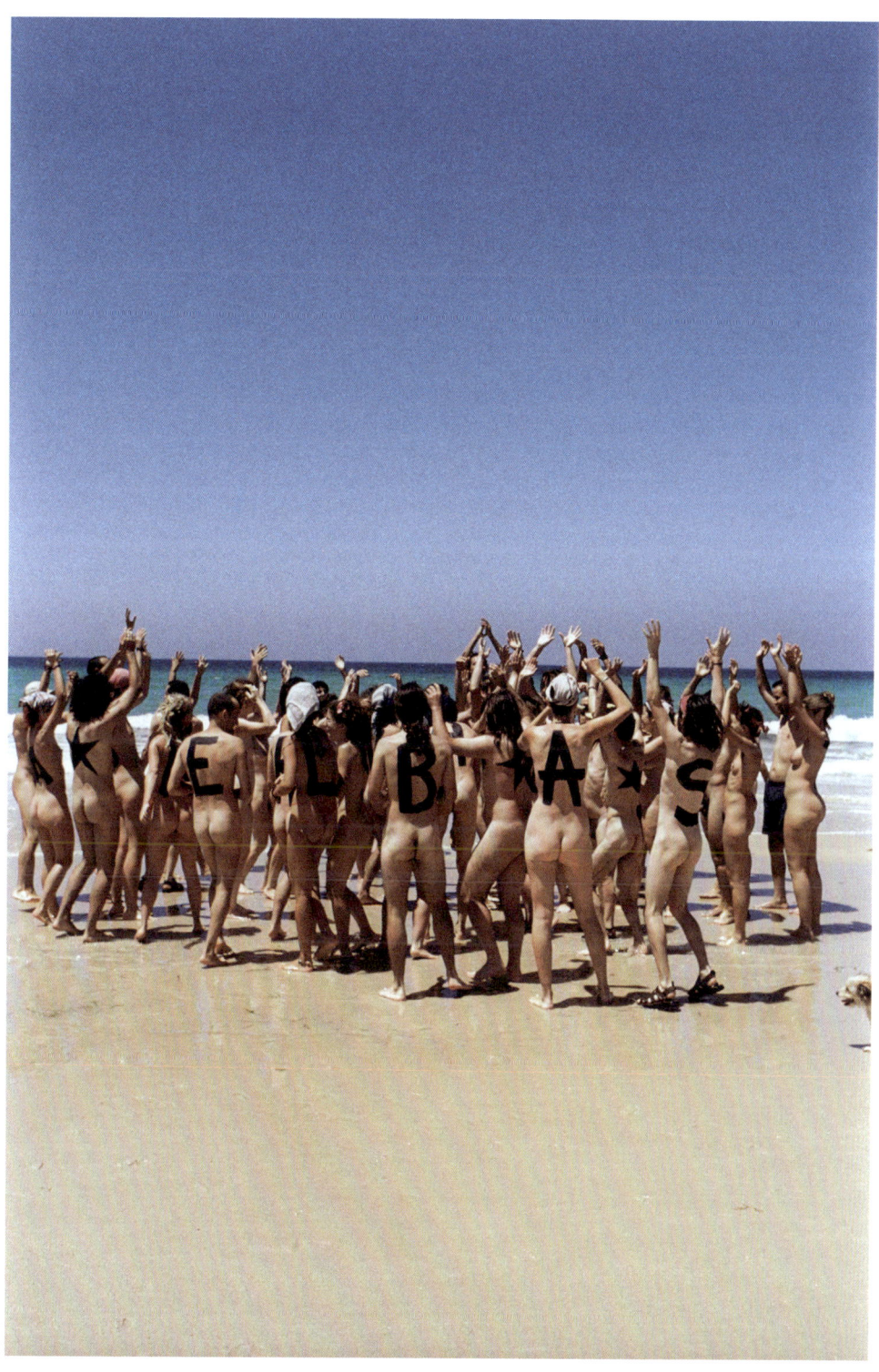

Borders Crossed: inflatable boat used by illegal immigrants on the shores of the Strait of Gibraltar. Photo Armin Smailovic

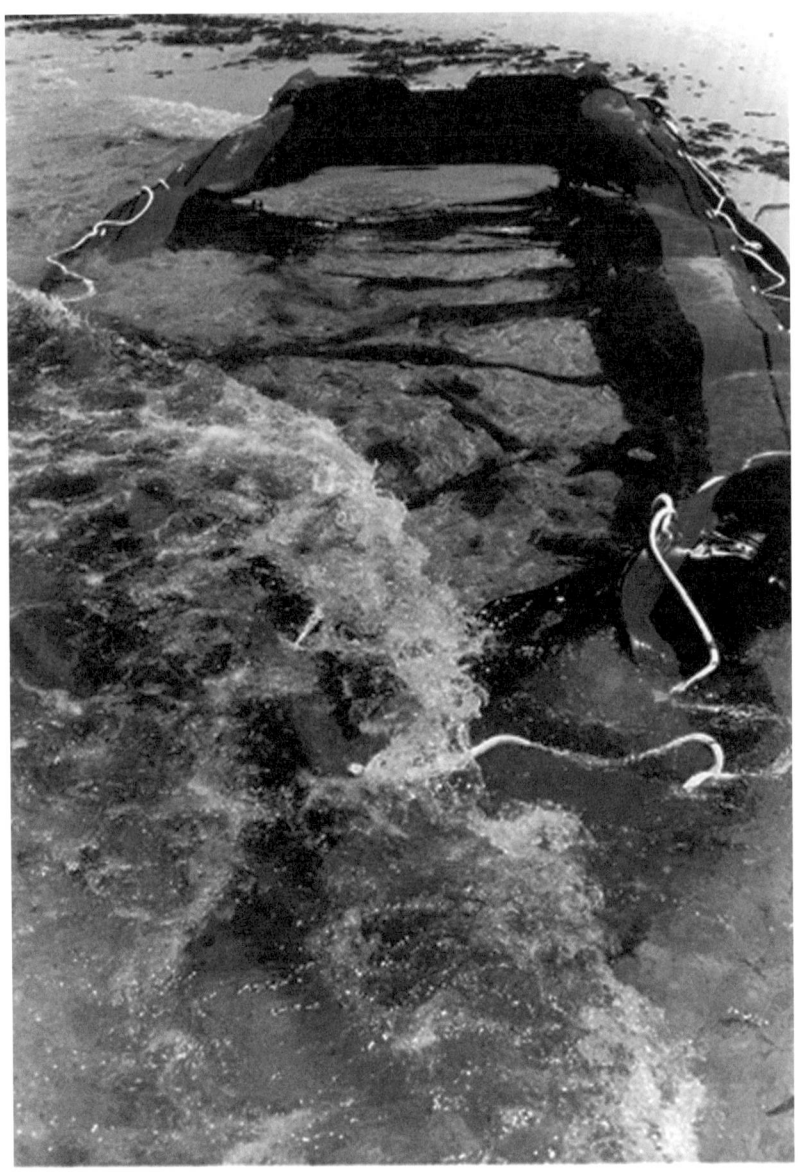

Transnationality

The only way out is a radically different approach. A theory of contemporary borders has to dare a maximum degree of abstraction as the only possibility to undo the picture puzzle. It needs to take into account a series of hypotheses.

First, the border is not the limit but the differentiator of mobility. In its postmodern condition it does not restrict freedom of movement as such: it modulates it. As soon as it is seen from a global perspective, a border appears as a circuit rather than as a line.

The border regime operates as an amplifier. In all its paradoxicality it marks a shift from actuality to potentiality. But it acts in a sense that always contains within it its own potential to not be. What is at stake at the border is a very specific notion of impossibility.

It is a border that manages its violations rather than ignores them, let alone prevents them from happening. It is subject to permanent experimentation in a vast laboratory set up to prove under varying circumstances that there is no absolute freedom of movement, only a relative one.

Nevertheless, the concept of freedom of movement needs to be understood as the derivative of both a desire for autonomy as well as of its limitless postponement in societies of control, amid ever more convoluted regimes of communication and mobility.

A notion of 'transnationality' could be the vanishing point in the distorted view of such a theory of borders. Somewhere out of the field, beyond the borders of framed reality, outside homogenized space and time, it anticipates something that is neither seen nor understood, but nevertheless perfectly present within the everyday life of both a mobile livelihood and social movements.

Transnationality is a radically different form of organizing and unorganizing that transcends the idea of the nation-state as the only reference of different degrees of mobility. Instead, it dares to imagine the fragments of an absolute freedom of movement.

John Thackara

The Gram Junkies

Change in the Way Mobility Is Thought about Is Essential

The many proposals advanced by policymakers and designers to tackle the ever more complex issue of mobility are merely spurious solutions, according to design critic John Thackara. We must radically change our thinking in this regard. In his view, we can learn a lot from the workings of the human brain, microprocessors and network topography.

Gram junkies are those fanatical hikers and climbers who fret about every gram of weight that might be carried – from titanium cook pans to toothbrush covers. Reading their online forums you discover that excess weight is not just a performance issue for these fanatics: they take excess weight *personally*.

In the matter of sustainable mobility, we all need to become gram junkies. Modern mobility doesn't just damage the biosphere, our only home. Global systems of air, rail and road travel are also greedy in their use of space, matter, energy and land. Economic structures perpetuate the problem. Few laws or tax regimes take account of these hidden costs. Sustainable mobility is more about changes to economic structures and cultural perceptions than about the development of exotic power sources for vehicles.

The hardest design challenge is the complexity of 'transport' and mobility as a policy or design issue. Many transportation interventions help solve one or two problems – but exacerbate others. The best-known example of such a rebound effect is the way that the expansion of highways reduces congestion for a time – but tends to increase total vehicle traffic. Another rebound effect is economic: increased vehicle fuel efficiency conserves energy, but because it reduces vehicle operating costs, it tends to increase total vehicle travel.

These negative on-costs are compounded through time. The growth of the us Interstate Highway System, for example, changed fundamental relationships between time, cost and space. We spend the same amount of time travelling today as we did 50 years ago – but we use that time to travel longer distances. The average German citizen today drives 15,000 km a year; in 1950 she covered just 2,000. A lot of our travel time these days is commuting and work-related travel which we believe we cannot avoid – but which we simply did not do 50 years ago, We also spend a lot of time travelling in order to shop and to take the kids to distant schools – 'essential' journeys that did not exist a generation or two ago.

These new patterns of use of space and time, which have been enabled by car ownership, have stimulated the growth, in turn, of a gigantic worldwide ecology of mutually dependent economic actors. It is not in the interest of these actors to reduce transport intensity; on the contrary, their economic survival depends on its perpetual growth.

Unsustainable transport is not, for the most part, the result of bad behaviour such as laziness. It's the result of human beings responding to economic stimuli. Todd Litman, who runs the Victoria Transport Policy Institute in Canada, explains one way in which simple tax arrangements amplify transport intensity. To a car owner, for example, depreciation, insurance, registration and residential parking are largely fixed costs – they are not directly affected by how much a vehicle is driven. Motorists therefore have an incentive to maximize their vehicle travel to get their money's worth from such expenditures. They receive no incentives to drive less. Litman describes these market distortions as 'economic traps' in which competition for resources creates conflicts between individual interests and the common good. Most insidious of all: the impacts of these economic traps are 'cumulative and synergistic: total impacts are greater than the sum of individual impacts', as Litman puts it. Seemingly innocuous fiscal distortions skew countless travel decisions and contribute to a long-term cycle of automobile dependency.

The damaging impacts of modern mobility on the biosphere tend to be indirect and hard to perceive. Curiously, the same goes for its impact on human bodies. Cars kill people too – but without causing much of a fuss. An average of 3,242 people die on the roads each day around the world[1] – a number similar to the total deaths in the 9-11 attacks. Children are especially vulnerable: traffic accident deaths account for 41 per cent of all child deaths by injury. But the carnage caused among children by cars barely registers on the public imagination. The threat of 'terrorism', on the other hand, has driven the growth of 'homeland security' as a new global industry.

1. injurytriallawyer.com/library/facts-figures-death-and-mortality-statistics-for-accidental-injury.cfm.

Even when it doesn't kill people outright, modern mobility is bad for our health – and the on-costs of that, too, are astronomical. The highest rates of obesity, for example, correlate 1:1 with the proportion of car journeys taken by children – and the costs of obesity are heading for 10 per cent of US GDP. Increased auto dependency and air pollution also contribute to escalating respiratory illnesses, cardiovascular disease and hospital admissions.[2]

2. sfphes.org/phes_transport.htm

The movement of stuff is as much a burden on the planet as the movement of people. The World Economic Forum estimates that 2,800 megatonnes of harmful emissions – or 5.5 per cent of the total – are contributed by the logistics and transport sector.[3] Even if

3. weforum.org/pdf/ip/Supply-ChainDecarbonization.pdf.

modern mobility were not a climate-change or social problem, the fact that global mobility depends on a finite energy source – oil – means it is fundamentally not resilient as a system. Whether oil and gas are at a peak or on a plateau, increasing consumption means that the nine million gallons of petrol people currently use in the US each day simply will not be available, in future, in the quantities desired. And because 95 per cent of all transportation depends on oil, life-critical systems that are transport-dependent – such as food – are also vulnerable to any disruption in the prevailing logistical system.[4]

4. jameshowardkunstler. typepad.com/clusterfuck_ nation/2008/11/presto-change-o.html.

A dazzling array of solutions is being considered to deal with these complex challenges. The website Newmobility.org, for example, has identified 177 different projects and approaches to sustainable mobility.[5] These range from bus rapid transit (BRT), car-free days and demand-responsive transport (DRT) to hitchhiking, pedestri-anization, smart parking strategies and vanpooling. The trouble is that every solution that assumes our present or increased levels of transport intensity turns out, on closer inspection, not to be viable.

5. ecoplan.org/wtpp/wt_index. htm.

Non-Solutions

To a car company, replacing the chrome wing mirror on an SUV with a carbon fibre one is a step towards sustainable transporta-tion. To a radical ecologist, all forms of motorized movement are unsustainable. So when is transportation sustainable and when is it not? Chris Bradshaw, a transport economist, emphasizes that 'light' transport systems are not, per se, sustainable – only less unsustainable than commuting by car.[6] 'Light rail supports far-flung suburbs; street cars support, well, street-car suburbs,' says Bradshaw. 'A smaller, more efficient, or alterna-tive-fuel vehicle is only less unsustainable than another private vehicle. It will still take up space on the road and in parking lots; it will still threaten the life and limb of others; it will still create noise, and it still will require lots of energy and resources to manufacture, transport to a dealer, and dispose of when its life ends.'

6. thecityfix.com/the-future-of-urban-sustainable-mobility-go-beyond-the-car/.

Bradshaw wants planners and designers to respect what he calls 'the scalar hierarchy'. This is when trips taken most frequently are short enough to be made on foot (even if pulling a small cart), while the next more frequent trips require a bike or street car, and so on. 'If one adheres to this, then there are so few trips to be made by car that owning one is foolish.'

Investments in high-speed trains such as the TGV are another non-solution. Europeans believe that high-speed trains are far more environmentally friendly than aircraft – but they're not.[7] When researchers at Martin Luther University studied the construction, use and disposal of high-speed rail infrastructure, they found that it takes 48 kg of solid primary resources for one passenger to travel 100 km by Germany's high-speed train.

7. changeobserver. designobserver.com/entry. html?entry=21768.

Is one answer to go by banana boat? Not really. The world's merchant fleet contributes nearly 4.5 per cent of all global emissions – a huge amount, up there with cars, housing, agriculture and industry.[8] (Like aviation, shipping emissions are omitted from European targets for cutting global warming.)

8. guardian.co.uk/environment/2008/feb/13/climate-change.pollution.

Electric cars are the biggest distraction of all. The assumption in European and US policy is that smart grids powered by renewable energy will power millions of electric or hybrid vehicles.[9] Unfortunately, these technology-driven solutions are not viable once the economics of electrical grid modernization, and sheer time, are factored in. The German branch of the World Wildlife Fund (WWF) published a study in May 2009 (conducted with IZES, a German institute for future energy systems) – electric cars reduce greenhouse gases only marginally, they found.[10] The manufacturing processes of both the hybrid and the fully electric car require more energy than those of any conventional petrol-powered car. A worst-case (and frankly most likely) scenario is that most electric cars will run on electricity from coal rather than from renewable sources.

9. ec.europa.eu/ resource-efficient-europe/.

10. zdnetasia.com/news/hardware /0,39042972,62053736,00.htm.

The least talked-about obstacle to electric transportation concerns the raw materials needed to manufacture the vehicles. Rare earth metals are key to global efforts to switch to cleaner energy and therefore cleaner transportation. But mining and processing these metals cause immense environmental damage. Each year, China's rare-earth industry produces more than five times the amount of waste gas, including deadly fluorine and sulfur dioxide, than the total flared annually by all miners and oil refiners in the US.[11] Alongside that 13 billion m^3 of gas are 25 million tonnes of waste water laced with cancer-causing heavy metals such as cadmium. And, just as we already have a problem with peak oil, a shortfall looks likely in the world's capacity to produce lithium. One rare-metals expert, William Tahil, claims the production of hybrid and electric cars will soon tax the world's production of lithium carbonate.[12]

11. noir.bloomberg.com/apps/
news?pid=20601010&sid=aGl5
xEold2d4.

12. tyler.blogware.com/lithium_
shortage.pdf.

Think More, Move Less

Politicians dissemble, or lie, or both, in response to a perceived dilemma: transportation damages the biosphere, costs a fortune and kills people – and yet transport, they believe, is essential to economic growth. This false belief is based on grossly inadequate ecological accounting and the power of the myriad industries involved. Every actor in the aviation industry, for example – airplane manufacturers, airlines, airports – is subsidized by direct grants and tax breaks. Remove these hidden subsidies, and also charge aviation the true costs of its environmental impact, and the whole enterprise becomes un-economic even on its own terms.[13]

13. ens-newswire.com/ens/
apr2003/2003-04-23-02.asp.

Politicians are also scared that no voter will tolerate a curtailment of air travel. A better way to put it is that no *rich* voter will. Only 5 per cent of the world's population has ever flown. Aviation is overwhelmingly an activity of the rich, and strong measures to combat the environmental impact of aviation would not adversely impact poor people.[14]

14. worldwatch.org/node/4346.

We once hoped that the Internet would replace trips to the mall, that air travel would give way to teleconferencing and that digital transmission would replace the physical delivery of books and videos. In the event, technology has indeed enabled some of these new kinds of mobility – but in addition to, not as replacements for, the old kinds. In the same way that roads built to relieve congestion have increased total traffic, the Internet has increased physical transport intensity in the economy as a whole. Rhetorics of a 'weightless' economy, the 'death of distance' and the 'displacement of matter by mind' sound ridiculous, in retrospect.

Rather than tinker with symptoms – such as inventing hydrogen-powered vehicles, or turning petrol stations into battery stations – the more interesting and pertinent design task is to *rethink the way we use time and space* and to reduce the movement of matter – whether goods or people – by changing the word 'faster' to 'closer'.

Our transportation challenge can be compared to distributed computing. The speed-obsessed computer world, in which network designers rail against delays measured in milliseconds, is years ahead of the rest of us in rethinking space-time issues. It can teach us how to rethink relationships between place and time in the real world, too. Embedded on microchips, computer operations entail a precise accounting for the speed of light. The problem geeks constantly struggle with is called *latency* – the delay caused by the time it takes for a remote request to be serviced or for a message to travel between two processing nodes. Another key word, *attenuation*, describes the loss of transmitted signal strength as a result of interference – a weakening of the signal as it travels farther from its source – much as the taste of strawberries grown in Spain weakens as they are trucked to faraway places. The brick walls of latency and attenuation have led computer designers to speak of a 'light-speed crisis' in microprocessor design.

The clever design solution to the light-speed crisis is to move processors closer to the data – in ecological terms, to relocalize the economy.

Network designers, striving to reduce *geodesic distance*, have developed the so-called storewidth paradigm or 'cache and carry'. They focus on copying, replicating and storing web pages as close as possible to their final destination, at content access points. Thus, if you go online to retrieve a large software update from a file library, you are often given a choice of countries from which to download it. This technique is called 'load balancing' – even though the loads in question, packets of information, don't actually weigh anything in real-world terms. Cache-and-carry companies maintain tens of thousands of such caches around the world.

By monitoring demand for each item downloaded, and making more copies available in its caches when demand rises and fewer when demand falls, operators help to smooth out huge fluctuations in traffic. Other companies combine the cache-and-carry approach with smart file sharing or 'portable shared memory parallel programming'. Users' own computers, anywhere on the Internet, are used as shared memory systems so that recently accessed content can be delivered quickly when needed to other users nearby on the network.

The Law of Locality

My favourite example of decentralized production concerns drinks. The weight of beer and other drinks, especially mineral water, trucked from one rich nation to another is a large component of the freight flood that threatens to overwhelm us. But first Coca-Cola and now a boom in microbreweries demonstrate a radically lighter approach: export the recipe, and sometimes the production equipment, but source raw material and distribute locally.

People and information *want* to be closer. When planning where to put capacity, network designers are guided by the *law of locality*. This law states that network traffic is at least 80 per cent local, 95 per cent continental and only 5 per cent intercontinental. Communication network designers use another rule we can learn from in the analogue world: 'The less the space, the more the room.' In silicon, the trade-off between speed and heat generated improves dramatically as size diminishes: small transistors run faster, cooler and cheaper. Hence the development of the so-called processor-in-memory (PIM) – an integrated circuit that contains both memory and logic on the same chip.

So, too, in the analogue world: radically decentralized architectures of production and distribution can radically reduce the material costs of production. We need to build systems that take advantage of the power of networks – but that do so in ways that optimize 'localness'.

Nowhere is this design principle – 'the less the space, the more the room' – better demonstrated than in the human brain. The brain, in Edward O. Wilson's words, is 'like 100 billion squids linked together' – an intricately wired system of nerve cells, each a few millionths of a metre wide, connected to other nerve cells by hundreds of thousands of endings. Information transfer in brains is improved when neuron circuits filling specialized functions are placed together in clusters.

Neurobiologists have discovered an extraordinary array of such functions: sensory relay stations, integrative centres, memory modules and emotional control centres, to name a few.

The ideal brain case is spherical, or close to it, Wilson observes, because a sphere has the smallest surface relative to volume of any geometric form. A sphere also allows more circuits to be placed close together; the average length of circuits can thus be minimized, which raises the speed of transmission while lowering the energy cost for their construction and maintenance.

The mobility dilemma is not as hard as it looks. I have tried here to look at the issue through a fresh lens and to borrow from other domains, such as microprocessor design, network topography and the geodesy of the human brain. The biosphere itself is the result of 3.8 billion years of iterative, trial-and-error design – so we can safely assume it's an optimized solution. As Janine Benyus explains in her wonderful book *Biomimicry*, biological communities, by and large, are localized or relatively closely connected in time and space.[15] Their energy flux is low; distances covered are proximate. With the exception of a few high-flying species, in other words, 'nature does not commute to work'.

15. Janine Benyus, *Biomimicry: Innovation Inspired by Nature* (New York: Perennial (Harper-Collins), 1998).

'The Wonder City You May Live to See. Buildings Half-Mile High and 4-deck Streets May Solve Congestion Problems', *Popular Science Monthly*, 1925.

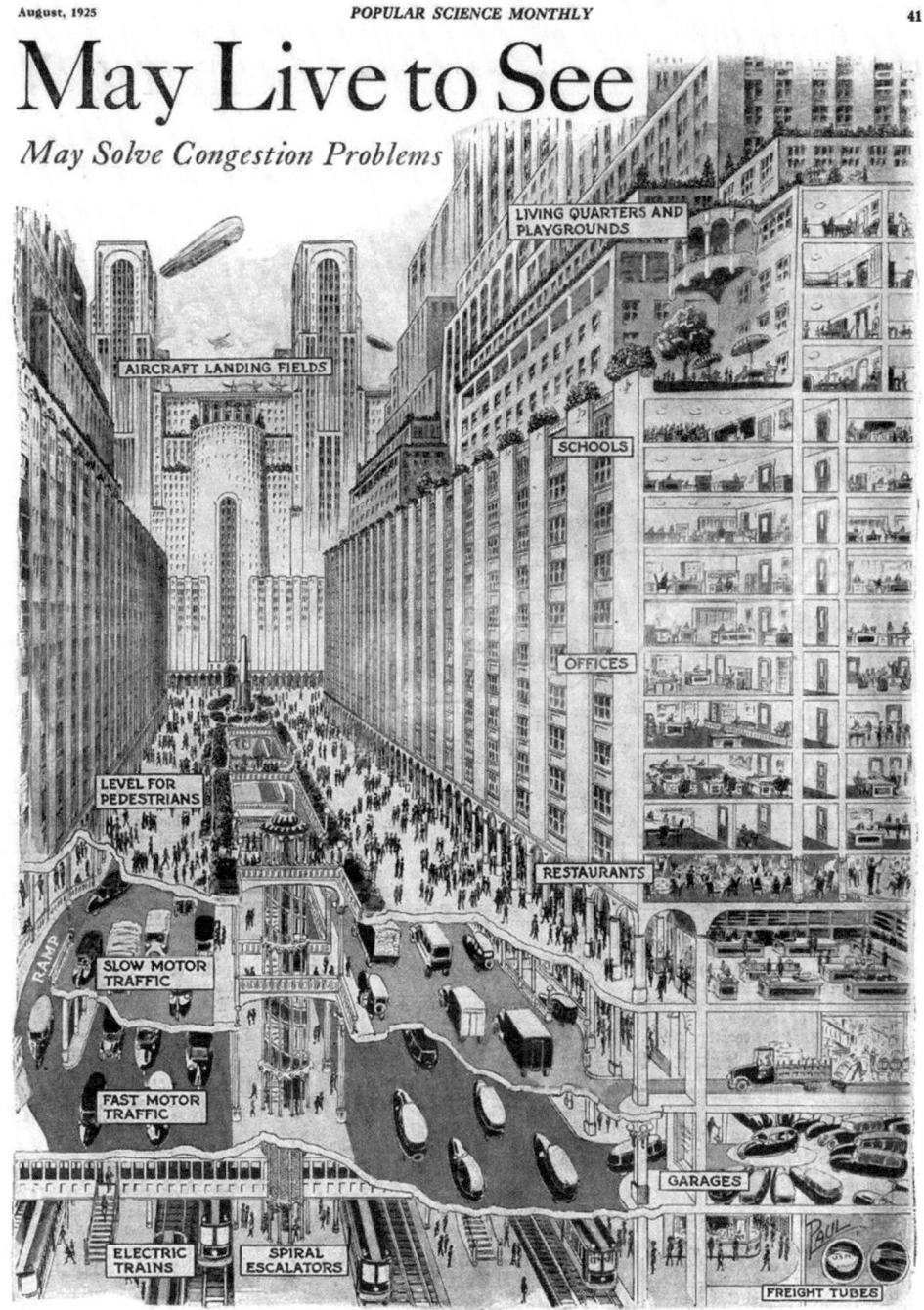

Tatiana Goryucheva

Food Mobility and Traceability

The Preconditions for the Democratic Design of Technology

Media theorist Tatiana Goryucheva investigates the logic behind the correlations between the traceability of food and the technological and social processes during its production. She advocates a democratic model of a socio-technological infrastructure for reconnecting people with their natural and social environment through food.

Tracing the origin of our food, its quality, conditions of production and other relevant data is a service we expect modern technology should be able to provide us with. Many personal mobile devices today can be updated with applications for scanning symbolical codes on products' packages. Production and delivery companies increasingly use advanced equipment and software to monitor their supply chains. At the same time, expert and activist organizations provide the public with plenty of information on different aspects of food's background and related issues. Yet we as consumers, standing in front of a shelf in a supermarket or local grocery shop, have no clear picture of where our food comes from, how is it produced or even what, exactly, is in it. What is the missing link?

So far most ongoing research and development reveals a predominantly technocratic approach towards the issue of food traceability, which is the elaboration of practically and economically efficient tools for monitoring and controlling food supply chains on national and international scales by companies and governmental authorities. The main argument against such an approach is that it omits the diversity of agendas embedded in the politics of the global food market, where relationships between food producers and consumers are increasingly determined by a variety of institutional arrangements. The problem with those arrangements in the situation of a globalized food market is that their settlement is often not transparent and the major players and beneficiaries are not fully accountable according to democratic criteria. Since the role of technologies in fostering both social and economic relationships within the global network society is increasingly important, it seems logical to question the politics of its development from a democratic perspective. What seems to be the most striking problem in the case of food traceability technology is that its objectives so far do not include an active role of the consumer as a critical political player, despite his economic significance.

In this article I would like to review the critical aspects of the logic of interrelationships between the issue of 'food traceability', objectified in a technological form, and the social process in the course of its production. The question that I seek to address in this regard is whether the current practices in the development and implementation of food traceability under the conditions of globalization adequately incorporate the growing demand for democratization, that is people's involvement with politics, especially when it concerns the mediatory role of technologies and the institutional arrangements on the global food market.

Towards a Non-Technocratic Approach

In the contemporary information politics of the food market notions of 'security' and 'safety' are the predominant incentives behind the idea of food traceability taking shape in public debates right now. Considering the increasing dynamics of the global food market in terms of the quantity of exported and imported products, the public concerns about guarantees of quality of food delivered from all over the world put more pressure on the food industry and governments to provide a proper control. At the same time, a range of other issues and concerns are being introduced into the public debate. In particular, ethical considerations are becoming an increasingly important factor in the economy of food production, trade and consumption. The authors of the research *Ethical Traceability and Communicating Food* advocate a shift in the regulatory agenda concerning food-related policies of the European authorities. It should incorporate a broader spectrum of the ethical concerns voiced by citizens, such as the preservation of the environment, social injustice, animal welfare and fair trade. The authors stipulate that this is a rather practical political matter that should be structurally addressed: 'From the political and institutional standpoint, the themes of governance, democratic citizenship, political participation and sustainable development are confronted with the compelling need to establish institutions that are capable of delivering efficacy and maintaining legitimacy both in the society and in the market.'[1] Further on the authors state that reviewing reforms of the food market regulation in the EU since 1997 reveals that 'the nature of EU governance has not changed to any notable extent in the food safety regulatory reforms' and remains 'essentially technocratic'.[2] In this context traceability is imbedded in EU food law (Regulation 178/2002) as its general principle and is in itself 'a precautionary and procedural instrument for food safety and risk management that is based on the model of liberal governance whose main purpose is the regulation and unification of the

1. Christian Coff, David Barling, Michiel Korthals and Thorkild Nielsen (eds.), *Ethical Traceability and Communicating Food* (Dordrecht: Springer Netherlands, 2008), 24.

2. Ibid.

European market'.[3] In response to that a different approach to traceability is suggested that, instead of a sheer regulatory instrument, should be turned into a means 'to promote and facilitate' an informed food choice, thus putting the consumer at the centre of the equation. 'In this way,' the authors argue, 'trust may be re-embedded in the European food system in a more sustainable fashion.'[4]

3. Ibid.

4. Ibid.

Sociotechnological Challenges of Globalization

If we assume that the idea proposed by the authors of the research and voiced by many others is to be a guiding principle for the implementation of food traceability, then it should concern itself with reassessing the spectrum of relationships between the public on the one side, and on the other the economic and political actors associated one way or another with the production of technological solutions for food traceability. Up until now the development of traceability technology has mostly addressed the internal needs of the food industry, such as managing supply chains and quality control, whereas the desires of consumers are presented discursively as a value-adding factor. Recently, more interest has been shown in the development of consumer technologies, mainly applications for portable devices such as IBM's 'Breadcrumps', publicized but not yet available, or currently distributed via iTunes 'HarvestMark' for iPhone. However, the developers of these and similar applications are destined to run into serious dilemmas when embarking on the task of food information supply, which one cannot simply crowdsource, or make fully open and voluntary. While the economic stakes are high on the food market, the implications of providing improper information linked to a product on a shelf are potentially too damaging for both consumers and industries. On a global scale one cannot organize a process of the required data management without reliable sociotechnological support structures, which would guarantee the accuracy and verifiability of information. In the situation of a competitive liberalized market with privately owned companies as major players, guided by legal arrangements that favour the means of reinforcement of competitiveness (of which commercial secrets and intellectual property protection are the most crucial), general public interests tend to be superseded by private interests in the course of designing commercial technology. This means that when the initiation of technology is left to the entrepreneurial will of competing companies, the ideal 'free market' approach to food traceability is not an appropriate solution, as it cannot provide the level of transparency and external control necessary for the sake of public interests.

The nature of traceability technology is such that it requires a complex infrastructure and elaborate arrangements, including the institutional ones mentioned above. Traceability is an example of a pervasive network technology, which does not have a finished stable form and requires multiple interrelated nodes through which data and metadata can be integrated and verified. A practical tool that can connect us to the history of the food that we consume is just a part of the arrangement. It needs to be built *in line with* the *prior* institutionally established standards regarding the whole *chain* of food production, delivery and informatization. The main problem with the design of the technological component of the broader issue of food traceability is that, unlike an autonomous device that has to comply with a limited amount of technical standards defining its functionality, it must be applied to the rather fluctuating unstable and heterogeneous reality of the global food market. It means that the process of setting up standards for food traceability technology should take into account the political challenges that the process of globalization involves, where the task of setting up standards is probably a smaller problem than their implementation and control. One of the most critical of those challenges is the democratization of the process of technological development.

Politics of Standards

For philosopher Andrew Feenberg, the way towards the democratization of technology lies in the reconsideration of the modes of technical design. The latter reflects a 'technical code', a set of standards that is the result of rather controversial social processes.[5] These processes are hidden in the technical object; a finished product does not reveal the controversies involved in the politics of setting up its standards once they are established through a 'technical code'. If we accept Feenberg's argument that setting up standards is the practice in which the politics of technology resides, then we should look for ideas of defining and

5. Andrew Feenberg, 'Democratic Rationalization: Technology, Power, and Freedom', in: Robert C. Scharff and Val Dusek (eds.), *Philosophy of Technology: The Technological Condition* (Oxford: Wiley-Blackwell, 2003).

implementing the standards that are more suitable for a demo-cratic process.

The recent movement towards the democratization of tech-nological development brought in the idea of 'open standards' along with 'open source' software design practices. The main premise for the introduction of open standards has a lot to do with the ideology of open and free communication, upon which the development of the Internet and the World Wide Web have been based so far. According to Tim Berners-Lee, the Web inventor and director of the World Wide Web Consor-tium, which plays a significant role in laying down guidelines for the introduction and implementation of standards for the Internet and Web-related technologies, 'open standards' are 'standards that can have any committed expert involved in the design, that have been widely reviewed as acceptable, that are available for free on the Web, and that are royalty-free (no need to pay) for developers and users'.[6] While the 'Internet era' of technology dramatically influenced the modes of its development to the extent that ideas of 'open standards' and 'open source' started to be adopted by govern-ments and proprietary companies, the critical issue of the democratiza-tion of technology is not resolved by its premises. The main question in this regard is: How are the social and political issues related to technological implementa-tion, but which exceed the scope of technological expertise, present in the process of setting up technological standards? So far, and Berners-Lee's definition complies with the prevailing assumption, the purview of technological standards remains a sanctuary of technology experts. Moreover, regardless of the definition of the standards, the tendency towards depoliticizing standards-setting procedures occurs particularly in the insti-tutional autonomization of the role of specialized professional communities in the standards-development process, and, partly related to this, the expansion of the privatization of standards. The latter is characterized as a 'digital enclosure' by Timothy Schoechle in his research *Standardization and Digital Enclosure. The Privatization of Standards Knowledge and Policy in the Age of Global Information Technology.*[7]

6. Tim Berners-Lee, 'Long Live the Web: A Call for Continued Open Standards and Neutrality', *Scientific American Magazine*, 22 November 2010. Available online at: http://www.scientificamerican. com/article.cfm?id=long-live-the-web&page=3, published 22 November 2010, accessed 5 January 2010.

7. Timothy Schoechle, *Stand-ardization and Digital Enclosure: The Privatization of Standards, Knowledge, and Policy in the Age of Global Information Technology (Advances in It Standards and Standardization Research)* (IGI Global Information Science Reference, 2009).

Schoechle's analysis is an attempt to shift the focus of discussions about standards from results to the process, where forms and conditions of participation should be of primary concern. In this respect, further deliberations about the democratization of practices regarding standards development should focus on reassessing the existing institutional arrangements.

The current stage of development of standards for food traceability is expressed in the ISO22005:2007(E) document. The document is designed within the procedural framework of the International Organization for Standardization and can by no means be characterized as an 'open standard'. Despite the fact that, according to the ISO statement, all interested parties affected by a standard can potentially be present in the committees responsible for its development, participation in the process is not transparent and even susceptible to dominance abuse, according to critics. While the development of traceability technologies can hardly follow the path of the Internet and Web technologies, developed mostly outside ISO, a critical review of the social mechanisms of standards setting for its implementation necessarily should take into account the expectations introduced by Internet communities regarding the openness of the process. At the same time the problem of democratization of technology cannot be reduced to the issues of openness and accessibility alone. There is an intricate dichotomy built into the practice of the development of standards, particularly within an international context. On the one hand, the design of most of the standards assumes their voluntarily adoption, unless a special, usually governmental, regulation enforces it. On the other, the very necessity of standards is created by a search for binding rules and, thus, controlling tools over technological development. It means that in order to ensure the development of technology with respect to the demands of the rest of society, the standardization procedure itself should be designed in such a way that it includes a broader social agenda at both levels, contribution and control. As the case of food traceability shows, enabling it goes far beyond the technological solution in a technodeterminist sense.

One of the major problems in the relationship between the development of technologies and democratic institutions was identified by philosopher John Dewey in his analysis of the democratic public sphere of the industrial age. He observed an inadequate institutional response to the industrial revolution, which he associated with 'democratic disturbances'.[8] The production of new technologies in the course of industrialization had a disruptive impact upon institutional arrangements. Instead of replacing old institutions by new ones, a rather contradictory readjustment occurred. Persistence of old institutions, the most important of which for industrial development had been the institute of private property, along with the introduction of new ones, accompanied by ideologies of utilitarian economic determinism and individualism, contributed, according to Dewey, to disturbances of democratic forms. It undermined the necessity of broad and direct public engagement with politics. One can see that the problem repeats itself in the case of the postindustrial informational revolution. While the Internet and social media enable people to be more engaged with matters of society and its political agenda in a direct and participatory way, the institutional political realm is still unable to structurally accommodate this remarkable sociotechnological shift in its practices. The food traceability case is an obvious example of this discrepancy. As more and more diverse groups and individuals begin to play a significant role in the information politics of the food market at a global scale, especially with the help of social media, the food industry becomes more dependent on peoples' knowledge about the products, based on information provided by third parties. The question is: How can the increasing social participation in food information politics be integrated with the implementation of food traceability at the technological level in a more open democratic way?

8. John Dewey, *The Public and Its Problems* (New York: Henry Holt & Co, 1927), republished in 1954 by Swallow Press and in 1991 by Ohio University Press.

The logic of the development of software applications for personal devices is such that together with their increasing role in the mediation of our engagement with everyday reality, the demand for more freedom regarding flexibility and customization of tools according to individual choice increases, too. This is what very likely would be an ideal food traceability application, according to one of the bloggers on the issue: 'Here is how I would envision the "shopping app" of the future. First, I can personalize my filter. I can do that based on standardized product attributes. I can set, whether I care about "organic", "locally grown", absence or presence of certain ingredients and other filters. Once this filter is being set, I would like to cross reference exactly those product attributes with my local grocery stores, I would like to see who carries products and potentially at what price. When I really would use my application on my smart phone to read a bar-code, I would like to be flagged, if any of my desired features is missing and which ones are present. I don't want to read a poem about the product where I need to find the information I care for by reading 90% of information I do not care about at all.'[9]

9. See: http://food-erp.com/blog/category/traceability/, published 31 May 2010, accessed 15 January 2011.

The next step is to envision a democratic model of a socio-technological infrastructure for reconnecting people with their natural and social environment through food. The problem of the democratization of technology is not the question of choosing a mode of social or practical engagement with technology, but rather the elaboration of principles for a proper inclusive, open and fair process of its development, and their practical implementation.

The NomadicMILK project by artist Esther Polak presents a poetic interpretation of landscape and mobility. The project follows the daily routes of two dairy economies in Nigeria. Tracked by GPS, the personal routes of nomadic dairy farmers and local truck drivers become an object of reflection.
© NomadicMILK project, Esther Polak and team, Nigerian version 2009, www.nomadicmilk.net

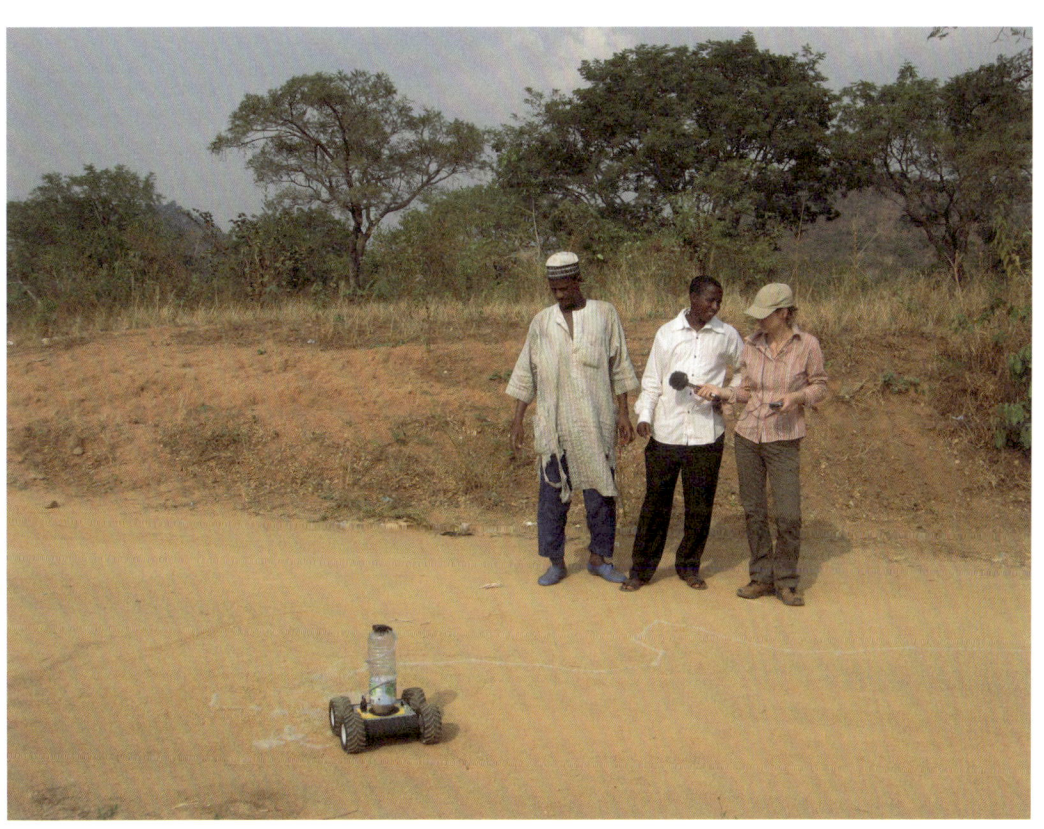

Metahaven

Mobile Money
(The Near Future)

Metahaven is an Amsterdam-based design studio, founded by Vinca Kruk and Daniel van der Velden. Metahaven creates and researches visual identity, which was the focus of their 2010 book *Uncorporate Identity*. For this issue on mobility, they draft a speculative future for 'mobile money', in which a faltering Euro currency is rescued by Facebook Credits

Mobile Money
(The Near Future)
Metahaven

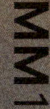

Fig. 1

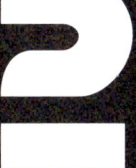

The euro crisis has seen rising inflation, an inability for countries to manage their budget deficits, and subsequent difficulties in addressing the bailout schemes provided. The euro is beginning to lose credibility via its broken promise of the original model, found detailed in the Maastricht criteria. An inevitable fragmentation of countries within the euro zone has begun. Economists are beginning to seriously question the future of the euro and it is becoming relevant to speculate on what may succeed the euro in the event of a collapse.

Despite calls to opt out of the euro and reintroduce national currencies, comeback national money would be quite baseless as a standard of value. Its moment of issue would need to be prepared long in advance. And its exchange rate would need to be established against the euro. Any freefall of the euro would inevitably affect the escape currency as well.

We turn to organizations that have the capacity to establish membership, value and exchange, but are not states. Facebook, the social networking platform, is a commercial firm that provides its users with free services. As its user

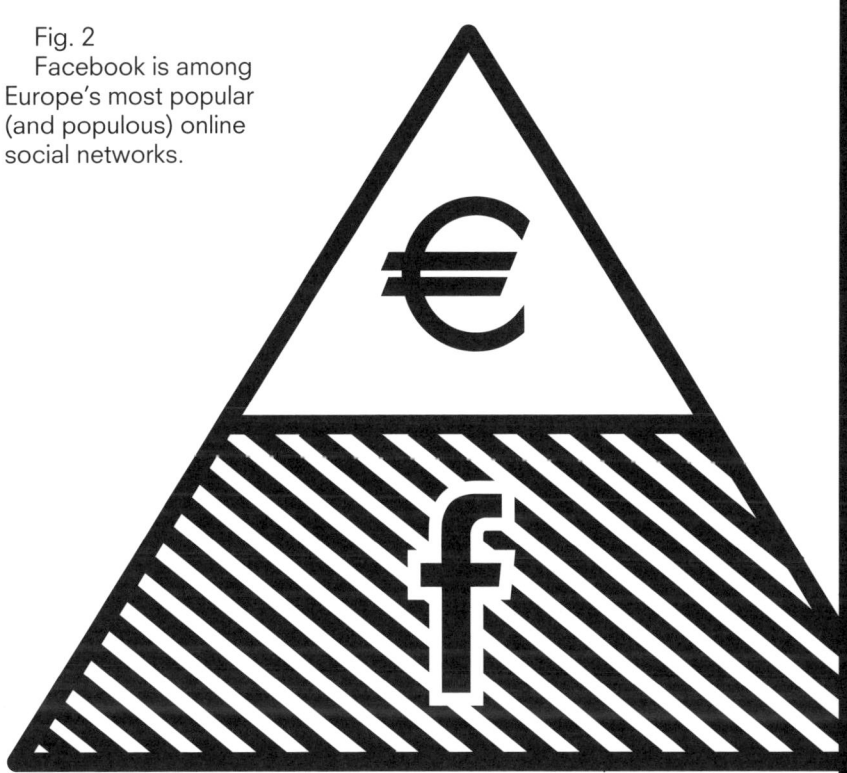

Fig. 2
Facebook is among Europe's most popular (and populous) online social networks.

Fig. 3
When scaling up, social networks face challenges similar to those of governments.

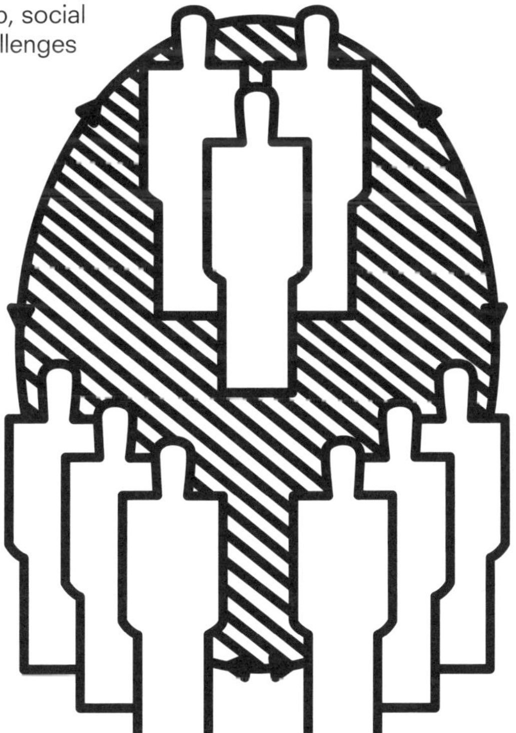

base continues to grow, Facebook may be considered a political association in an early stage of development. It is governed undemocratically, yet by the consent of voluntary membership. Facebook has over 600 million users, allowing the possibility for its credit system to become a dominant form of online payment. As Facebook gains further users, online merchants will become increasingly pressured to accept Facebook credits as a customary form of payment. Facebook credits have a fixed universal exchange rate, which decreases the chance of complications when purchasing goods. Despite rapid expansion, Facebook also continues to demonstrate reliability and security.

However, just as Facebook has the power to accommodate growing online purchases, it is equally likely to use access to purchasing data for increased target advertising and overall control.

With further expansion, there is reason to assume that Facebook credits may eventually become a plausible form of currency outside of the virtual realm, nursing the fractured currencies of the world through global oversight.

Facebook credits would present a more immediately feasible alternative

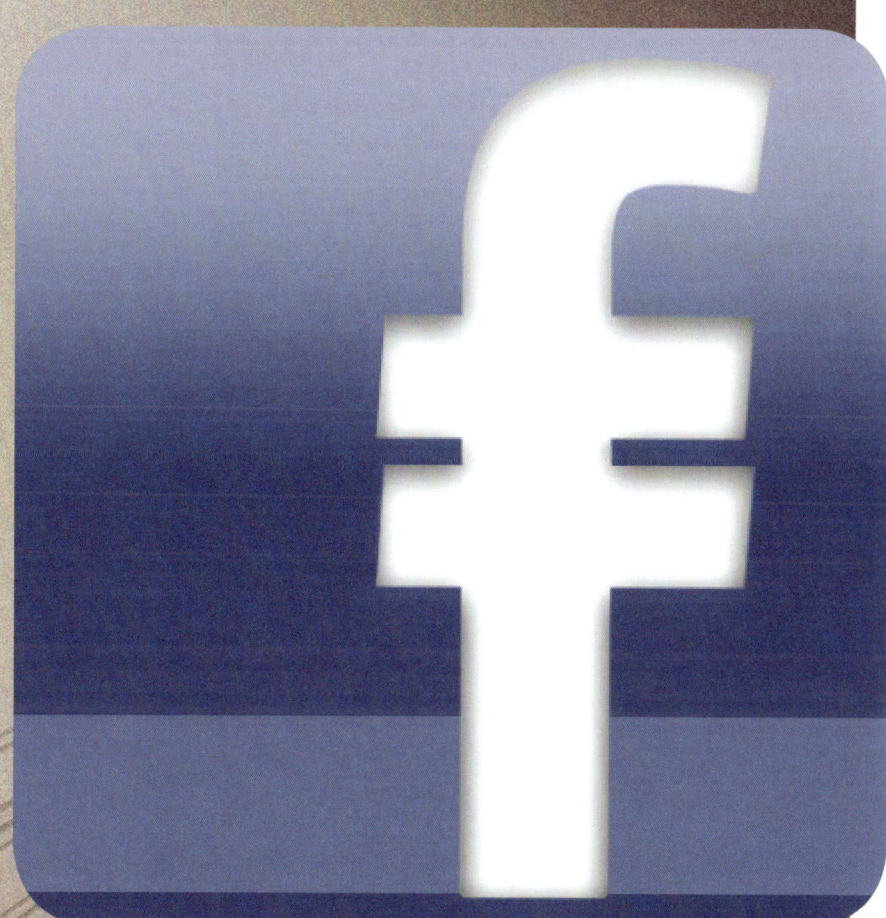

MM5

Fig. 4
The ubiquitous
Facebook lower case
"f" logo is a single stroke
away from becoming a
currency symbol.

to the euro in the event of a collapse, as many euro-zone citizens already have Facebook accounts, spandexed between national jurisdiction by birth, and social network participation by choice.

A response to this situation should be expected from France and Germany, prone to present national alternatives to a simple fallback to Facebook. Germany's likely response to a folding euro would not be a new Deutsche Mark, but a national virtual currency. Such an 'e-Mark' would meet a perceived desire for national jurisdiction and control, but at the same time express technological innovation. Conversely, France is expected to think through the problem on its own, more fundamental terms, and propose a European social network as an alternative to Facebook, just as it once tried to challenge the Google search engine.

The success of both efforts is expected to be partial, with Facebook still coming out as the dominant currency standard.

The euro-Facebook assemblage is makeshift and precarious. It includes not just money and finance but the entire social livelihood of citizen subjects. The monetization of social ties is

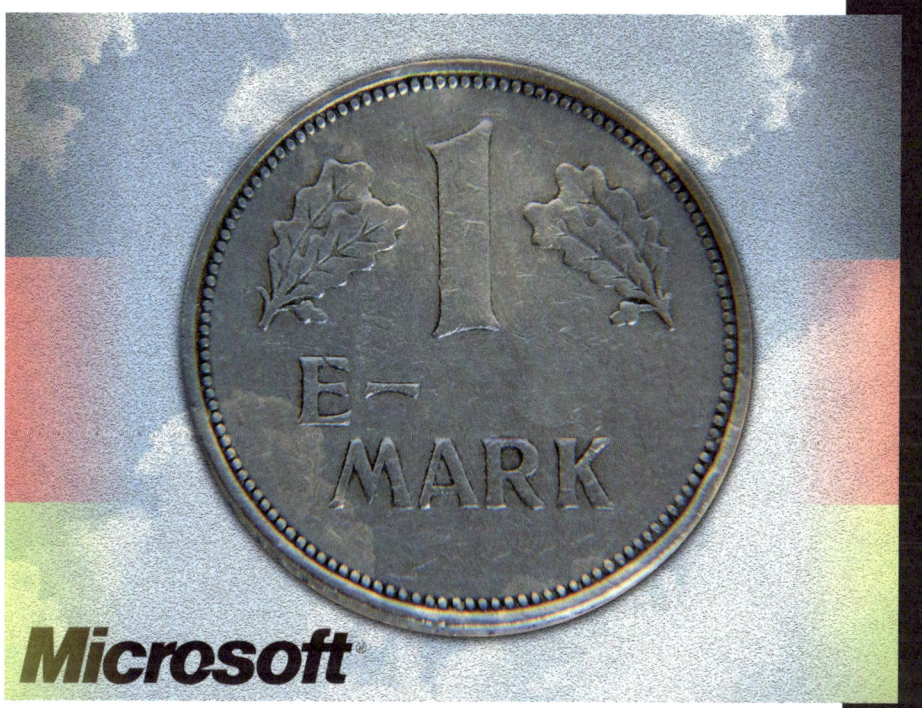

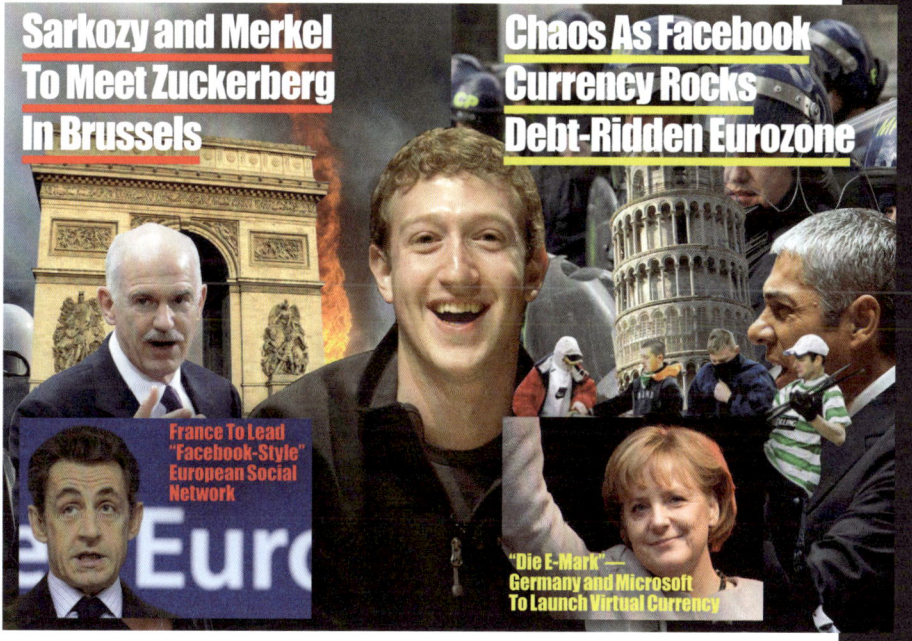

Fig. 5 & 6
Always keen on
innovation, Germany's
most likely move would
be to launch a virtual
currency of its own
design, helping Microsoft
to get up to speed.

both a treasure trove of Silicon Valley investment, and a last resort to faltering postindustrial economies trying to live off immaterial goods. Social reputation as credit is conclusively exemplified by the term 'Whuffie'. Originally conceived by the author Cory Doctorow as a fictional index of on personal reputation, Whuffie is now shorthand for the type of value exchanged in social transactions and consequently 'stored' in the user base of successful social media platforms.

The social gold rush is eventually expected to exploit hitherto ungraspable occurrences, such as the making of eye contact.

Facebook, in its relentless pursuit of the social domain, has recently made moves to brand protect not just its own company name but even the word 'face' itself.

Facestate is the ultimate combination of government and social media. Under the combined regime of public spending cutbacks and participation in social networks, Facestate is expected to, in the mid to long term, supplant the welfare state. Facestate is the social superpower.

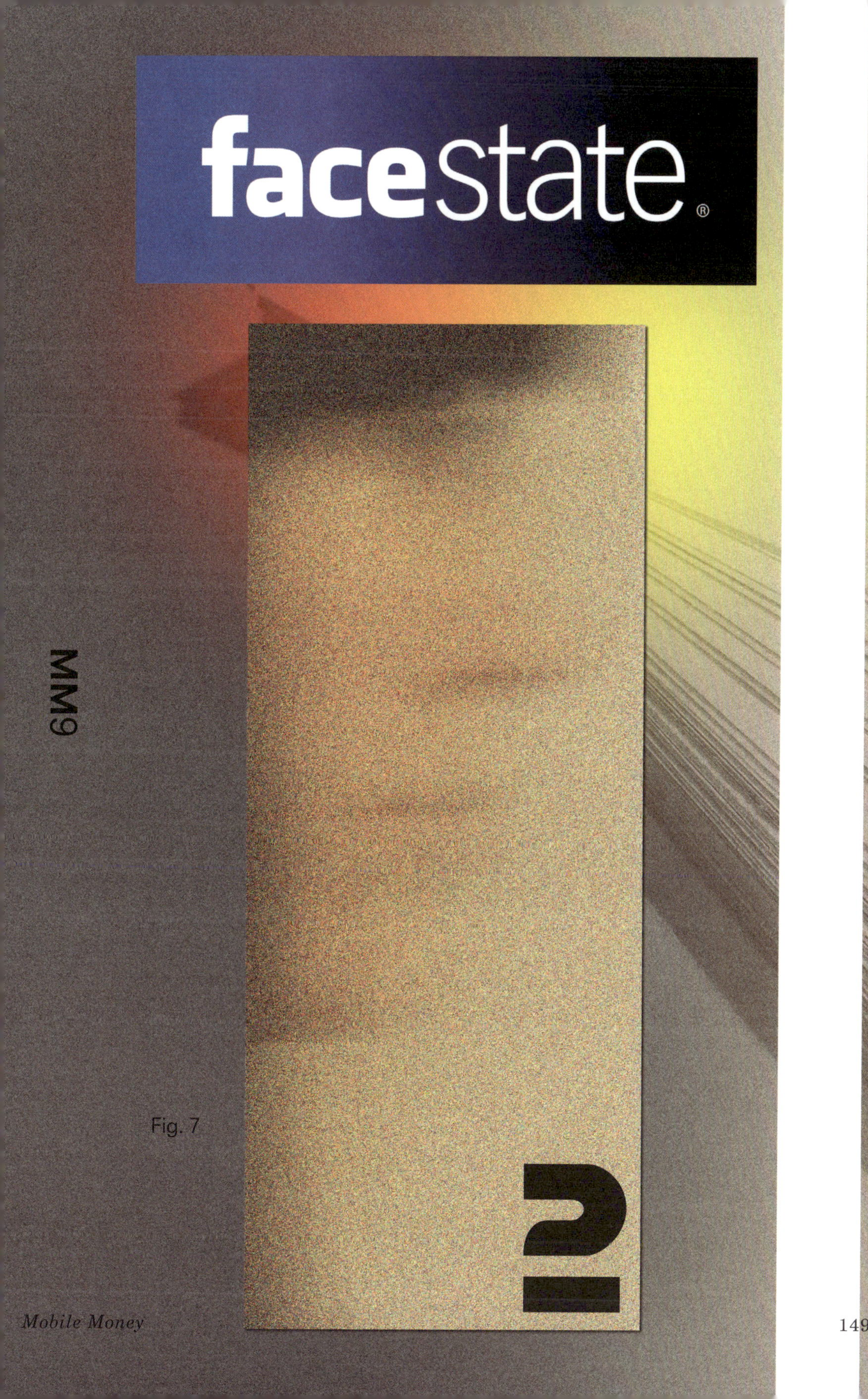

facestate®

MM9

Fig. 7

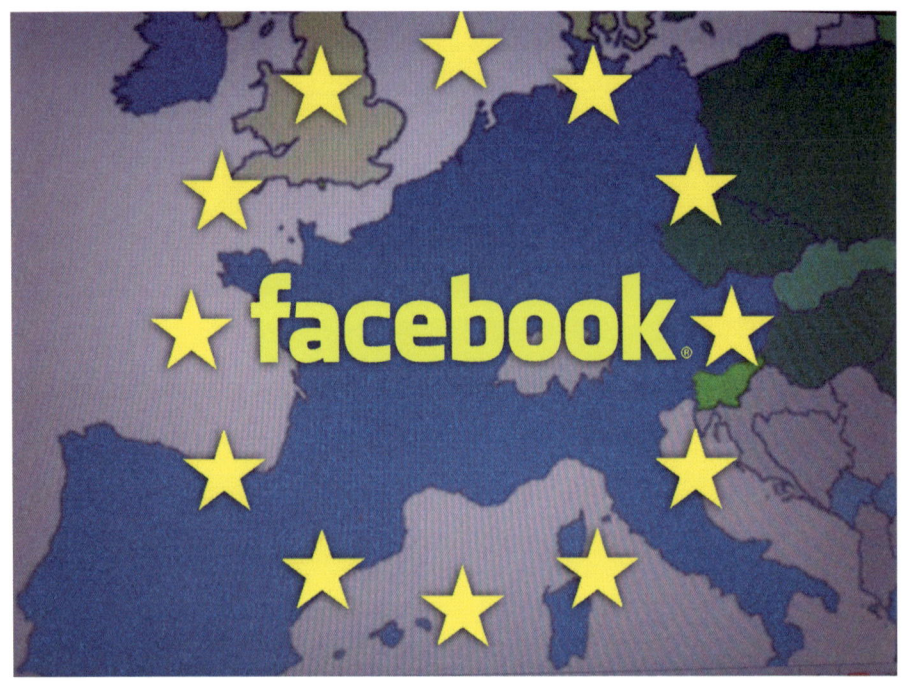

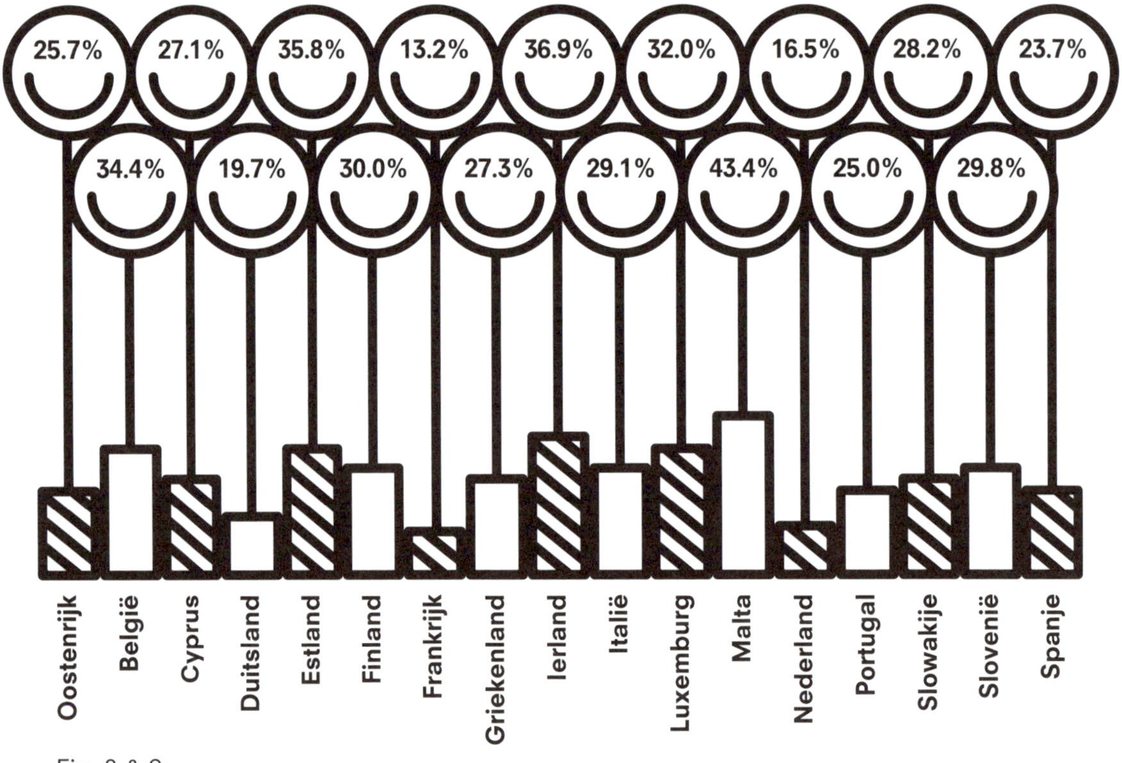

| 25.7% | 27.1% | 35.8% | 13.2% | 36.9% | 32.0% | 16.5% | 28.2% | 23.7% |

| 34.4% | 19.7% | 30.0% | 27.3% | 29.1% | 43.4% | 25.0% | 29.8% |

Oostenrijk · Belgïe · Cyprus · Duitsland · Estland · Finland · Frankrijk · Griekenland · Ierland · Italïe · Luxemburg · Malta · Nederland · Portugal · Slowakije · Slovenïe · Spanje

Fig. 8 & 9
Facebook usage in the Eurozone, percentage of population per country, September 2010, source: internetworldstats.com

Nerea Calvillo

Colored Data Clouds

Ubiquitous Ambient Technologies as Public Urban Infrastructures

With the project _In the Air_,[1] Spanish architect Nerea Calvillo wants to make the citizens of Madrid more aware of the city's official monitoring systems for measuring air pollution and get them involved. Through the development of interfaces, collective action can be initiated that is aimed at exchanging experiences and raising community consciousness.

1. _In the Air_ is an ongoing project initiated in 2008 by the author of this text, and has been developed through collaborative workshops with 30 international collaborators. See www.intheair.es.

This text aims to question some of the aspects of Madrid's aerial ecosystem through the project *In the Air*. By visualizing the substances in the air as non-human, invisible agents, it sets out to identify their physical, social and political relation to the urban environment, with effects ranging from the interior of the human body to the image of the city. Visibility of this symmetrical relationship between humans and non humans makes it possible to shed light on its controversies and to include these in the social political debate.

In 1967 Reyner Banham described Los Angeles, identifying four ecologies that integrated the geographical, infrastructural, architectonical, social and political aspects of the city.[2] This eco-systemic perspective allowed him to comprehend the interrelation and contextualization of urban systems, as well as how they are embedded in their physical and social context.

2. Reyner Banham, *The Architecture of Four Ecologies* (Berkeley, CA: California University Press, 1995).

The urban milieu has been documented in almost all of its aspects, from the built environment to traffic and energy flows. However, there are equally active invisible agents, whose functioning and properties we ignore because they are invisible from a certain point of view. An example of these invisible actors is provided by the microscopic and non-human substances in the air, which are agents of the aerial ecosystem, a new ecology that could be added to Reyner Banham's urban analysis.

The specific case of Madrid is relevant here because of its symbolic and public health implications. First, it is one of the most contaminated cities in Europe, to the extent that it has been fined several times by the European Commission. And secondly, because traditionally the city has been represented by its sky, from Velazquez's royal equestrian paintings to contemporary pictures, accompanied by the seventeenth-century proverb and present urban marketing slogan: 'From Madrid to the sky.'

However, the sky of the city has changed from a deep blue to a light brown, so either action must be taken to restore its previous qualities or the city may need to find new representations.

In Madrid's official air-quality monitoring system, sensors are hosted in green steel boxes in the middle of boulevards or roundabouts, hidden by plants or trees, camouflaged to the eyes of passers-by. They become invisible devices, and their data remains invisible in the public space.

The results of these measurements are published on the City Council's web page. As they are published in a non-computable format they can't be used by citizens, and the highly specific data they provide make it impossible to combine different data sets and make comparisons. Therefore the analysis of this public data is relegated to experts, who are the only ones able to understand the implications.

Having seen that data in all its formats is black-boxed, the project *In the Air* proposes different ways of making these data public. It does so by testing prototypes of mediation devices that allow the citizen to access and understand the information emitted by means of various levels of communication.

Maps as Interactive Machines

The first level of communication that was tested by the project is a virtual map, conceived as an inscription device that allows different sets of quantified data to interrelate. The map is conceived as a machine that can be activated in different ways. There are institutions that publish two-dimensional or three-dimensional air-quality maps, but they are almost never interactive, and therefore have only one way of being read.[3] The application permits many of the visualization parameters to be controlled, so that the user can construct his or her own map, his own construction of reality. In this way not just one visualization is offered, but a tool that facilitates multiple interpretations.

3. A main reference for the project was provided by the maps of the London Air Quality Network. See www.londonair.org.uk.

In The Air uses a geo-localized topographical mesh as an instrument to interrelate data obtained hourly in each measuring station. With it, the user can localize his or her position within the city and see the density of each of the substances, as well as their relative quantities in comparison to other points of the city.[4]

4. This topography doesn't resemble a gas and doesn't move as a fluid, because it pretends that people become part (mentally or physically) of the model. This strategy is called 'simulation' in AI studies, as opposed to 'mimesis'. In a mimetic process the attention is centred on the aspect of things, in a simulation process the attention is centred on the identification with the object. In mimesis there is an emphasis on fiction, and on the contrary in a simulation the interest is to transform fiction into reality. In: Claudia Gianetti, *Estética digital* (Barcelona: L'angelot, 2002).

Each mesh corresponds to one of the five substances selected: Carbon Monoxide (CO), Nitrogen Dioxide (NO_2), Sulphur Dioxide (SO_2), Ozone (O_3) and Particulate Matter (PM_{10}). This distinction allows the user to identify the different emission sources, the repercussions to human health and the possible implications of each substance, as well as the actions that can be taken to reduce their densities. In this way, the difficulty of understanding the data as a whole is mitigated by reducing it to smaller and more comprehensible fragments.

However, these maps are still online and in a virtual

Online digital application, 2008

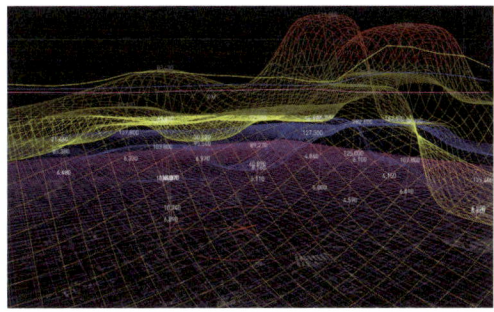

Madrid in the Air I and II, 2008 and 2009.

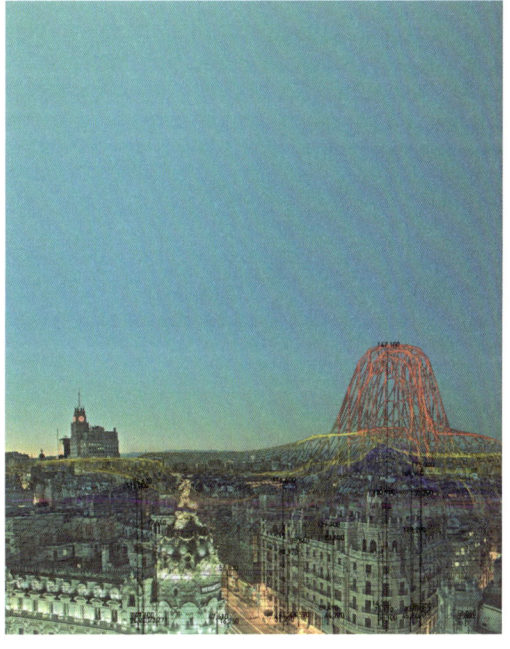

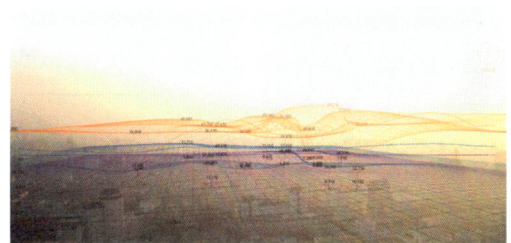

Contamination compass prototype. Kitchen Budapest, 2009

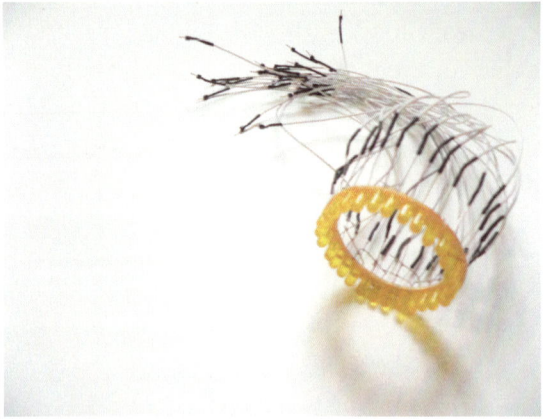

Digital façade application. Medialab-Prado, 2009

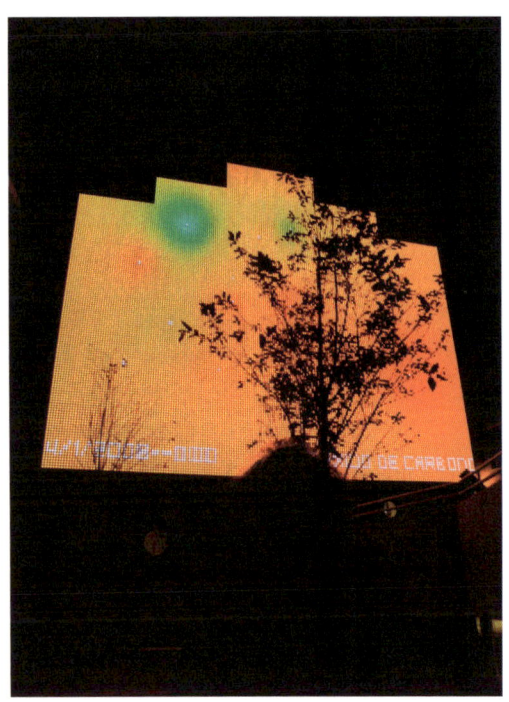
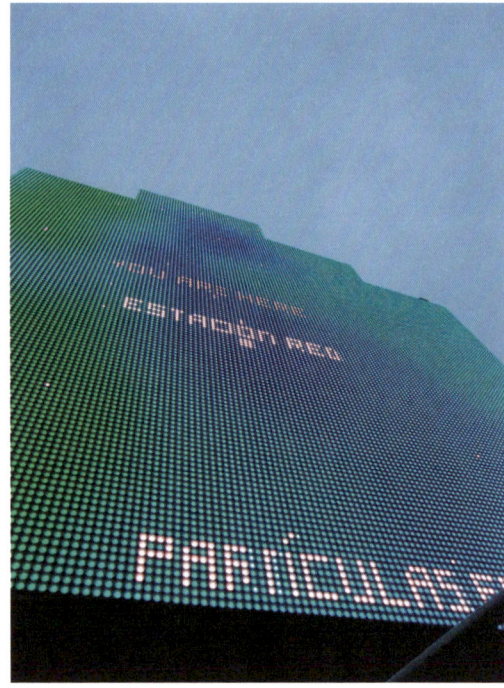

environment, and it is necessary to have equipment and an Internet connection to access them. Even the proliferation of 3G mobile phones can't yet guarantee a wide access to digital information in the public realm. So it is necessary to identify possible devices that could provide access to those data in the public space, to make it possible for people to move through the city according to the density of contaminants, or to convert the public space into a public arena where urban topics can be discussed.

Urban Displays

A second level of communication is the construction of devices that emit information in the urban space.

In Madrid small digital screens are used in one plaza (paradoxically at the Tourist Information Centre), where air quality is shown together with meteorological conditions. However, as has been argued above, these means are insufficient for an understanding of the general system or the local situation at any specific point in time. Instead, large digital screens could be a possible platform because they make it possible to communicate more information in a more complex way. These screens, attached to or integrated into a building, transform urban space, blurring the boundaries of architecture, juxtaposing its reflections and opening windows to multiple worlds simultaneously, as can be perceived in Times Square in New York.

Such screens generally broadcast advertisements, but are potentially public infrastructures.[5] What kinds of relationships can be established between the screens and the public still needs to be evaluated with this new type of content, as it contains information of public interest it alters the spectacular relationship of advertisement and constructs a relationship of interactive reciprocity, transforming the spectator into a user. *In the Air* has developed an application for this format, in which the citizen can choose pollution paths through the city by using heat maps.

5. As could be tested at the Media Facades Festival 2010: www.mediafacades.eu.

Also, another type of screen has been designed and proto-typed. It consists of coloured water vapour, and uses the elements of analysis as a visualization medium. The intensity, colour and rhythm of vapour emissions encode the various substances, their density and their trend. This display is a prototype of what has been called a 'diffused façade', because it builds a blurred interface between a solid façade and the urban space around it. This ephemeral interface has several functions: first, it contains and provides information on the air

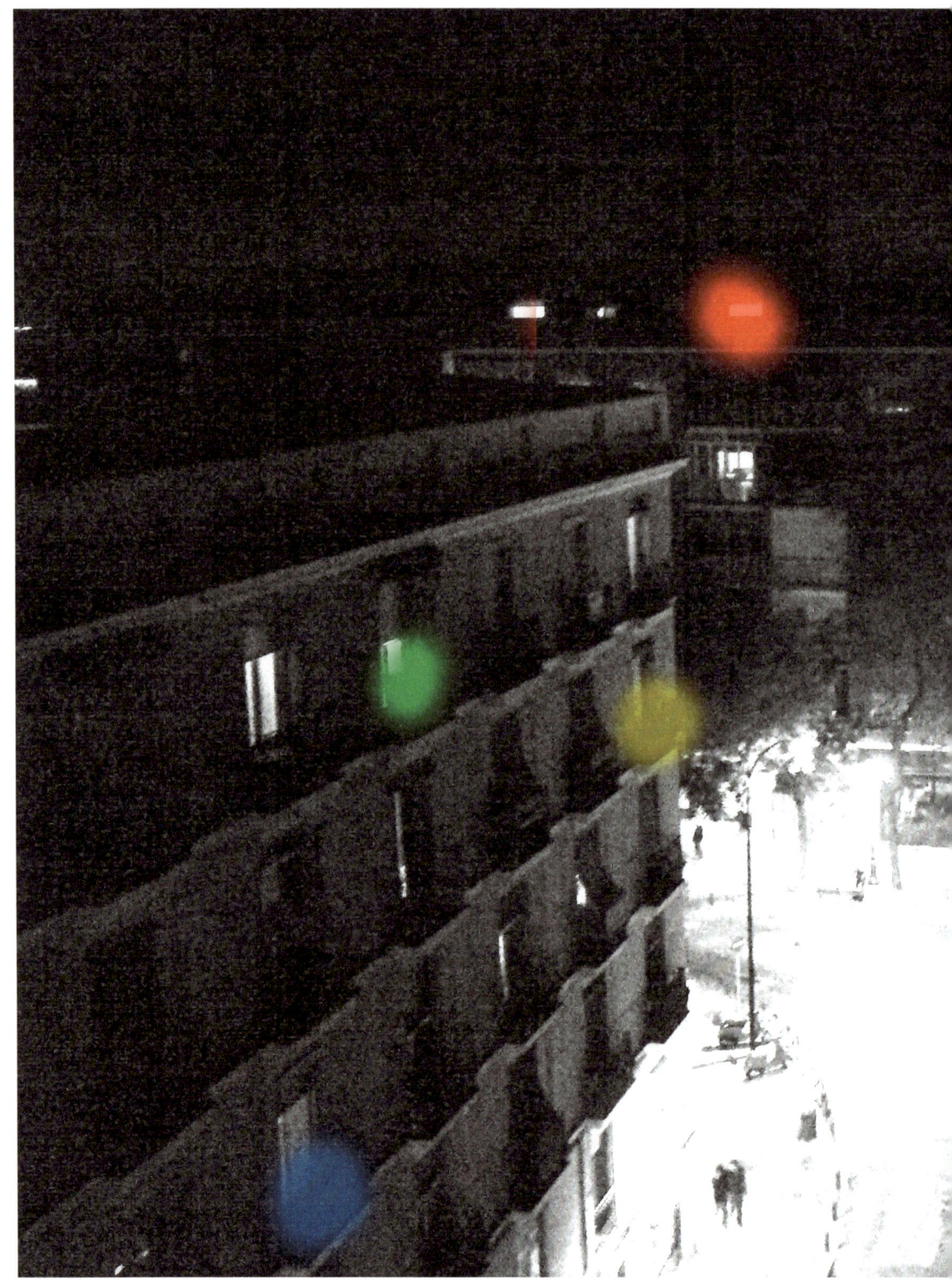

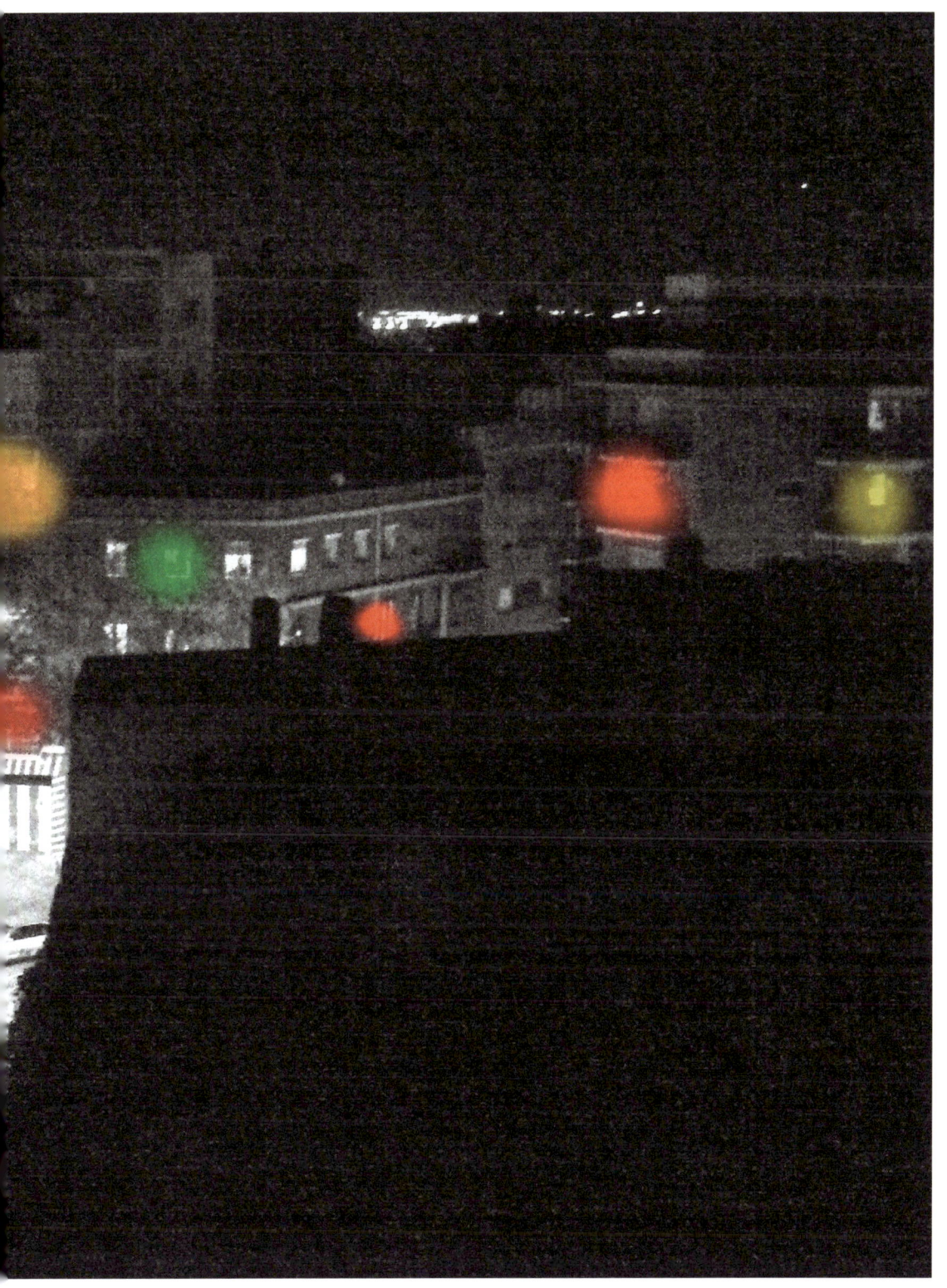

Colored Data Clouds

Diffused façade prototype during the day, revealing the density of SO_2 measured in the closest measuring station.

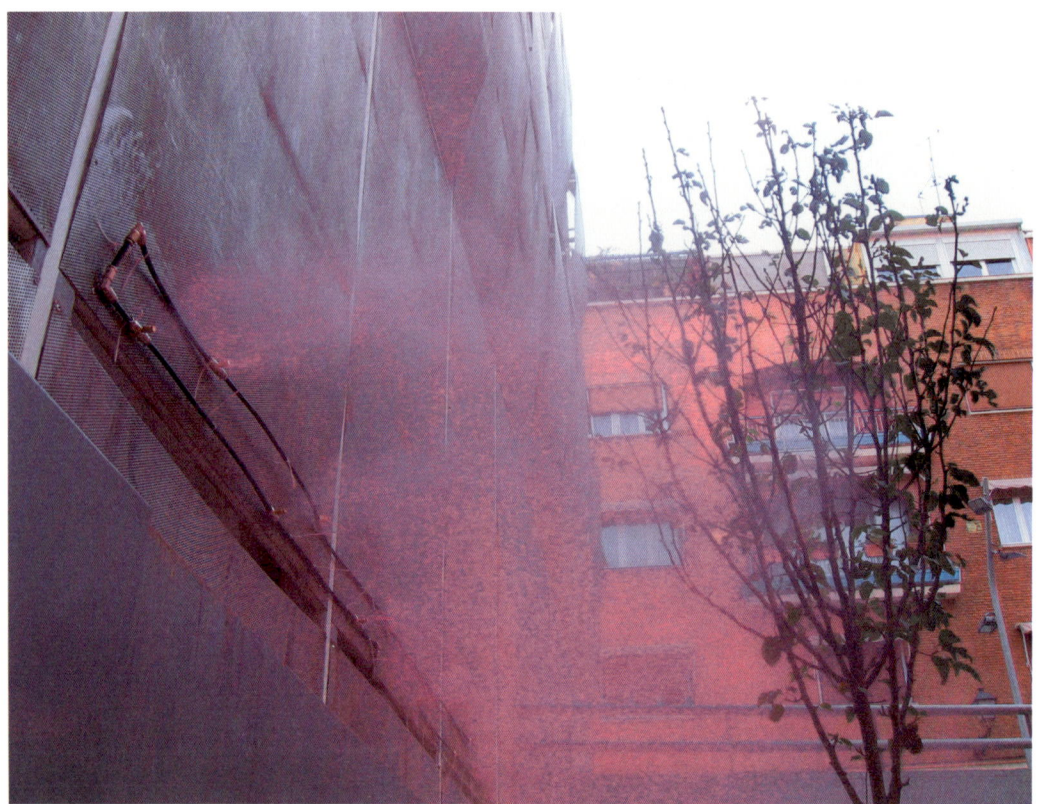

quality in real time, then it transforms urban space by reducing the temperature and increasing the humidity, and finally it reduces the levels of pollution because it causes sedimentation of the chemical substances. It therefore constitutes a giant air-quality indicator, consisting of a coloured cloud that blends architecture with the atmosphere it has invaded and that mediates with the bodies it surrounds.

Mobile Displays

Another family of displays that the project has tested are small mobile devices that convert the citizen into a data visualizer. These can be just pollution visualizers in the shape of led-pins, or devices that can provide more complex information, like a compass, which identifies pollution densities and their direction with respect to the users' position, as if it were an emergency exit indicator.

One could say that sensor networks are likely to be infrastructural to the extent that they facilitate the production or use of other systems, although they have different properties than what is traditionally called 'hard infrastructure', such as communication and transport systems, materials or fluids. It is a network of discrete, small-scale and low-budget technological elements, as opposed to continuous and large-scale ones. Infrastructures could also be understood as a series of artefacts. But it would be interesting to broaden the spectrum and to understand them as well as cultural production objects with spatial content, as 'soft infrastructures'.[6]

6. Alexander D'Hooghe, *The Objectification of Infrastructure: The Cultural Project of Suburban Infrastructure Design* (Berlin: Jovis Verlag GmbH, 2010).

So what is proposed by *In the Air* is to integrate these hard and soft properties, in which the infrastructure is not only the detection network, but includes all data visualization systems, and to expand, as far as possible, the potential use of each of its parts by the general public. That is, the public infrastructure would consist of the whole data management system, from its sensor networks to its reception and public use.

Although the construction of the monitoring and detection networks are implemented mostly by public institutions (in the European Union this has already been mandatory for three decades), research on its implementation, display and on sensor types are taking place these days mainly in universities and small businesses with environmental interests.[7]

7. Large-scale environmental sensing projects are being developed by the Centre for Embedded Network Sensing, University of California; wireless monitoring networks applied to cities by Harvard Sensor Networks Lab, Harvard School of Engineering and Applied Sciences; the identification of new parameters or indicators by SENSEable City

In the case of Madrid the first network to measure air quality was implemented in 1968 by the Department to Combat Pollution of the city council. Since then it has been updating and renewing the equipment and the network. As of today the Integrated System of Monitoring, Prediction and Information of Air Pollution consists of 28 measuring stations, making it one of the largest in the European Union (Paris has seven, Budapest nine, for example, although London has more than 50). Research on sensors takes place at the UNED University, and the GMSMA department of the Polytechnic University of Madrid develops the visualization and simulation systems in collaboration with specialized companies. Finally, projects that seek to embrace all of these fields, like *In the Air*, have been developed by unregulated and informal groups around media labs or art centres based on 'antidisciplinary' design.[8]

Lab, MIT; or the production of visualization systems and participation by xDesign Environmental Health Clinic, NYU, among others.

8. Andrew Pickering, *The Cybernetic Brain* (Chicago and London: The Chicago University Press, 2010).

One purpose of an infrastructure is to organize the coexistence of different modes and speeds of presence in the urban space as one of the first ways to make it public. That is why the ambition of *In the Air* is to become a platform for individual and collective consciousness and a tool for decision making, because it recognizes the political implications of the production of significance. In order to achieve this it will need to be activated by citizens, and therefore various intensities of participation are proposed.

The display of data in both digital devices and in the urban space can be used in real time to navigate the city. The topography and heat maps that reveal routes of low pollution might facilitate a bike ride or a walk with children or elderly people. Although these are just a few examples, since they suggest multiple readings and multiple actions.

The accumulation of historical data can be used as a database for urban planning. For the exhibition 'Habitar', some maps were produced that integrated data from areas in which in 2008 the limits of Particulate Matter were exceeded with data on the urban fabric, such as population density or land prices.[9] These data can be used by citizens (to buy a home, for example), and by planners (to locate future infrastructures, regulate traffic, etcetera). Also, historical data can be interpreted as indicators of urban life, where football matches, holidays, traffic jams or demonstrations can be identified so that the data not only has a quantitative

9. 'Habitar' exhibition. Curator: Jose Luis de Vicente, held at the Laboral Centro de Arte y Creación Industrial, Gijón, 2010.

application, but also a qualitative one, allowing the construction of new urban narratives.

In parallel, the project proposes another way of participation when it comes to data production. A domestic detector-visualizer kit is being developed that citizens will be able to assemble and put on their balconies or rooftops. On the one hand this would allow the production of data on a larger scale, increasing the resolution of the mesh. On the other hand the production of independent data would make it possible to make comparisons with official data, to ensure political transparency and to measure air quality at strategic points with no measuring devices. This massive domestic production of data would collectivize the maintenance and care of public infrastructure by replacing expensive equipment and specialized monitoring with voluntary control and caretaking, moving its perception from an external right to a common good.

The effects of these management systems are not only behavioural, but also relate to perception. As infrastructures they do construct subjectivity, conditioning the relations and the 'care between strangers'. They seek to produce experience and community, not only by proposing alternative imaginaries, but mostly by developing situations that enhance encounters and intensified exchanges of experience.

However, research still needs to be done on what might be achieved by the interaction of all these materials, human and non-human, as an evolutionary cybernetic design. Or what it means, in definitive, to inhabit coloured data clouds in the city.

book reviews

BAVO, *Too Active to Act. Cultureel activisme na het einde van de geschiedenis* (with a visual essay by Hendrik-Jan Grievink)

Merijn Oudenampsen

Amsterdam, Valiz, 2010, ISBN 978-90-78088-38-7, 128 p., € 15.-

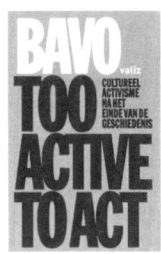

'Never before has so much explicitly socially engaged art been produced as there is now.' After this opening observation, the authors of *Too Active to Act. Cultureel activisme na het einde van de geschiedenis* (Cultural activism after the end of history) then proceed to thoroughly demolish this new type of engagement in the following 128 pages of their book.

Gideon Boie and Mathias Pauwels of BAVO analyse the growing involvement of cultural players in all sorts of spatial projects and compare this with the practice of embedded journalism: 'Just as embedded journalists report about today's battlefields from the perspective of the occupying forces, so does a motley army of diverse cultural players nowadays make itself useful on the margins of far-reaching government measures and market operations.' This, argue the authors, makes the new engagement fundamentally different from the old engagement that we are familiar with from the historical avant-garde. Whereas the avant-garde used its aesthetic know-how to undermine the status quo and try to go

beyond it, the new engagement stays carefully in line with prevailing policy agendas.

In a series of short, sharply formulated essays, we travel at breakneck speed through the landscape of the new engagement, with the authors bombarding a few emblematic projects with some pretty heavy criticism along the way. The first victim is Wouter van Stiphout and the WIMBY! project in Hoogvliet, which he helped design. The authors quote Wouter van Stiphout's plea to set aside 'critical attitudes' in order to 'be realistic' and do 'something useful'. According to BAVO, this is illustrative of the new engagement, which switches off its critical intellectual capacity in order to at least be able to sit at the controls again for a while. The result – so goes the critique – is that WIMBY! does not have its own story about the modernization of Hoogvliet but mostly supplies the existing, neoliberal-oriented programme of renewal with architectural acupuncture and marketing buzzwords.

We race onward, past the conceptual design company

Schie 2.0, which thinks that architects should not want to change anything; past Jeanne van Heeswijk, who therapeutically reconciles neighbourhood residents with the demolition of their neighbourhood; and past Rem Koolhaas and the idea that we should view marginal groups as 'voluntary prisoners' who ought not to be emancipated through architecture, but acknowledged for their 'differentness'. In short, not much of the new engagement is left intact.

BAVO's radical criticism makes few attempts to extend a hand to less politicized readers, in whom it might at times elicit indignation, even incomprehension. On the other side, the uncompromising, polemic tone of the book is a quality that distinguishes it from the often woolly discourse on renewal we are accustomed to reading. This style means that the subtleties are sometimes lost and the contrasts exaggerated. But logically enough, an attack on the polder mentality is never formulated in polder terms. This little book is the proverbial fox in the chicken coop, and in my opinion, one of the better foxes. What above all comes across is a thoroughgoing disappointment as to contemporary architecture's refusal to formulate its own (emancipatory) programme. Strangely enough, this is also the strongest criticism that can be made against the book.

The alternative that BAVO propose is the technique of over-identification. They derive this from the practice of the Slovenian avant-garde punk band Laibach, who developed a new way of rebelling against Tito's Yugoslavian regime by propagating his logic in an overblown manner and playing the advocate of the devil. A more recent example also mentioned is that of a number of Swedish artists who managed to torpedo an unpopular megaproject by presenting an even more megalomaniac version of the project, which was believed to be authentic and accordingly generated a storm of controversy. For the successful use of a comparable principle of provocation, BAVO laud American filmmaker Michael Moore, the recently deceased Austrian theatre maker Christoph Schlingensief, and Dutch artist Martijn Engelbregt.

'Instead of placing themselves outside the existing order,' state BAVO in closing, 'cultural players must without reservation embed themselves in the present order, of the end of history. They must totally assimilate the dominant logic of representative democracy and the free market, and from this radical inside position confront their supporters and adversaries with their unacknowledged devotion to these principles, as well as their all-too-fatalistic attitude toward the possibility of fundamental change.'

By adopting this technique, BAVO shrewdly manage to evade the responsibility of formulating their own programme; after all, they only have to caricature that of the opponent. This gives them the possibility of shooting away at will, without ever having to expose themselves. Their recent proposal to appoint someone as a *kunstmarinier* (literally Art Marine, figuratively comparable to an Art Czar) in Rotterdam shows that BAVO meanwhile have got so caught up in this game of assimilation that even their supporters no longer know where over-identification stops and sincerity begins. The aim of such a practice, we read, is 'to provoke the reputed critical forces in society', which shows that the practice of over-identification is always limited by its dependence on 'critical forces' that do have a programme and dare to come out for it. Moreover, it turns out that BAVO themselves are extremely cynical about these 'reputed' forces, a cynicism that also refers to the fundamental change for which BAVO say they are striving, but in which they evidently do not entirely believe. 'If it walks like a duck and quacks like a duck, we can call it a duck,' as the saying goes. With the ironic engagement that BAVO adopts, that's still very much the question.

None of this alters the fact that *Too Active to Act* and the practice developed by BAVO in recent years are hard to beat when it comes to the power and sharpness of their criticism.

Markus Miessen
The Nightmare of Participation (Crossbench Praxis as a Mode of Criticality)

Christel Vesters

New York/Berlin, Sternberg Press, 2010, ISBN 978-1934105-07-8, 304 p., € 22.-

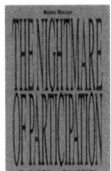

In his most recent publication, *The Nightmare of Participation (Crossbench Praxis as a Mode of Criticality)*, Markus Miessen postulates an alternative scenario for what Douglas Gordon describes on the back flap as 'pseudo-democracy . . . in which cynical globalized Muppets, drained of all joy, enact outdated hollow rituals grounded in unquestioned capitalism, zombie-style political correctness and poll-driven mock democracy'. The only way out of this status quo ruled by consensus and pseudo-participation is through the nonviolent intervention of an uninvited outsider: the 'crossbench practitioner'.

The Nightmare of Participation is the third volume in a series of publications in which Markus Miessen critically scrutinizes the phenomenon of participation. The first volume, in which he collaborated with Shumon Basar, titled *Did Someone Say Participate? An Atlas of Spatial Practice*, consists of a collection of short essays and descriptions of activist projects in which the boundaries of social, cultural, political and spatial conventions are sought. The contributions come from a diversity of people, ranging from Hans-Ulrich Obrist, Bas Princen and Armin Linke to Peter Weibel. The second book, *The Violence of Participation*, again with contributions by a varied group of thinkers and doers, investigates alternative forms of participation and different interpretations of the concept of democracy against the background of present-day Europe. In *The Nightmare of Participation*, Markus Miessen himself is the main narrator. He first of all observes and analyses the sphere of influence in which participation operates in all sorts of areas, in order to then formulate an alternative modus operandi of how we can act from a critical involvement in this sphere of influence and bring about changes, without being manoeuvred into the position of stakeholder.

Miessen – trained as an architect, but now working as a curator, educator, writer and consultant in the areas of urban planning, art and design – confronts us in the introduction with his twofold hypothesis: 'Sometimes. All-inclusive democracy has to be avoided at all cost,' and 'in order to make decisions . . . conflicts can ultimately only be overcome and turned into practice if someone assumes responsibility.' In order to clear the way for what Miessen calls the 'post-consensus model', he first looks at our conventional interpretation of the concept of participation and strips it of its apparent innocence. Participation is an empty concept; it refers to an action or process that in itself has no content. Nevertheless, the concept is permeated with false nostalgia and romantic longings with respect to inclusion (everybody has a say) advocacy and equality. In conventional notions of the democratic process, participation is equivalent to 'every vote counts' and 'the majority has a monopoly on truth'. Despite the fact that participation is an 'empty' concept, in no context is it neutral. As an example, Miessen describes the other side of the referendum: participatory methods such as referendums are especially popular as political instruments with parties who do not want to burn their fingers on sensitive decisions. By deferring the choice to the public, they not only postpone the decision, but also let slide the responsibility with which that same public had entrusted them at the elections. In the meantime, however, they determine what can be chosen, and how. As such, the referendum undermines the fundamentals of our democratic system from within.

Another way in which pseudo-participation is instrumentalized in order to maintain certain power balances is the game of musical chairs played by leaders and powerbrokers. For example: the government or management asks the public for its opinion on this or that proposal (think for example of the layout of public space), the public gets involved and perhaps even thinks its voice is heard. But by taking part in this procedure, the public is deprived in the following stages of every ground for being able to criticize the realization of the plan. Apart from the fact that these public participation procedures never result in new policies or ideas, they are above all imbued with creating consensus and limiting or even eliminating friction. Reading Miessen's critical exposition, it is easy to imagine how these sham procedures are implemented by authoritarian managements or an authoritarian government and can lead to pseudo-democracy.

This brings us to Miessen's third critical comment on the bankruptcy of participation – an argument that also has frequently been brought up over the last few years in discussions on participatory art, community art and relational aesthetics – namely that in spatial design practices, the design process is indeed participatory in terms of form, but the intention of the work (and therefore its critical significance in terms of engagement) is not. In other words, if you look further, you come to the conclusion that participation is anything but a rose-coloured dream, and sooner a nightmare of power politics and conflicts of interest.

Miessen draws two important conclusions from this. First of all: consensus can never lead to change or innovation – whether in the development of knowledge, the design process, or in a society. And secondly: every form of participation always carries a conflict within it. In short, *participation is war.* Drawing upon the political theory of Chantal Mouffe, among others, on the potential of the agonistic democratic model, Miessen substantiates the necessity of conflict in order to effectuate change and innovation, as well as the crucial role that the involved outsider plays in order to start this conflict. Whereas Eyal Weizman, in his prologue titled 'The Paradox of Collaboration', propagates a radical refusal to participate as a last way out of political and ideological instrumentalization, the answer according to Miessen lies in dilettantism new style: infiltrating the system from the sidelines with critical involvement and unlimited interest, and by introducing conflicting information, ideas or methods, creating friction, thus disrupting the status quo.

The Nightmare of Participation is comprised of short dissertations, e-mail correspondence and interviews with third parties on seemingly divergent topics. Miessen himself describes this ambiguous approach as a 'galactic model', whereby each chapter can be seen as a planet revolving around an undefined void. Miessen's argument moves through intellectual excursions from Stoic philosophy to an analysis of the developments that have led to the ideological crisis in the Left, a discussion of two management methodologies and their outlooks on intervention in a dysfunctional situation, a commentary on the commercialization of education and the disappearance of sanctuaries for radical thinking, and a critical analysis of the current state of affairs in architecture. Ultimately he arrives at the 'crossbench practitioner', the uninvited outsider who intervenes in a nonviolent manner in political structures, systems, situations or otherwise. This 'involved outsider' is the answer to the question of how architecture and other spatial and cultural practices can give form to this new modus operandi and create the necessary conditions for meaningful change.

If we ignore the seven mile boots with which Miessen at times runs through history or other fields and forgive him the hopscotch jumps in his argumentation, this little red book reads as a challenging and inspiring manifesto. *The Nightmare of Participation* not only makes us aware of our moral responsibility to critically examine the (political) power relations of every situation in which we participate – or let others participate! – it also formulates an ideological and working model for operating in an engaged manner in these situations without falling into the trap of consensus and pseudo-participation. Whether you are an architect, artist, curator or involved citizen.

Elena Filipovic, Marieke van Hal and Solveig Øvstebø (eds.)
The Biennial Reader: An Anthology on Large-Scale Perennial Exhibitions of Contemporary Art

Pascal Gielen

Bergen: Kunsthall Bergen, 2010,
ISBN 978-3-7757-2610-8,
512 p., € 35.-

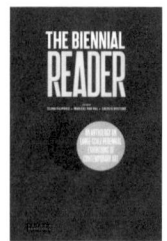

The Biennial Reader was created in response to the desire of the municipal government of the Norwegian city of Bergen to organize a biennial of their own. The Kunsthall Bergen, which the city had approached in this regard, had the courage to turn the question around. At the height of the proliferation of biennials and similar events throughout the world, the Bergen art hall first wanted to thoroughly examine the biennial phenomenon and its implications. What was intended to have been the first Bergen biennial in the autumn of 2009 was therefore tactically replaced by an international conference with the telling motto, 'To biennial or not to biennial?' During the preparations for this event, the lack of substantial literature, analysis and theorizing on the biennial phenomenon became evident, so the art hall decided to compile this reader. Both the conference and the book are a confirmation of 'the discursive turn', the shift from practice to discourse within the visual arts described by Paul O'Neill in this anthology (pages 240 to 259).

The Biennial Reader is divided into five sections logically following one another. The first is a selection of essays analysing the history of the phenomenon ('Histories, Precedents and Origins'). The second section ('What Is a Biennial? Potentials, Functions, and Ideals') examines the role of biennials and the expectations that people have of such large-scale exhibitions. The third ('The Curatorial') covers the protagonist of the contemporary biennial world, namely the (independent) curator. The authors included in section four ('Rethinking Biennials: Models and Formats'), indicate possible new models and strategies for this type of international exhibition. The last section ('The Politics of a Global Art') places the phenomenon of 'biennialization' within the perspective of increasing globalization.

From the very first essay, it is obvious that the editors have not taken the easy path of unequivocal interpretations or consensus. A reading of the first section, for instance, makes us aware that the genesis of the contemporary biennial can be described in different ways, and that the first art biennials in Havana may actually be more representative of the current exhibition format than the prototypical Venice Biennale. The uncertainty generated by the combination of essays in the first section continues throughout the rest of the book. The reader is caught up in a pendulum swing between proponents and opponents, pros and cons. In this dichotomous chain of standpoints, the biennial at one moment is merely a part of the market and an instrument of crass capitalism, while at another the phenomenon offers a platform for political engagement and cultural responsibility. One time, the mega exhibition stands for Debord's 'society of the spectacle', in which the visiting masses are benumbed with simple entertainment; another time it offers a veritable public space for dissensus and democracy. The biennial is the ideal example of cultural homogenization driven by the West on the one hand; on the other, it is the ultimate place for artistic pluralism and cultural diversity. It can be an ideal means of promoting the egos of curators, only the next moment to be a noble vehicle for teaching and even emancipating people. Are curators more like bloodthirsty colonizers who occupy as-yet-unexplored artistic territories or cleverly claim ideas to build up their own careers, or are they peace-loving anthropologists who want to promote more understanding of other cultures and artistic practices? Does the rampant 'biennialization' phenomenon mean the imposing of Western universalism, or a decentralization of the artistic power centre?

The plethora of polyphonic and contrapuntal voices does not mean that this 512-page reader lacks nuance. What especially stands out is its broad scope, which extends far beyond the realm of the artistic. The writers in *The Biennial Reader* readily discuss economic, social, political and aesthetic issues such as commoditization, representation, democracy, neoliberalization, identity politics or geopolitics. Nowadays, art or artists hardly have a part in this debate. In this book, they have even less of a voice. Of the 32 writers whose essays have been included, only 1.5 of them are artists. Not that that half of an artist is mediocre, but he only counts for half because in addition to his artistic practice he is also a curator and writer. This proportion raises the question of whether artists today no longer have a critical voice in the world in which they operate. And what about the opinions of autonomous critics? This anthology confirms the present hegemony in the globalized art world. Nowadays

it is not the artist or independent critic who determines the prevailing discourse, but the so-called 'independent' curator. The professional label of the latter covers a lot of territory, however. For ages now, the image of this – preferably nomadic – art professional has in no way resembled that of the somewhat withdrawn caretaker of museum art works. Curators today are aestheticians, diplomats, economists, critics, historians, politicians, audience developers and promoters, as Michael Brenson indicates in his contribution to the book (page 223). In short, curators are generalists, who moreover regard their own activities with the necessary reflexivity. Thanks to this broad interest shown by curators, the reader is treated to a rich and intelligent discourse that not only attests to their wide-ranging social knowledge but also to their involvement and engagement. For those who want to keep abreast of the relevant discourse in today's biennial world, this anthology is required reading. The fact that this book is also the first extensive publication on large-

scale international art exhibitions only makes it a more vital resource.

Yet the dominant voice that curators have in this book is not unproblematic. The advantage of involvement and practical experience simultaneously holds the risk of over-involvement or too little distance. This is also true of the selection of essays in this anthology. Although by now the biennial has a history of more than 100 years, the selected essays examine a notably recent period. Moreover, the majority of these curator-authors are part of the same sub-network, familiar to insiders. In other words, just like the present art world, this reader suffers from the *doxa* of contemporaneity. But the position of curators, who simultaneously are organizers, promoters and their own critics, raises a more fundamental question. From this hybrid position, in which criticism to a considerable extent is reduced to self-criticism, can you still speak of a genuine agony and thus of a true public space? Or do curators have enough independence to shatter their own crystal palaces?

Boris Groys
Going Public, e-flux journal

Jorinde Seijdel

Berlin/New York, Sternberg
Press, 2010,
ISBN 978-1-934105-30-6,
168 p., € 12.-
www.sternberg-press.com/

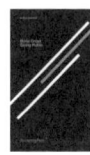

The philosopher, media theorist and art critic Boris Groys (b. East Berlin, 1947) has published substantial theoretical studies, such as *Über das Neue. Versuch einer Kulturökonomie* (1992), *Unter Verdacht. Eine Phänomenologie der Medien* (2000), *Topologie der Kunst* (2003), *Das kommunistische Postskriptum* (2006) and *History Becomes Form: Moscow Conceptualism* (2010). Serious literature, whose influence on various discourses is justly deserved. But Groys is by no means a withdrawn sitting-room scholar or a university-ensconced academic: he is an active presence in the art world that he reflects upon in his books. He teaches, gives frequent public lectures, makes video films (*Thinking in Loop: Three Videos on Iconoclasm, Ritual and Immortality,* ZKM, Karlsruhe, 2008) and exhibitions – this year, Groys, a native Russian, was appointed curator of the Russian Pavilion of the Venice Biennale. Recently, short essays of his have been coming out at a fast clip, both online and off-line, usually written on commission for an exhibition, conference or theme publication. They testify both to Groys's 'complicity' and his established renown.

In 2008, MIT Press published *Art Power*, a miscellaneous collection of essays in which Groys describes and analyses the modern work of art from various perspectives and contexts (including newness, the curator, biopolitics, digitalization, war, social realism, Europe) as a 'paradox-object' that simultaneously functions as a commodity and as ideological propaganda – also and particularly, contemporary Western art – and that wields power in those capacities. Quite recently, Sternberg Press brought out *Going Public*, a compilation of essays Groys wrote for various issues of the monthly online publication *e-flux journal*, the editorial project of Anton Vidokle and company (www.e-flux.com/journal). *Going Public* is the first of a series of printed *e-flux journal* readers, each of which will comprise work by only one author.

Just as in his previous books, in *Going Public* Groys positions contemporary art, its institutions and protagonists specifically within modernism/the historic avant-garde, the media culture and the post-communist era. In these discursive contexts, he considers common concepts such as the installation, the project, design, the museum, the body, etcetera, which he examines as constructions of this age and turns inside-out. Groys's essayism is authentic, and at times sooner prosaic than academic. He writes in a concrete manner, eschewing ideological rhetoric or fashionable philosophical vocabulary. This apparent lightness and his accessibility do not alter the fact that he indeed considers and analyses art in terms of its ideological function. Groys's art and cultural criticism excels in sharp thought experiments that arise from paradoxes and inversions of ready-made ideas, in which established identities and power structures are exploded through their own internal logic. His clear insights challenge the reader to formulate new questions.

In *Going Public*, the central issue is the changed relation between the viewer/public and the artist. With the advent of visual media, of the Internet and its social networks, art must no longer be considered aesthetically, but 'poetically'; that is to say, from the perspective of the art producer instead of the consumer, according to Groys. (The word 'poetry' stems from the Greek *poiesis*: creation or production). In the age of digital media and the globalized presentation-and-distribution platform of the Internet, the focus is increasingly on 'autopoiese', the production of one's own public self – 'autopoiese' literally means self-production. He argues for a change of perspective: moving away from the modern aesthetic or hermeneutical analysis of the work of art, which encourages a consumptive attitude, and returning to a more technical and poetical concept of art. Only from the position of the producer can we get a grip on the implications of current shifts in terms of the public and the private, the consumer and the producer, the amateur and the professional, the physical and the virtual. At the same time, according to Groys, from this non-aesthetic perspective, art can become visible beyond capitalism and the art market, and thus broaden its range and significance. Only when considered from the point of view of the producer can there be a question of a 'politics of art', argues Groys, seeing as this concerns a dimension that has nothing to do with a work of art's impact on the viewer – which produces an aesthetic experience – but with the actual decisions that precede the creation of a work.

More specifically, this compilation of essays further considers the art installation as a private autonomous zone within the museum, the (im)possibility of the collective social project in art, design and self-design, religion in the age of digital reproduction and Beuys's statement 'Jeder Mensch ist ein Künstler' in relation to the supposed de-professionalization of the artist. The underlying question in all of these essays is whether art and the artist are losing their exclusivity and professionality, and thereby also their privileged position, now that everyone has become a producer and can publicly manifest themselves in the networks and the media.

Groys tries to perpetrate a 'creative' form of criticism that is not about the subversion of contemporary art and the art world, nor the superficiality of the public media culture, but about the broadening of ideas and new relations. And about similarities rather than differences. Taken concretely and materially, what actually are the similarities between contemporary works of art and the visual products of media users? And what do artists have in common with other 'producers'? Nor is it about giving up art, or completely eradicating the differences between identities and domains, between high and low culture. Groys sooner appears to be seeking what is left of art and artistry outside the established categories and eroded value systems. In the introduction to *Going Public*, he writes that from the perspective of aesthetics, art does not have a privileged position, because after all there are so many things and phenomena in the world that can be considered or experienced as aesthetic (page 13). It could be that with his pushing forward of the perspective of the producer, Groys wants to recuperate that privileged position by taking an opposite tack, out of cool romanticism, via a different legitimization. But knowing Groys's way of thinking, he would never consolidate that, let alone consume it.

Nerea Calvillo is an architect educated at the universities of Madrid, Venice and Columbia. She is a professor at the Universidad Europea de Madrid and the Universidad de Alicante, and her work ranges from architectural to research projects related to digital tools and visualization.

Pascal Gielen is affiliated with the University of Groningen (RUG) as an art sociologist and holds the Arts in Society chair at the Fontys University of Applied Sciences in Tilburg. His last three publications are: *The Murmuring of the Artistic Multitude: Global Art, Memory and Post-Fordism* (2009), *Arts in Society: Being an Artist in Post-Fordist Times* (2009, co-edited with Paul De Bruyne) and *Community Art: The Politics of Trespassing* (2011, co-edited with Paul De Bruyne).

Tatiana Goryucheva is a media theorist, curator and lecturer based in Amsterdam. In her research and projects, she explores the politics of technological design, the culture of democracy and social engagement in relation to technology.

Joss Hands is the author of *@ is for Activism: Dissent, Resistance and Rebellion in a Digital Culture* (2010). He teaches media and communication at Anglia Ruskin University, Cambridge where he is also co-director of the Anglia Research Centre in Digital Culture.

Brian Holmes is a culture critic living at present in Chicago. He is the author of *Escape the Overcode: Activist Art in the Control Society* (2010) and is now working on crisis theory and technopolitics. All his texts are obtainable free of charge at http://brianholmes.wordpress.com.

Eric Kluitenberg is an independent theorist, writer and curator who focuses on culture, media and technology. He was head of the media programme of De Balie, centre for culture and politics in Amsterdam, and teaches and lectures regularly throughout Europe and beyond. Recent publications include the theme issue 'Hybrid Space' (*Open* no. 11, 2006), of which he was guest editor; *Book of Imaginary Media* (2006) and *Delusive Spaces* (essays, 2008).

Charlotte Lebbe is reading European Studies at the University of Bath. She graduated last year from the University of Leuven as an architect. Her Master's thesis, *De terugkeer van harde grenzen. Een biopolitieke blik op Fort Europa*, (The Return of Hard Borders. A Biopolitical Look at Fortress Europe) received the Karel Verleye award.

Metahaven is an Amsterdam-based design studio founded by Vinca Kruk and Daniel van der Velden. Apart from commissions, Metahaven works on research projects on visual identity, such as as the *Sealand Identity Project* (2004), *Transparency Inc.* (2010-2011), and the *Museum of Conflict* (2006). Metahaven's work was shown at 'Forms of Inquiry' (London, 2007), 'Manifesta 8' (Murcia and Cartagena, 2010) and 'Graphic Design Worlds' (Milan, 2011). Solo exhibitions by Metahaven were 'Affiche Frontière' (Bordeaux, 2008) and 'Stadtstaat' (Stuttgart and Utrecht, 2009). Metahaven's book *Uncorporate Identity* (2010) is an anthology of design projects and critical writings. See further: www. metahaven.net.

Wim Nijenhuis is an independent architect/writer on the history and theory of architecture, urban design and art, and presently lectures at the ArtEZ Institute for the Arts. He introduced Paul Virilio in the Netherlands and wrote *De diabolische snelweg* (The Diabolical Highway, 2007). See: home. hccnet.nl/j.w.nijenhuis/bestand/ curriculum.pdf.

Merijn Oudenampsen is a political scientist and sociologist. He is affiliated with the University of Tilburg, where he is working on his doctorate in populism and cultural studies. His texts can be read on- and offline in *de Groene Amster-dammer*, *Metropolis M*, *Denktank Waterland*, *Archined* and *Mute Magazine*.

Miguel Robles-Durán, urbanist, is co-founder of 'Cohabitation Strategies', a cooperative for sociospatial development based in New York and Rotterdam. He directs the Urban Ecologies Graduate Program at the New School/Parsons in New York.

Florian Schneider is a filmmaker and media artist based in Munich and Brussels. He is one of the initiators of the campaign 'kein mensch ist illegal' and curated the performance project 'Dictionary of War'. He teaches at the Trondheim Academy of Fine Art and the Jan van Eyck Academy, Maastricht.

Marc Schuilenburg teaches in the criminology department of the VU University in Amsterdam. Previously, he (co-)published *Mediapolis. Popular Culture and the City* (2007), the *Deleuze Compendium* (2009) and *De nieuwe Franse filosofie* (2011). His website: www.marcschuilenburg.nl and e-mail address: m.b.schuilenburg@vu.nl.

John Thackara is a writer, educator and design producer. He is the author of *In the Bubble: Designing in a Complex World* (2005) and of a widely-read blog at designobserver.com.

Christel Vesters is a critic and independent curator. She studied art history and curating in Amsterdam, New York and London. She has curated various exhibitions and discursive projects on art and architecture and regularly contributes to interna-tional art magazines and art publi-cations.

CREDITS

Cover Left: Allan Sekula en Noël Burch, *The Forgotten Space*. Right: © Chiara Tamburni, Brussels.

Open Cahier on Art and the Public Domain
Volume 10 (2011) no. 21

Editors Jorinde Seijdel (editor in chief), Liesbeth Melis (final editing)
Contributing editor Eric Kluitenberg
Advisory council Nicolas Bourriaud, Brian Holmes, Sven Lütticken and Gerald Raunig
English copy editor D'Laine Camp

Dutch-English translations
Jane Bemont (editorial, texts by Charlotte Lebbe, Eric Kluitenberg, book reviews by Merijn Oudenampsen, Pascal Gielen, Jorinde Seijdel, Christel Vesters); Pierre Bouvier (text by Wim Nijenhuis); Andrew May (text by Marc Schuilenburg)

Graphic design Thomas Buxó and Klaartje van Eijk , Amsterdam
Printing and lithography Die Keure, Brugge
Project coordinator Marieke van Giersbergen, NAi Publishers

Publisher Eelco van Welie, NAi Publishers

Open is published twice a year
Open 22 will be published in November 2011

Editorial address
SKOR
Ruysdaelkade 2
1072 AG Amsterdam
the Netherlands
Tel +31 (0)20 6722525
Fax +31 (0)20 3792809
open@skor.nl
www.opencahier.nl

SUBSCRIPTIONS

Abonnementenland
Postbus 20
1910 AA Uitgeest
the Netherlands
0900-2265263 – € 0,10 per minute)
Fax +31 (0)251 310405
www.aboland.nl.

PRICE PER ISSUE
€ 23.50

SUBSCRIPTION PRICES
(postage included)
the Netherlands: € 32.50
Within Europe: € 39.50
Outside Europe: € 45.00
Students: € 24.50

SUBSCRIPTION CANCELLATION
Cancellations (in writing only) must be received by Abonnementenland eight weeks prior to the end of the subscription period. Subscriptions not cancelled in time are automatically renewed for one year.

For a comprehensive overview
of contents according to
author, article and theme,
see www.opencahier.nl

open

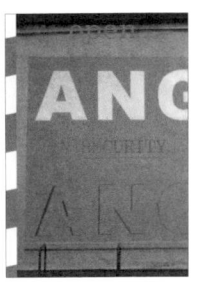

(IN)SECURITY

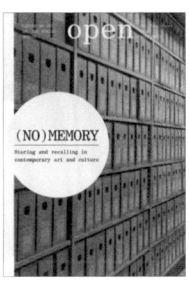

(NO) MEMORY

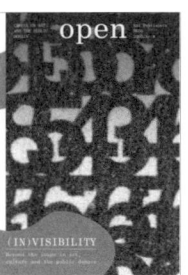

(IN)VISIBILITY

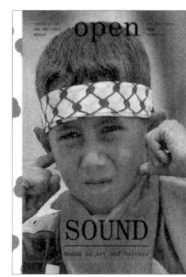

SOUND

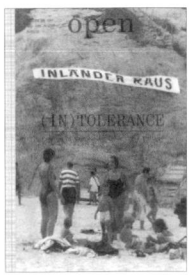

(IN)TOLERANCE

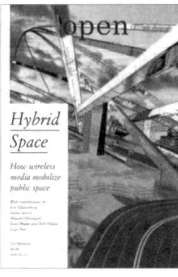

HYBRID SPACE

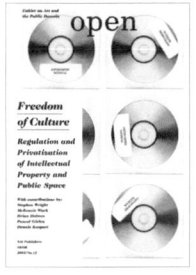

FREEDOM
OF CULTURE

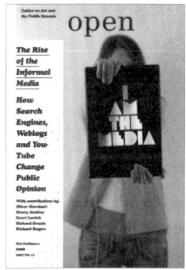

THE RISE OF THE
INFORMAL MEDIA

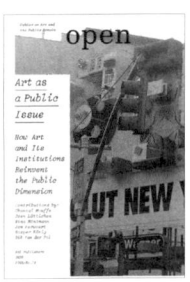

ART AS
A PUBLIC ISSUE

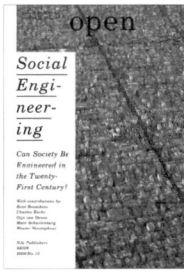

SOCIAL
ENGINEERING

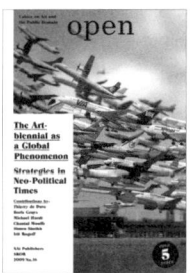

THE ART BIENNIAL
AS GLOBAL
PHENOMENON

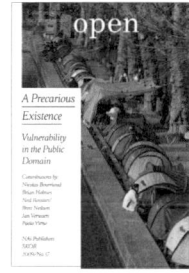

A PRECARIOUS
EXISTENCE

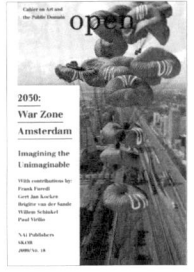

2030: WAR ZONE

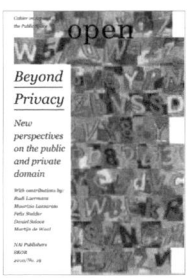

BEYOND PRIVACY

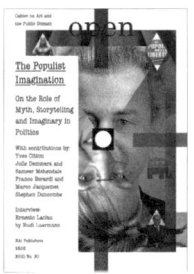

THE POPULIST
IMAGINATION

For works of visual artists affiliated with a CISAC-
organization the copyrights have been settled with
Pictoright in Amsterdam. © 2010 c/o Pictoright
Amsterdam

NAi Publishers is an internationally orientated
publisher specialized in developing, producing and
distributing books on architecture, visual arts and
related disciplines.
www.naipublishers.nl info@naipublishers.nl

It was not possible to find all the copyright holders
of the illustrations used. Interested parties are
requested to contact NAi Publishers, Mauritsweg 23,
3012 JR Rotterdam, the Netherlands.

Available in North, South and Central America through
D.A.P./Distributed Art Publishers Inc, 155 Sixth
Avenue 2nd Floor, New York, NY 10013-1507, Tel 212
6271999, Fax 212 6279484.

Available in the United Kingdom and Ireland through
Art Data, 12 Bell Industrial Estate, 50 Cunnington
Street, London W4 5HB, Tel 208 7471061, Fax 208
7422319.

SKOR (Foundation for Art and the Public Domain) is an
organization whose objective is to realize special art
projects in public and semi-public settings
www.skor.nl info@skor.nl

Printed and bound in Belgium

ISSN 1570-4181
ISBN 978-90-5662-814-7